Know Your SHIPS

Guide to Boats & Boatwatching
Great Lakes & St. Lawrence Seaway

© 2000 — Updated Annually

(No part of this book may be published, broadcast, rewritten or
redistributed by any means, including electronic.)

ISBN: 1-891849-02-6
ISSN: 0190-5562

Marine Publishing Co. Inc.

Box 68, Sault Ste. Marie, MI 49783

Editor & Publisher: Roger LeLievre

Listings Researchers: Philip A. Clayton, John Vournakis

Contributing Researchers: Jody Aho, Rod Burdick,
Angela S. Clayton, Al Miller, Neil Schultheiss, George Wharton

Founder: Tom Manse, 1915-1994

www.knowyourships.com

Front cover: **Cason J. Callaway and a saltwater vessel at anchor
in the St. Mary's River.** *Back cover:* **Marion Green
leaves Lock 1 on the Welland Canal.** *(Roger LeLievre - both photos)*

CARGO

---

*The information contained herein was obtained from the United States
Coast Pilot (Vol. 6), the St. Lawrence Seaway Authority, the Lake Carriers'
Association, the Institute for Great Lakes Research, Jane's Merchant Ships,
the American Merchant Seaman's Manual, Lloyd's Register of Shipping,
the U.S. Army Corps of Engineers, 'Great Lakes Log' and publications of the
Great Lakes Maritime Institute, the Toronto Marine Historical Society and
the Marine Historical Society of Detroit.*

CSL Niagara meets Algosound in the Welland Canal. (Roger LeLievre)

WELCOME ABOARD

As we sail full speed ahead into the next 100 years, it is worth remembering that Great Lakes shipping also stands at the end of century of great change. Lakers today are sizes undreamed of 100 years ago. Vessel tonnages are 15 times what they were in 1900. Mariners have at their disposal an array of navigation and communications gear that would astonish their 1900s counterparts. Great Lakes sailors are safer than any time in history. Still, familiar challenges remain. Storms are forces to reckon with. Water levels continue to fluctuate. Economies ebb and flow.

To kick off the 2000 'Know Your Ships,' regular contributor Jody Aho reviews some of the changes in the shipping industry and in the vessels themselves during the past 100 years. In addition, marine historian Al Miller tells the story of a trio of familiar sisterships — **Arthur M. Anderson, Philip R. Clarke** and **Cason J. Callaway** — featured collectively as this year's Vessel of the Year. The popular Vessel Spotlights return with profiles of even more familiar lakers, and as usual, marine photographers from around the Great Lakes and Seaway document the busy shipping scene from Montreal to Duluth with their superb photos.

So what's on the horizon? Will more powered steamers be converted to barges? Can 1,300-foot vessels be far behind if a new, bigger lock is ever built at the Soo? Will imported steel continue to threaten the vitality of the Great Lakes shipping industry? What familiar vessels will be scrapped next? Will the **Edward L. Ryerson** ever get that self-unloading boom? We're not pretending to know the answers ... but don't you agree it will be fun to watch it all unfold?

— The 'Know Your Ships' staff

3

A CENTURY OF CHANGE

Marine Milestones 1900 - 2000

It's no exaggeration to say there have been more changes in Great Lakes shipping in the past 100 years than in any other period since the first recorded attempts at navigating the lakes more than 300 years ago. Many of the changes have been positive, such as improved working conditions and advances in technology. To the boatwatcher, other changes may not be viewed as favorably, such as the reduction in the number of the vessels and the evolution in design from the attractive lines of the coal-fired straight-deckers with tall stacks to the all-cabins-aft self-unloaders to tug-barge units. Here's a look at some of the milestones achieved during the last 100 years.

The 560-foot Augustus B. Wolvin was Queen of the Lakes in 1904. (Rev. Edward J. Dowling S.J. Marine Collection, University of Detroit Mercy)

Paul R. Tregurtha is the longest laker as the century ends. (Roger LeLievre)

Vessel size

The 500-foot threshold in vessel length was being approached in 1900, as the **James J. Hill** and her three sisterships entered service. The first decade of the 20th century saw a rapid increase in size. The **Augustus B. Wolvin** entered service in 1904 with an overall length of 560 feet, and two years later the first group of 600-footers made their debuts. During the next few decades there were smaller increases in size, culminating with the 638-foot **Carl D.** ▶

4

Bradley in 1927. Although the "Supers," or **Leon Fraser** class, surpassed the Bradley by 18 inches in overall length when they came out in 1942, the next large jump in size would not take place until several years later. The **Wilfred Sykes** of 1949 is largely regarded as the prototype of post-World War II lakers, and her 678-foot overall length made her almost 40 feet longer than the next largest vessel of the time.

When the **Edmund Fitzgerald** entered service in 1958, the maximum-size Seaway vessel was born, although slight additional increases in size would be added into subsequent vessels over the next 14 years. The largest increase in vessel size at any point in Great Lakes history occurred in 1972 when the **Stewart J. Cort**, the lakes' first 1000-footer, entered service. A few more increases in size were incorporated in subsequent vessels; at the end of the century **Paul R. Tregurtha** remains the longest Great Lakes vessel at 1,013 feet 6 inches overall. The Tregurtha has held this honor since

Carl D. Bradley opened the MacArthur Lock at Sault Ste. Marie on 11 July 1943. She was lost in Lake Michigan in 1958. (Manse Collection)

she entered service in 1981 — longer than any other vessel in Great Lakes history.

Corresponding increases took place in cargo capacity. In 1900, the average iron ore cargo shipped on the Great Lakes was 3,783 tons. By 1909, this had grown to 7,777 tons. As more vessels in the 600-foot class entered service, the figure steadily grew until 1930, when the average cargo reached 9,595 tons. Although few vessels were added in the 1930s, more than 20 large vessels entered service in 1942 and 1943 to add to the fleet's capacity. With dozens of smaller units retired immediately after World War II, the average iron ore cargo reached 10,446 tons in 1950. The pace continued to grow through the active shipbuilding years of the 1950s and 1960s, with the average ore cargo reaching 13,555 tons by 1960 and 16,063 tons in 1970. The addition of the 1000-footers to the ore-carrying fleet resulted in a sharp increase in the average cargo, to 25,693 tons by 1980. In 1990, the average was 31,265 tons, and in 1998, the average peaked at 32,112 ▶

5

Wyandotte, launched in 1908, was the first vessel built as a self-unloader. *(Rev. Edward J. Dowling S.J. Marine Collection, University of Detroit Mercy)*

tons. It is likely that the figure will remain nearly flat, with perhaps slight growth, as the 21st century begins with no new vessels planned and the few smaller vessels remaining in the iron ore trade retired.

Size of the Great Lakes fleet

The Lake Carriers' Association has long served as the group representing the interests of the majority of American-flagged Great Lakes fleets. Its membership rolls clearly show the changes in the number of vessels on the lakes. In 1909, there were 597 vessels registered with LCA, not counting the several hundred Canadian vessels at that time or many of the small, one-ship fleets. In 1920, this figure dropped to 382, although a building boom in the 1920s resulted in an increase to 408 enrolled vessels by 1930. The Great Depression took its toll, though, as 1940 LCA membership fell to 341 vessels, with the total, including Canadian vessels, at 817. In 1950, there were 313 vessels registered with LCA, and, counting Canadian vessels, there were 665 vessels on the Lakes. In 1960, LCA membership decreased to 293, but the overall total climbed for the last time to 675 as the Canadians began a major rebuilding program in their fleets. The advent of the Seaway-sized bulk carrier made many of the old "canaller"-type vessels of Canadian fleets obsolete, and by 1970 this made a huge impact. LCA membership stood at 194, while the overall total fell to 425 vessels. Many of the classic lakers from the first couple of decades of the 20th century went for scrap during the 1970s, and by 1980 the rolls were down to 126 vessels registered with LCA and 302 vessels overall in the U.S. and Canadian fleets. The recession of the 1980s caused one more purge of excess capacity, and by 1990 LCA membership stood at only 64 vessels, with only 176 Great Lakes vessels remaining between U.S. and Canada. As the 2000 shipping starts, fleets are at their optimum sizes, where enough vessels exist to handle demand with a few boats held in reserve. LCA membership stands at 61 vessels, while the combined U.S. and Canada total is 157. Excluding the growth decade of the 1920s, the 1990s has the interesting ▶

Stewart J. Cort, the lakes' first 1000-footer, navigates early spring ice. (John L. Wagner, www.michiganlighthouse.com)

distinction of experiencing the smallest reduction in size in the U.S. Great Lakes fleets during this century. Boatwatchers are bracing for the start of another purge of surplus tonnage as non-self-unloading Canadian-flag bulkers built in the 1960s and '70s near the end of their economically useful lives.

Changes in cargo handling

Iron ore has remained the primary Great Lakes cargo throughout the century, but there have been changes in how the cargo is loaded and unloaded. The large, new vessels of the early 20th century necessitated a quick loading system, and soon the gravity chute iron ore dock became common in the many ore-loading ports on Lake Superior. Trains loaded with iron ore would go on the dock, and the ore cars would be centered over pockets to dump the ore into. When a boat pulled into the dock, chutes — typically placed on 12-foot centers to match the arrangement of the vessels' hatches — would be lowered against the side of an open hatch, and the iron ore slid down the chutes and into the holds. The **D.G. Kerr** set the record for the fastest iron ore load at a gravity chute dock in Two Harbors on 7 September 1921 when the vessel took on 12,508 tons of iron ore in 16.5 minutes. The chutes remain an effective means to load a boat, and these docks still see frequent use in Duluth, Two Harbors and Marquette, however with the introduction of taconite pellets in 1956, conveyor systems became the loading method of choice. Most of the iron ore today is loaded by conveyor. While an average 60,000 ton cargo for a 1000-footer takes between 10 and 12 hours to load, cargoes close to this size have been loaded in less than four hours at conveyor docks.

The record-setting William A. Irvin. (Manse Collection)

Unloading systems have seen the greatest change during the century and have had wider reaching effects. Early in the century, the Brown electric automatic hoist was a common machine used for unloading ore, while the Hulett unloader quickly grew in popularity. The Hulett consisted of a large mechanical arm with a set of jaws at the end. The jaws reached through an open hatch, picked up 15 to 20 tons of iron ore out of the hold, lifted it out of the vessel, and released the cargo on shore. With three or four Huletts working at once, the 600-footers usually required around eight hours to unload. The **William A. Irvin** holds the record for the fastest unloading of a cargo using Huletts. On 27 August 1940, the Irvin unloaded 13,856 tons of iron ore in two hours, 55 minutes, in ▶

Conneaut, OH. With the disappearance of shoreside unloading equipment, the Irvin will likely retain the record.

Self-unloading systems made their entrance during the first decade of the century, with the **Wyandotte**, of 1908, credited with being the first vessel built specifically as a self-unloader. Although specific mechanisms used in the system have changed, particularly those used to lift the cargo from hold to spar deck, the basic principle is the same. Gates are opened in the bottom of the holds to allow cargo to empty onto conveyors beneath. Conveyors carry the cargo underneath the holds to the lifting mechanism. Currently, a loop-belt system is the most common form of lifting mechanism; Cargo is sandwiched

T.W. Robinson — the first Great Lakes vessel powered by a turbine. (Manse Collection)

between belts under tension and carried upward. The cargo then falls through a hopper onto the conveyor belt on a boom on the spar deck. The boom swings out over the side, and the cargo comes off the boom. The self-unloader is extremely versatile, since the vessel does not need to be at a dock to unload. Self-unloaders have been used in vessel-to-vessel transfers, in lightering situations when the self-unloader runs aground, and in other unusual situations. Self-unloaders helped build the underwater foundations for the Mackinac Bridge in the mid-1950s, dumping limestone directly into the water. The **H. M. Griffith** used its self-unloading system as a sort of fire extinguisher on Lake Superior in 1996 when her coal cargo started burning in her holds. The Griffith unloaded about 3,000 tons of burning cargo over the side, thus preventing the loss of the entire cargo and vessel. Early self-unloaders were used mainly in the coal and limestone trades, although iron ore gradually became compatible with the systems. **Canadian Ranger** even has a self-unloading system for grain. As nearly every cargo can now be handled by these vessels, some form of self-unloading system should be expected in any future vessel.

Improved propulsion systems

The reciprocating engine was used in steam-powered vessels at the turn of the century. Most of these were the triple expansion type, with three cylinders, although several vessels used quadruple expansion engines with four cylinders. The latter type was often used in vessels towing barges. Steam for reciprocating engines was produced in coal-fired Scotch, or fire-tube, boilers.

The first diesel-powered vessels were the **Benson Ford** and **Henry Ford II**, ▶

which entered service for the Ford Motor Company in 1924. Although it would be many years before additional diesel-powered boats entered service, the engine would eventually become the primary propulsion system used in most Great Lakes vessels.

The first turbine installation occurred on the **T.W. Robinson** in 1925. The vessel used a turbo-electric system, where steam turbines ran electric generators. The electricity produced would then power motors that turned the propeller. The turbo-electric system never became popular, though, and a direct drive to the propeller via reduction gear would be used in almost all other steam turbine plants on Great Lakes vessels. The **John Hulst, Governor Miller, William A. Irvin** and **Ralph H. Watson** became the first class of vessel to use the direct-drive steam turbine when the four entered service in the summer of 1938.

In 1943, two notable events concerning propulsion systems occurred. The "Maritime" class vessels — 16 of them — entered service. Ten were powered by traditional triple expansion engines, and they became the last new Great Lakes vessels to be so-powered. The other six members of the class received Lentz Poppet steam engines. No other Great Lakes vessels were fitted with this engine, and time proved the power plant a failure, prone to breakdown and power loss. The last Lentz engine was retired over the winter of 1999-2000 when the **Cuyahoga**, formerly **J. Burton Ayers**, was repowered with a diesel.

The Skinner Uniflow steam engine was also introduced to the Great Lakes in the 1940s, and a few dozen vessels were either built with the engines or repowered with them well into the 1950s. This engine never gained dominance either, and few remain on the Great Lakes.

During the 1950s, steam turbines were the most popular choice for new propulsion. In addition, many of the newer vessels were oil-fired, with some older coal-burners converted to oil fuel. This trend continued over the next four decades, until the carferry **Badger** became the lone coal-burner in 1995. **Feux Follets** (now **Canadian Leader**) was the last new steam-powered vessel on the Great Lakes when it came out on 12 October 1967. All new vessels built since have been powered with diesel engines. A more recent development, popularized with the conversion of the **Joseph H. Thompson** in 1990, is the integrated tug-barge unit, in which a laker's engines are removed and a notch cut in the stern for a tug to fit. The resulting vessel needs a much smaller crew and has the novelty of a power plant that can be separated from the cargo-carrying hull for refueling and other tasks. While several older, smaller vessels have seen their lives continue in this form, they are unpopular with most Great Lakes boatwatchers. As the 1990s closed, several repowering projects were being considered, most notably with the "AAA" class vessels of U.S. Steel and the **John G. Munson**.

New tools in the pilothouse

The pilothouses of Great Lakes vessels in 1900 were small and had minimal equipment. The open-air pilothouse was a popular arrangement in the first several years of the century, but by 1920, pilothouses were fully enclosed. Besides the wheel, a magnetic compass, and the all-important barometer to help captains make weather forecasts, there were few other aids to navigation. The gyrocompass was invented in 1911, although it did not become commonplace on vessels until a couple of decades later. Radio became the first widespread accessory added to vessels, and most were so equipped by the 1920s. At about the same time, radio direction finders were added to help refine navigation. ▶

Joseph H. Thompson as a steamer in 1973. She was converted to a barge in 1990. (Roger LeLievre)

Collisions between vessels in fog caused a great many casualties in the years before and during World War II. In 1943, the first radar set on a Great Lakes vessel was installed aboard the **James A. Farrell**; by 1950 most of the Great Lakes fleet was radar-equipped. The 1990s saw the development of more advanced sets that automatically plot targets and give readouts of target courses, speeds and other information.

Even more precise forms of electronic navigation have been used in the last 20 years. Loran service for the Great Lakes was completed in 1979, and became the method of choice for the next 15 years. GPS, or Global Positioning System, is even more precise; in 1993 GPS receivers started making their way aboard commercial Great Lakes vessels. GPS is also more dependable, because it works off of satellites, while Loran works off of shore-based antennas that can be affected by weather at the antenna site. Outmoded radio direction finders were removed from many vessels beginning in the late 1980s.

The lakers of tomorrow

With no apparent plans for new construction by the Great Lakes fleets, and with a dwindling number of vessels in a reserve capacity, the future of Great Lakes shipping in the next 100 (or even 10) years becomes difficult to predict. Will tug-barge units become the predominant form of transportation, with many existing vessels being converted to this format? Will we see a return to shipbuilding to replace aging vessels or even increase the size of the fleet? Certainly many of the developments experienced toward the end of this century were not foreseen at its start; the same can certainly be said about the upcoming century.

— Jody Aho

Jody Aho, a resident of Duluth and a former Great Lakes sailor, is author of the book "William A. Irvin: Queen of the Silver Stackers."

AAA CLASS ACT

Vessel of the Year

Philip R. Clarke
Cason J. Callaway
Arthur M. Anderson

They are among the most widely recognized boats on the Great Lakes. The AAA class vessels of USS Great Lakes Fleet Inc. — **Arthur M. Anderson, Cason J. Callaway** and **Philip R. Clarke** - have been favorites among boatwatchers for nearly 50 years. Yet despite their age, they remain a key part of the Great Lakes Fleet because of modifications that have increased their versatility and efficiency to meet changing market demands.

Prompted by a growing need for steel and the promise of a new iron product called taconite, U.S. Steel's Pittsburgh Steamship Company announced in 1950 that it would build three ore carriers. These would be the fleet's first vessels built after World War II, and the largest it had ever constructed. They also would turn out to be the last straight-deckers the company ever built, ending a tradition that stretched back to its introduction of the famed Gary-class vessels in 1905.

The AAA class boats represented a new vessel design for the fleet. Hull streamlining introduced in lakers built during World War II was refined in these boats. The stern was designed to be asymetrical to improve the flow of water into the propeller, and the rudder was offset slightly to perform more efficiently. The boats also were the first in the fleet to use AC electrical power and to have built-in sewage treatment systems.

Arthur M. Anderson at Toledo. *(Jim Hoffman)*

The Clarke and Anderson were built by the American Ship Building Company at its yard in Lorain, OH. These vessels were true sisters, taking shape as consecutive hull numbers and having an identical gross registered tonnage of 11,623 tons. The Callaway was built at Great Lakes Engineering Works in Ecorse, MI, and was completed at 11,591 gross registered tons. Despite the variation in tonnage, all three shared the same dimensions: 647 feet in overall length; 620 feet long at the keel, 70 feet of beam and 36 feet in depth.

The Clarke was launched first on 26 November 1951, and the Anderson and Callaway soon followed. All three vessels entered service in 1952, and they quickly made their presence felt. Longer, wider and deeper than anything else ▶ in the Pittsburgh fleet, the Anderson, Callaway and Clarke could carry about

Cason J. Callaway is the first boat of the season at Sault Ste. Marie on 8 April 1971. The Clarke and Anderson follow close astern. (Roger LeLievre)

19,000 tons of ore — a substantial increase over their older fleetmates. In addition, their 7,000-horsepower Westinghouse turbine engines could drive the boats at 16 miles per hour, enabling them to make more trips in a season than the older boats. These advantages became evident in 1953, when the Anderson made 46 round-trips and carried a single-season record of 866,855 tons of cargo.

The Anderson, Callaway and Clarke were only about 10 years old when the fleet began to modify them.

Arthur M. Anderson under the unloading Huletts at Conneaut, OH. *(Tom Manse)*

They were among 13 Pittsburgh vessels altered in the early '60s to operate in saltwater so they could steam down the St. Lawrence River to haul iron ore from Canada. The Anderson was the fleet's first boat to make the trip, departing Conneaut, OH, on 14 August 1962, to load ore at Port Cartier, QC, for delivery to Gary, IN.

Next, the fleet added bowthrusters to the boats in 1966. A vessel with a bowthruster was less likely to need tugs and could reduce time spent maneuvering in port.

In 1974 and 1975, the fleet lengthened the boats to increase their capacity. Each was taken to Fraser Shipyards in Superior, WI, where it was put in drydock and cut in half. The stern was then floated out of the dock and a 120-foot, prefabricated mid-body section was inserted, giving each boat an overall length of 767 feet. The resulting gain in tonnage was impressive. On its first trip after lengthening, the Callaway loaded 26,634 gross tons of ore.

The biggest modification was their conversion to self-unloaders during the fall of 1981 and winter of 1982. Again, the work was done at the Fraser yard. Aboard each boat, sections of prefabricated hopper bottom were lowered through the hatches and installed in the holds. Conveyor systems were added and a 250-foot unloading boom was installed just in front of the aft deckhouse. The additional steel reduced cargo capacity to about 25,300 gross tons of taconite pellets, but they could now unload that cargo at a rate of 6,000 tons an hour. The increased speed in unloading and the ability to serve a wider range of customers more than compensated for the loss of capacity. ▶

Cason J. Callaway (above) is lengthened by 120 feet at Fraser Shipyards in 1974.

A welder works on converting one of the three vessels to a self-unloader in 1982 (left).

(Manse Collection)

In 1987, the Callaway received a sternthruster. The Clarke followed in 1988 and the Anderson received one the following year. With thrusters fore and aft, the boats became even more maneuverable in small harbors.

The modifications to the Anderson, Callaway and Clarke reflected their changing roles and the new challenges facing the fleet. As originally conceived, these vessels were to spend their lives hauling natural iron ore and taconite pellets from the head of Lake Superior to U.S. Steel's mills on the lower lakes. They performed admirably in that role through the 1970s. During the experiments with extending the navigation season, the AAA boats were true workhorses. The Clarke made 56 trips during the '74-'75 season, hauling 1.4 million tons of cargo. On most of those trips it carried natural ore "fines," or taconite pellets, loaded in Duluth or Two Harbors, MN, for delivery to Conneaut, Gary and occasionally South Chicago. It ended the season on 16 March 1975, when it arrived in Gary, and started the '75-'76 season later the same day when it departed for Two Harbors.

The boats' roles began to change in the 1980s, however, as the nation's steel industry suffered through a major economic recession that led to widespread mill closings and drastic reductions in demand for ore. The Pittsburgh fleet was first spun off from U.S. Steel in 1981, then sold outright in 1988, emerging as USS Great Lakes Fleet Inc. As an independent fleet, the company continued to serve U.S. Steel, but it also had to find new customers. USS Great Lakes Fleet expanded its customer base by using the AAA boats to carry cargoes such as stone, coal and sand to a wide range of ports where the vessels had never previously called. Because they were self-unloaders, they could unload at virtually any dock. With the advantage of having both bowthrusters and sternthrusters, they could safely negotiate narrow rivers and small harbors.

Throughout their years of service, the Anderson, Callaway and Clarke have remained favorites among boatwatchers. With their expanding roles, they are now seen in more places than ever. Each vessel also has made its unique mark on Great Lakes history. Philip R. Clarke was the first vessel to transit the new Poe Lock when it officially opened in 1969. The Callaway has always been a stalwart of the extended navigation season, setting several marks for the latest trip of the season. Arthur M. Anderson, of course, achieved a macabre immortality when it became the last vessel to have contact with the **Edmund Fitzgerald** before it disappeared near Whitefish Point in 1975.

The next big modifications anticipated for the Anderson, Callaway and Clarke are the overhaul or replacement of their engines. The vessels' hulls reportedly are capable of serving another 25 years, but their turbines and boilers are showing their age. USS Great Lakes Fleet has proposed repowering the boats with diesel engines. This would be less costly and result in more efficient vessels than rebuilding the turbines or converting the vessels to barges.

Whatever the outcome of the repowering proposal, the Arthur M. Anderson, Philip R. Clarke and Cason J. Callaway are likely to remain in the roles they've developed during the past two decades: versatile boats capable of carrying virtually any type of bulk cargo to a wide range of ports. As such, they're likely to be familiar sights around the Great Lakes for years to come.

— Al Miller

Al Miller is author of the book "Tinstackers: The History of the Pittsburgh Steamship Co.," published by Wayne State University Press in 1999.

Philip R. Clarke, downbound on the St. Clair River. *(Bob Campbell)*

PASSAGES

Changes in the shipping scene since our last edition

Fleets & Vessels

The 1999 shipping season will be remembered for low water levels and reduced demand for commodities around the Great Lakes. The loss of one foot of water depth meant 3,240 tons less cargo carried per trip by a typical 1,000-footer, leading to more trips to make up the difference. The influx of imported steel products continued to depress the domestic market, with the corresponding outflow of grain in the same saltwater ships that brought the steel into the lakes reducing business for Great Lakes grain boats. In fleet activity, Algoma Central Corp. and Upper Lakes Group pooled their roster of vessels (21 self-unloaders and 22 straight deck bulk carriers) into one huge corporate unit, **Seaway Marine Transport**, early in January, 2000.

A rainy christening day for the new Saginaw. (Ryan Kinney)

The American Steamship Co.'s 1953-vintage self-unloader **John J. Boland** got a welcome new lease on life in late 1999, thanks to Lower Lakes Towing Co., of Port Dover, ON, which bought the idle steamer and placed her in service in December under the name **Saginaw**. Consequently, American Steamship Co. renamed its 1973-built **Charles E. Wilson** the **John J. Boland** early this spring. This is the fourth laker to bear that name.

Interlake's new tug-barge combination, **Dorothy** ▶

Tug Roger Stahl tows Saginaw into Sarnia. (Don Geske)

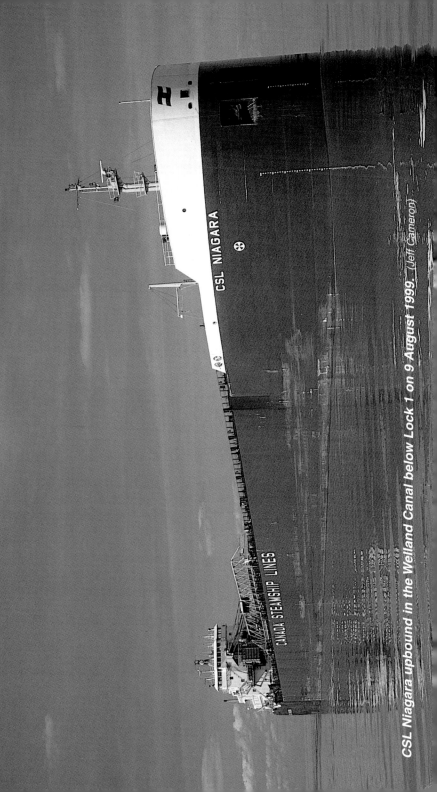

CSL Niagara upbound in the Welland Canal below Lock 1 on 9 August 1999. (Jeff Cameron)

The newly-named Southdown Challenger.
(Richard I. Weiss)

Ann/Pathfinder, was christened at Cleveland 28 June 1999 (see Vessel Spotlight, Page 24).

The former Medusa Cement vessels **Medusa Challenger** and **Medusa Conquest** were renamed **Southdown Challenger** and **Southdown Conquest** just after the 1999 shipping season began. The new names are a result of Medusa's 1998 sale to Southdown Inc.

Algoma Tankers renamed its 1999-acquired **Enerchem Catalyst** in late spring. The vessel, which saw only sporadic service in 1999, now sails as **Algocatalyst**. The **Enerchem Trader**, also acquired in the deal, is laid up with return to service unlikely, while **Enerchem Refiner** was sold for use on saltwater.

Construction Conversions Scrappings

The new, 740-foot self-unloading barge **Great Lakes Trader**, integrated with the tug **Joyce L. Van Enkevort**, enters service sometime this season. The Great Lakes Trader was built at the Halter Marine Group in Mississippi.

The 740' x 78' **CSL Niagara** was christened by Canada Steamship Lines 28 July 1999, the end result of a project that mated the aft end (engine room and accommodations) module of the fleet's **J.W. McGiffin** with an entirely new forebody built to take advantage of larger maximum dimensions on the St. Lawrence Seaway. The fleet's **H.M. Griffith** had similar surgery during the winter of 1999-2000, and resumes service under the name **Hon. Paul J. Martin** this season.

Canada Steamship Lines disposed of its 1965-built self-unloader **Tarantau** during 1999. She was towed up the Welland Canal to International Marine Salvage's scrapyard at Port Colborne at the end of October. The Tarantau last sailed in December 1996. Her demise leaves CSL with just one remaining steamer, **Halifax**.

▶

Retired self-unloader Tarantau is towed up the Welland Canal to a Port Colborne scrapyard. (Jeff Cameron)

Algoma Tankers' 1977-built **Algoeast** spent the winter of 1999-2000 having a new double bottom installed at Port Weller Drydocks, thus prolonging her career by many years

Lower Lakes Towing Co.'s 1943-built **Cuyahoga** had her historic (and problem-plagued) Lentz Poppet steam engine, last of its kind in service on the lakes, replaced over the winter with a new, 3,084 hp Caterpillar diesel engine. The operation is expected to add many years to the life of this classic laker.

Casualties

Low water around the Great Lakes lead to numerous groundings during the 1999 season. The most serious happened on 5 April 1999, when Algoma Central's **Algontario**, upbound with a load of about 19,000 tons of cement, struck a boulder in the lower St. Mary's River near Johnson's Point, incurring $1 million in damages. The vessel was taken to Thunder Bay, ON, where she was laid up. A decision on repairs is still pending.

On 6 April, the **Arthur M. Anderson**, outbound from Rogers City, MI, hit a rock in the channel. Repairs were made immediately at Sturgeon Bay, WI. **Jean Parisien** also required shipyard repairs at Thunder Bay after a 23 April grounding in the St. Mary's River.

Records

CSL Niagara loaded 29,707 metric tons of wheat (1,091,545 bushels) at Thunder Bay, 27 November 1999. This bests the previous record set by **Paterson** of 29,016 metric tons of the same commodity.

Lay-up Log

Edward L. Ryerson spent 1999 in idleness at Sturgeon Bay, WI, and remains tied up in 2000 as well. Rumors she will be converted to a self-unloader continue to circulate. The grain boat **Kinsman Enterprise** is still in use as a storage hull at Buffalo, NY, while the status of the long-idle **John Sherwin** remains unchanged at Superior, WI. The cement carrier **S.T. Crapo** is still laid up at Green Bay, WI, along with her former fleetmate **Lewis G. Harriman**. The 101-year-old **E.M. Ford** is still tied up as a cement storage hull at Saginaw, MI (hopes are high she may sail in 2000), while the retired cement carrier **J.B. Ford**, used for storage near Chicago the past several years, will be moved during 2000 to an as-yet-unnamed port. The long lay-up for the passenger liner **Aquarama** continues at Lackawanna, NY, while the historic, former Detroit River passenger steamers **Columbia** and **Ste. Claire** continue to deteriorate at Detroit. (Discussions in 1999 indicated Ste. Claire could become part of a waterfront development at Amherstburg, ON.). The intact hull of the former Inland Steel steamer **L.E. Block** is still sitting at Escanaba, MI, where she has been since 1981. The carferry **Viking** continues in idleness at Erie, PA; she was joined in 1999 by the former Detroit River carferry and restaurant **Lansdowne**. On the Canadian side, Paterson's **Comeaudoc** remains in reserve at Montreal, as do the **Vandoc** and **Quedoc** at Thunder Bay. **Algontario** is also at the Canadian lakehead, laid up there after a serious grounding last spring. The Maritime-class steamer **Willowglen** is still earning her keep as a grain storage hull at Goderich, ON, where she has been since 1993.

The latest John J. Boland at Duluth, shortly after renaming. (Patrick Lapinski)

DOROTHY ANN — PATHFINDER

Vessel Spotlight

With the crack of the traditional bottle of champagne, Interlake's new tug **Dorothy Ann** was christened at a ceremony in Cleveland, 28 June 1999. Susan Tregurtha Marshall, daughter of shipowner Paul R. Tregurtha, successfully broke the bottle on the tug's hull with one swing. Shortly after, April S. Barker, daughter of James R. Barker, repeated the task for the barge **Pathfinder**.

Dorothy Ann is the largest Z-drive tug built to date in North America. Her twin Ulstein Z-drives enable her to turn on her own axis, stop within her own length, and move easily in any direction. Alone, Dorothy Ann can travel at 16 mph; when pushing the loaded barge, open lake speed is 11.5 mph. She is fitted with a Great Lakes-specific, articulated pin-type connection system for engaging Pathfinder's notched stern. Dorothy Ann's elevated pilot house — outfitted with state-of-the-art navigation and communication equipment — has a height of 70 feet, with a vented tower designed to spoil trailing air drafts. Accommodations include air-conditioned private cabins with semi-private bathroom facilities for 12 crew members, a lounge and an owner's stateroom.

April S. Barker cracks the traditional champagne bottle across Pathfinder's bow. (Neil Schultheiss)

The namesake of Dorothy Ann is Dorothy Ann Tregurtha Croskey of Minneapolis, MN.

The Pathfinder is the former steam-powered Great Lakes bulk carrier **J.L. Mauthe**, built by Great Lakes Engineering Works, River Rouge, MI, in 1953. After 40 years of service in the Interlake Steamship fleet, she was idled in 1993. In January 1997, the Mauthe was towed to Bay Shipbuilding company for conversion to a self-unloading barge.

Designed by Northeast Technical Services Company, Inc., conversion involved eliminating forward cabins, removing propulsion machinery, replacing the original stern with a notch to accommodate the Dorothy Ann, and installing an automated unloading system that includes a 260-foot, aft-mounted unloading boom. Intended primarily to serve the bulk stone and aggregate trade, Pathfinder can easily handle a wide variety of bulk cargoes and material sizes.

Pathfinder loaded her first cargo at Escanaba on 12 March 1998, and has since become the largest tug-barge to transit Cleveland's Cuyahoga River. Her cargo capacity is 21,260 gross tons. She delivered 112 cargoes totaling nearly two million tons in 1998, her first season of operation.

— Neil Schultheiss

Dorothy Ann (left) and Pathfinder on christening day, 28 June 1999. (Neil Schultheiss)

GREAT LAKES GLOSSARY

AAA CLASS - New vessel design popular on the Great Lakes in the early 1950s. **Arthur M. Anderson** is one example.

AFT - Toward the back, or stern, of a ship.

AHEAD - Forward.

AMIDSHIPS - The middle point of a vessel, referring to either length or width.

ARTICULATED TUG-BARGE (or ATB) - Tug-barge combination. The two vessels are mechanically linked in one axis, but with the tug free to move, or articulate, on another axis. **Jacklyn M/Integrity** is one example.

BACKHAUL - The practice of carrying a revenue-producing cargo (rather than ballast) on a return trip from hauling a primary cargo.

BARGE - Vessel with no engine, either pushed or pulled by a tug.

BEAM - The width of a vessel measured at the widest point.

BILGE - The lowest part of a hold or compartment, generally where the rounded side of a ship curves from the keel to the vertical sides.

BOOMER - Great Lakes slang for self-unloader.

BOW - The front of a vessel.

BOWTHRUSTER - Propeller mounted transversely in a vessel's bow under the waterline to assist in moving sideways. A sternthruster may also be installed.

BRIDGE - The platform above the main deck from which a ship is steered or navigated. Also **PILOTHOUSE** or **WHEELHOUSE.**

BULKHEAD - A wall or partition that separates rooms, holds or tanks within the hull of a ship.

BULWARK - The part of the ship that extends fore and aft above the main deck to form a rail.

DEADWEIGHT TONNAGE - The actual carrying capacity of a vessel, equal to the difference between the light displacement tonnage and the heavy displacement tonnage, expressed in long tons (2,240 pounds or 1,016.1 kg).

DISPLACEMENT TONNAGE - The actual weight of the vessel and everything aboard her, measured in long tons. The displacement is equal to the weight of the water displaced by the vessel. Displacement tonnage may be qualified as light, indicating the weight of the vessel without cargo, fuels, stores; or heavy, indicating the weight of the vessel loaded with cargo, fuel and stores.

DRAFT - The depth of water a ship needs to float. Also the distance from keel to waterline.

FIT-OUT - The process of preparing a vessel for service after a period of inactivity.

FOOTER - Slang for 1,000-foot vessel.

FORECASTLE - (FOHK s'l) Area at the forward part of the ship and beneath the main cabins, often used for crew's quarters or storage.

FOREPEAK - The space below the forecastle.

FORWARD - Toward the front of an object on a ship.

FREEBOARD - The distance from the waterline to the main deck.

GROSS TONNAGE - The internal space of a vessel, measured in units of 100 cubic feet (2.83 cubic meters) = a gross ton.

HATCH - An opening in the deck through which cargo is lowered or raised. A hatch is closed by securing a hatch cover over it.

HOLD - The space below decks where cargo is stored.

HULL - The body of a ship, not including its superstructure, masts or machinery.

INBOARD - Toward the center of the ship.

INTEGRATED TUG-BARGE (or ITB) - Tug-barge combination in which the tug is rigidly mated to the barge. **Presque Isle** is one example.

JONES ACT - U.S. law that requires cargos moved between American ports to be carried by U.S. flag, U.S. built and U.S.-crewed vessels.

KEEL - A ship's steel backbone. It runs along the lowest part of the hull.

LAID UP - Out of service. Also: at the wall.

MARITIME CLASS - Style of lake vessel built during World War II as part of the nation's war effort. The **Richard Reiss** is one example.

NET REGISTERED TONNAGE - The internal capacity of a vessel available for carrying cargo. It does not include the space occupied by boilers, engines, shaft alleys, chain lockers, officers' and crew's quarters. Net registered tonnage is usually referred to as registered tonnage or net tonnage and is used to figure taxes, tolls and port charges.

PELLETS - See TACONITE.

PORT - The left side of the ship facing the bow.

RIVER-CLASS SELF-UNLOADER - Group of vessels built in the '70s to service smaller ports and negotiate narrow rivers such as Cleveland's Cuyahoga. **David Z. Norton** is one example.

SELF-UNLOADER - Vessel able to discharge its own cargo using a system of conveyor belts and a moveable boom.

STARBOARD - The right side of the ship facing forward.

STEM - The extreme forward end of the bow.

STERN - The back of the ship.

STRAIGHT-DECKER - A non-self-unloading vessel. **Edward L. Ryerson** is one example.

TACONITE - Processed, pelletized iron ore. Easy to load and unload, this is the primary method of shipping ore on the Great Lakes and St. Lawrence Seaway.

TRACTOR TUG - Newer style of highly maneuverable tug propelled by either a z-drive or cycloidal system rather than the traditional screw propeller.

Vessel Index

Edward L. Ryerson
departs Marquette
on 27 April 1997.

(Richard I. Weiss)

Vessel Name / Fleet Number	Vessel Name / Fleet Number	Vessel Name / Fleet Number
APJ Angad IS-33	Armada Trader IP-1	Bagotville..........C-6
APJ Anjli IS-33	Armco..........O-3	Baker, M. H. III..........C-38
APJ Karan IS-33	Armonikos IS-6	Bakradze..........IG-4
APJ Sushma..........IS-33	Arosa IS-16	Balaban I IE-5
APL France..........IP-1	Arosette..........IC-5	Baldy B. S-7
APL Germany..........IP-1	Artaki IM-6	Balkan IN-6
APL Indonesia..........IP-1	Artisgracht IS-28	Baltia IO-5
Apollo C IS-10	Asher, Chas...........R-5	Baltic Confidence..........IV-6
Apollogracht IS-28	Asher, John R. R-5	Baltic Sif IK-2
Appledore B-7	Asher, Stephen M. R-5	Baltic Trader IH-10
Aptmariner..........IC-12	Aslan-1 ....IA-11	Baltimar Boreas..........IB-4
Aquatique IA-7	Aspen U-4	Baltimar Euros..........IB-4
Arabella IA-12	Asta..........IL-5	Baltimar Notos..........IB-4
Arabian Express..........ID-1	Astrea IF-6	Baltimar Orion IB-4
Aramae..........IP-1	Astron IP-6	Baltimar Saturn IB-4
Arcadia IH-8	Athinais P IC-16	Baltimar Sirius IB-4
Archangelgracht IS-28	Atkinson, Arthur K...........C-30	Baltimar Venus IB-4
Arctic..........F-4	ATL 2301..........I-8	Barbara Ann {1}..........A-9
Arctic Kalvik..........F-4	ATL 2302..........I-8	Barbara Rita A-14
Arctic Viking..........C-1	ATL 2401..........I-8	Barbarossa IM-8
Arethusa IS-16	ATL 2402..........I-8	Barentzgracht IS-28
Argonaut..........IS-26	Atlantic Adler..........I-8	Barker, James R. I-6
Argut IF-4	Atlantic Beech I-8	Barker, Kaye E...........I-6
Ariel..........J-1	Atlantic Birch..........I-8	Barry J..........K-7
Arion IW-1	Atlantic Cedar I-8	Basse-Cote L-11
Aristotelis..........IA-12	Atlantic Elm..........I-8	Bataafgracht IS-28
Arizona..........G-16	Atlantic Erie C-3	Batna IS-23
Arkansas {2}..........G-16	Atlantic Freighter..........M-8	Bayfield M-3
Arktis Atlantic IE-2	Atlantic Hemlock I-8	Bayfield..........MU-3
Arktis Blue IE-2	Atlantic Hickory G-22	Bayship B-6
Arktis Breeze IE-2	Atlantic Huron {2}..........C-3	Beaver A-17, U-7
Arktis Carrier IE-2	Atlantic Maple I-8	Beaver D. M-19
Arktis Crystal IE-2	Atlantic Oak I-8	Beaver Islander B-9
Arktis Dream IE-2	Atlantic Poplar..........I-8	Becky E. E-6
Arktis Fantasy..........IE-2	Atlantic Spruce {2}..........I-8	Bee Jay G-3
Arktis Fighter..........IE-2	Atlantic Teak..........I-8	Beeghly, Charles M...........I-6
Arktis Future..........IE-2	Atlantic Willow..........I-8	Beluga IL-4
Arktis Grace..........IE-2	Atlantis Charm..........IA-13	Beluga Obsession IB-6
Arktis Hope..........IE-2	Atlantis Joy IA-13	Beluga Performer IB-6
Arktis Hunter IE-2	Atlantis Spirit IA-13	Bergen Bay IB-7
Arktis Light IE-2	Atlas G-17	Bergen Sea IB-7
Arktis Mariner IE-2	Atlas IA-9	Bergon IB-2
Arktis Mayflower IE-2	Atlasgracht IS-28	Bert, Donald..........M-2
Arktis Meadow..........IE-2	Atomic..........M-19	Betsiamites L-11
Arktis Meridian IE-2	Atria IH-3	Betty D...........D-14
Arktis Mirage IE-2	Attica ID-8	Beursgracht IS-28
Arktis Mistral IE-2	Atticos IR-7	Bge 6704 ....S-24
Arktis Ocean IE-2	Audacious..........IP-17	Bickersgracht IS-28
Arktis Pearl IE-2	Auriga IA-7	Bide-A-Wee {3}..........S-18
Arktis Pride IE-2	Aurora IO-2	Bigane, Jos. F. B-12
Arktis Princess IE-2	Aurora Borealis C-27	Bilice..........IS-21
Arktis Queen IE-2	Aurora Gold IA-15	Billie M. M-19
Arktis River IE-2	Aurora Jade IA-15	Billmaier, D. L. U-3
Arktis Sea IE-2	Aurora Topaz IA-15	Biograd IS-21
Arktis Sirius IE-2	Avantage T-6	Birthe Boye..........IH-11
Arktis Sky IE-2	Avdeevka IA-16	Biscayne Bay..........U-4
Arktis Spring IE-2	Avenger IV P-14	Bison IS-24
Arktis Star..........IE-2	Ayse Ana IA-3	Bittern C-5
Arktis Sun IE-2		Bizerte IC-18
Arktis Trader IE-2	**B**	Black Carrier M-19
Arktis Venture IE-2	Baalbeck IL-3	Black, Martha L. C-5
Arktis Vision..........IE-2	Badger [43] {2}..........L-2	Blackie B. G-1

29

Vessel Name / Fleet Number	Vessel Name / Fleet Number	Vessel Name / Fleet Number
Blake, Henry........................U-4	Canadian Enterprise......U-15/S-5	Cavalier Maxim C-33
Block, Jospeh L...................C-13	Canadian Leader..........U-15/S-5	Cavalier Royal C-33
Block, L. E. B-2	Canadian Mariner........U-15/S-5	Cay.....................................IN-1
Bloemgracht IS-28	Canadian Miner U-15/S-5	Celebrezze, Anthony J. C-24
Blough, Roger U-18	Canadian Navigator......U-15/S-5	Celtic Sif IK-2
Blue Bay IS-17	Canadian Olympic U-15/S-5	Cemba..................................D-4
Blue Heron U-11	Canadian Pioneer.................A-4	CG 119.................................C-5
Blue Heron V B-16	Canadian Progress.......U-15/S-5	CGB-12000 ....U-4
Blue Lagoon IS-17	Canadian Prospector.....U-15/S-5	CGB-12001 ....U-4
Blue Marine IS-17	Canadian Provider........U-15/S-5	CGR-100 ....C-5
Blue Moon IC-3	Canadian Ranger U-15/S-5	Chada Naree........................IG-11
Blue Moon IS-17	Canadian Trader U-15/S-5	Challenge.............................G-20
Bluebill IM-1	Canadian Transfer U-15/S-5	Chalothorn Naree IG-11
Boatman No. 3 ....M-19	Canadian Transport {2}.U-15/S-5	Champion {1} C-14
Boatman No. 4 ....M-19	Canadian Venture U-15/S-5	Champion {3} D-14
Boatman No. 6 ....M-19	Canadian Voyager U-15/S-5	Charlevoix {1}......................C-15
Bob Lo Islander I-10	Canadiana MU-23	Chavchavadze......................IG-4
Bol IS-29	Canmar Bravery IC-1	Cheetah IV-1
Boland, John J....................A-13	Canmar Conquest................IC-1	Chelsea Bridge IV-1
Bolder IA-7	Canmar Courage..................IC-1	Chembulk Fortitude IM-2
Bontegracht IS-28	Canmar Fortune IC-1	Chembulk Singapore IM-2
Bounty V-5	Canmar Glory.......................IC-1	Cheraw.................................U-3
Boyd, David.........................G-21	Canmar Honour IC-1	Cheremkhovo IF-4
Boyer, Willis B....................MU17	Canmar Pride IC-1	Cherokee {2} B-1
Bramble U-4	Canmar Spirit IC-1	Cherokee {3}.......................L-3
Brandon E. C-31	Canmar Triumph...................IC-1	Cheryl C IC-4
Bray, James M.....................U-3	Canmar Valour IC-1	Chetek.................................U-3
Bremon IB-2	Canmar Venture IC-1	Chicago II.............................C-16
Brenda L..............................F-6	Canmar Victory IC-1	Chicago Peace......................I-1
Bribir...................................IC-22	Cantankerous E-11	Chicago's First Lady M-22
Bristol Bay U-4	Cap Aux Meules...................C-5	Chicago's Little Lady...........M-22
Brochu F-4	Cap Goelands C-5	Chi-Cheemaun.....................O-8
Brown, John W. P-13	Cape Confidence IH-4	Chief Shingwauk..................L-13
Brunto IW-3	Cape Hurd............................C-5	Chief Wawatam P-14
Buccaneer W-1	Cape Kennedy IC-2	Chios Charity IH-6
Buckeye {3}.........................O-3	Cape Syros IC-2	Chios Charm IH-6
Buckley K-6	Capetan Michalis..................IU-2	Chios Glory IH-6
Buckthorn U-4	Capt. Roy.............................B-20	Chios Harmony IH-6
Buffalo U-3	Capt. Shepler.......................S-12	Chios Pride IH-6
Buffalo {3}...........................A-13	Captain Barnaby...................K-1	Chios Spirit IH-6
Bunyan, Paul U-3	Captain Christos IG-1	Chippewa {5}.......................G-8
Burns Harbor {2} B-11	Captain George F-8	Chippewa {6} A-17
Burro M-7	Carey, Emmet J....................O-7	Chris Ann H-9
Burton, Courtney..................O-3	Cargo Carrier #1 ....M-19	Christiaan IA-7
Busch, Gregory J. B-23	Cargo Carrier #2.................M-19	Cicero C-23
Busse, Fred A. C-18	Cargo Master M-19	Cisco U-5
Buzet IC-22	Caribbean Express I ID-1	City of Algonac.....................D-1
	Caribou M-8	City of Milwaukee...............MU-25
C	Caribou Isle C-5	Clarke, Philip R. U-18
c. Columbus IH-5	Carl M..................................C-11	Clifford, A. E. S-15
C.T.C. No.1 ....S-19	Carl Metz IL-3	Clinton C-26
Cabot...................................C-23	Carleton, George N.............G-14	Clipper Adventurer N-7
Cadillac {5}.........................S-25	Caro IO-5	Clipper Amaryllis IP-17
Calanus II............................C-5	Carol Ann K-7	Clipper Antares....................IP-17
Calcite II..............................U-18	Carola I.................................IH-2	Clipper Arita.........................ID-8
California G-16	Carolyn Jo N-2	Clipper Atlantic....................IM-10
Callaway, Cason J. U-18	Carroll Jean A-9	Clipper Cheyenne IC-20
Calliope IA-5	Cartier, Jacques C-35	Clipper Cowbridge IG-10
Calliroe Patronicola..............IO-4	Cartierdoc {2}......................N-1	Clipper Eagle IP-10
Canadian.............................C-11	Catherine-Legardeur S-16	Clipper Falcon IP-10
Canadian Century U-15/S-6	Cavalier.................................M-19	Clipper Fidelity.....................IS-4
Canadian Challenger.............A-4	Cavalier des Mers C-33	Clipper Mandarin..................ID-8
Canadian Empress...............S-22	Cavalier Grand Fleuve C-33	Clipper Odyssey....................N-7

CANADIAN LEADER

Vessel Spotlight

When the **Canadian Leader** was launched in in 1967, few knew the vessel was making history. Built by the famous, now closed, Collingwood Shipyards in Collingwood, ON, this traditional-styled Seaway-sized straight-decker was the last Great Lakes vessel launched with steam propulsion.

CANADIAN LEADER	
Length	730'
Beam	75'
Depth	39'08"
Built	1967
Tonnage	28,300

Built as **Feux-Follets** (meaning Will of the Wisp) for Papachristidis Co, Ltd. of Montreal, QC, the vessel entered service 12 October 1967. She is powered by a Canadian General Electric 9,000 horsepower steam turbine engine. Her 17 hatches feed into 6 holds, which can carry 28,300 tons at a maximum St. Lawrence Seaway draft of 26 feet.

Sailing as a unit of the Papachristidis fleet, the majority of the vessel's cargos consisted of grain from lakehead ports to elevators along the St. Lawrence River, and backhauls of iron ore from Gulf of St. Lawrence ports to American steel companies. In 1972, she was bought by Upper Lakes Shipping (now Upper Lakes Group) and renamed Canadian Leader.

Now sailing as a part of Seaway Marine Transport (partnership of Algoma Central and Upper Lakes Group), the Canadian Leader is active in the grain and iron ore trades. A grounding in 1998 due to steering gear failure didn't sideline this handsome steamer; she was immediately repaired and returned to duty. As with other vessels of her kind, Canadian Leader is subject to periodic lay-ups due to changing demands in the grain industry.

— *Rod Burdick*

Canadian Leader, the last steamer built for Seaway service, upbound in the St. Mary's River, 28 June 1999. (Roger LeLievre)

Vessel Name / Fleet Number	Vessel Name / Fleet Number	Vessel Name / Fleet Number
Clipper Pacific IM-10		Dongeborg...........................IW-1
Clipper Spirit IC-13	**D**	Donner, William H. G-23
Clipper Westoe..................IG-10	Da Hua IC-12	Dora....................................IA-5
Cloud Chaser H-12	Daan IA-7	Dorothy Ann I-6
Clyde....................................M-9	Daldean B-18	Dover M-2
CMBT Esprit..........................IT-4	Dali IR-6	Dover Light...........................G-19
Coastal Cruiser T-7	Dalmig...................................D-2	Drnis....................................IS-21
Cobb, George......................U-4	Danah IW-2	Drummond Islander...............E-2
Cobia..............................MU-30	Danicia..................................B-2	Drummond Islander II M-1
Cod...................................MU-6	Daniel E................................E-6	Drummond Islander III..........E-2
Cohen, Wilfred M.................P-14	Daniella IJ-12	Drummond Islander IV E-2
Coleman B-13	Danis Koper.........................IS-32	DS Pioneer..........................ID-2
Colinette..............................M-19	Darya Devi IC-9	Duc d' Orleans D-13
Colombe, J. E.....................U-7	Darya Kamal IC-9	Duchess V............................M-19
Colorado G-16	Darya Ma IC-9	Duden..................................IS-25
Columbia {2} MU-26	Dauntless.............................M-20	Dufresne M-58.....................M-19
Columbia Star O-3	Daviken IT-3	Duga.....................................T-6
Comeaudoc..........................N-1	Davitaja IG-4	Duluth B-13, U-3
Commuter N-5	Dawnlight C-10	Durmitor IJ-10
Comorant F-3	DC 710 ....D-12	Durocher, Ray D-14
Compaen..............................IA-7	Dean, Americo D-6	Dynamic J-1
Concord...............................IB-2	Dean, Annie M. D-6	Dzintari..................................IL-1
Concorde.............................IS-20	Dean, Wayne D-6	
Concordia.............................IO-5	Debbie Lyn...........................M-2	**E**
Confederation {2} N-9	Deer Lake.............................A-5	E. P. Le Quebecois C-5
Connie E..............................M-19	Defiance A-12	E-63.....................................D-12
Conny IS-8	Delaware {4} G-16	Eagle IC-14
Consensus Manitou ID-4	Denise E...............................E-6	Eagle Island.........................A-16
Constructor...........................D-11	Dennis Danielsen IN-2	Eagle Quick IP-17
Containerships III IH-3	Derek E................................E-6	Eber......................................IS-25
Containerships IV.................IH-3	Derrick No. 4 ....R-7	Echo Pioneer........................IA-1
Containerships V IH-3	Des Groseilliers C-5	Eclipse..................................N-3
Contship Endeavour.............IC-1	Des Plaines..........................C-2	Edamgracht IS-28
Contship Success IC-1	Deschenes, Jos....................S-16	Edda.....................................IH-10
Cooper, J. W. C-32	Desgagnes, Amelia T-13	Eddie Mac I B-3
Cooper, Wyn M-19	Desgagnes, Anna T-13	Edelweiss I E-3
Corithian Trader....................IT-2	Desgagnes, Catherine T-13	Edelweiss II E-3
Cornelius, Adam E. {4}.........A-13	Desgagnes, Cecelia T-13	Edisongracht IS-28
Corner Brook........................IB-2	Desgagnes, Jacques.............T-13	Edith J. E-4
Cornett, J. A. H-7	Desgagnes, Maria T-13	Edna G. MU-12
Corsair..................................A-17	Desgagnes, Mathilda T-13	Eemsgracht IS-28
Cort, Stewart J. B-11	Desgagnes, Melissa..............T-13	Eemshorn IA-7
Costesti IC-19	Desgagnes, Petrolia..............T-13	Egbert Wagenborg IW-1
Cotter, Edwin M....................B-22	Desgagnes, Thalassa T-13	Egelantiersgracht IS-28
Coulet, Louis J......................P-2	Desmarais, Louis R...............C-3	Egmondgracht IS-28
Courtney-O...........................B-19	Detroit {1}.............................N-8	Eighth Sea............................S-24
Cove Isle C-5	Diamant IA-7	Eileen C I-1
Crapo, S. T. I-4	Diamond Belle.......................D-9	El Kef...................................IC-18
Credo...................................IR-2	Diamond Jack D-9	Elandsgracht IS-28
Creed, Frederick G................C-5	Diamond Queen D-9	Eleanor R. C-8
Crio IO-5	Diamond Star R-3	Elena G IP-15
Croaker................................MU-2	Dilmuan Shearwater..............ID-6	Elikon IH-8
Crow E-6	Dilmun Fulmar......................ID-6	Elisabeth Boye IH-11
Crystal-O..............................B-19	Dilmun Tern ID-6	Elisabeth Clipper...................IJ-11
CSL Atlas C-38	Dimitra..................................IG-1	Elisabeth G...........................IA-7
CSL Cabo..............................C-38	Dinara..................................IS-21	Elise Oldendorff....................IE-1
CSL Niagara..........................C-3	Dintelborg IW-1	Elite B IB-5
CSL Trailblazer C-38	Dmitriy Donskoi....................IM-12	Elizabeth C...........................IC-4
CSL Trillium...........................M-19	Dmitriy Pozharskiy IM-12	Ellen Knutsen IK-4
Curly B. L-3	Dobrush...............................IA-16	Ellinis P. IC-16
Cuyahoga L-14	Dona.....................................A-3	Elm......................................ID-5
Cygnus IS-19	Donald Mac...........................G-14	Elmglen {2} L-11
Cypress U-4	Donaustern...........................IR-8	Elpida...................................IH-6

Charles M. Beeghly unloads at South Chicago. (Gary R. Clark)

TOP: *German passenger liner c. Columbus, as seen from its shore tender, at anchor off Manitoulin Island.* BOTTOM: *Morning on the Detroit River from Columbus' deck. The Ambassador Bridge, between Detroit and Windsor, is at right.* (Roger LeLievre)

Vessel Name / Fleet Number	Vessel Name / Fleet Number	Vessel Name / Fleet Number
Marysville...............................G-1	Millenium Eagle IM-10	Mott, Charlie...........................U-7
Massachusetts....................G-16	Millenium Falcon.................IM-10	Mountain Blossom.................L-8
Matador VI.............................K-3	Millenium Golden Hind.......IM-10	Mr. Micky...............................H-1
Mather, William G. {2}........MU-8	Millenium Harmony.............IM-10	Mrs. C.................................C-32
Mathilde Oldendorff..............IE-1	Millenium Hawk...................IM-10	MSC Boston.........................IG-2
MBT 10................................M-24	Millenium Leader................IM-10	MSC Houston.......................IG-2
MBT 20................................M-24	Millenium Majestic..............IM-10	MSC New York......................IG-3
MBT 33................................M-24	Millenium Osprey................IM-10	Multiflex Brisk......................IP-17
McAllister 132........................A-2	Millenium Raptor.................IM-10	Multiflex Dart.......................IP-17
McAllister 252......................M-19	Millenium Yama...................IM-10	Multiflex Thrust....................IP-17
McAllister No. 3....................L-11	Milroy, Phil............................F-6	Munksund............................IG-12
McAllister No. 50..................L-11	Milwaukee Clipper...............MU-5	Munson, John G. {2}..........U-18
McAllister, Cathy..................L-11	Mimer...................................IG-5	Munteborg...........................IW-1
McAllister, Daniel.................MU-1	Mina Cebi..............................IP-5	Murray R................................F-6
McAsphalt 401.....................M-17	Miners Castle.........................P-6	Muskegon {2}........................K-7
McBride, Sam.......................T-12	Mini Lace.............................IC-7	Musky II.................................U-5
McCarthy, Walter J. Jr..........A-13	Mini Star..............................IG-5	Musselborg..........................IW-1
McCauley..............................U-3	Miniforest.............................IG-5	
McGrath, James E...............U-15	Minka C...............................IC-4	**N**
McGuirl, May.........................R-2	Minnesota {1}......................G-16	Nadro Clipper........................N-2
McKee Sons.........................U-14	Miseford................................N-2	Nancy Ann...........................M-12
McKeil, Doug {2}.................M-19	Mishe-Mokwa.........................M-6	Nancy Anne..........................D-14
McKeil, Evans......................M-19	Miska...................................IA-7	Nanook.................................L-11
McKeil, Florence..................M-19	Miss Brockville......................U-13	Nanticoke..............................C-3
McKeil, Jarrett.....................M-19	Miss Brockville IV.................U-13	Nantucket Clipper..................N-7
McKeil, Wyatt......................M-19	Miss Brockville V..................U-13	Narragansett........................IB-3
McKeller...............................P-14	Miss Brockville VI.................U-13	Nathan S.............................M-10
McLane.............................MU-29	Miss Brockville VII................U-13	Nautica Queen.......................J-3
Meagan Beth.......................D-14	Miss Brockville VIII...............U-13	Navcomar #1........................L-11
Mecta Sea.............................IE-3	Miss Buffalo........................B-21	Navigo..................................IR-2
Med Glory..............................IT-1	Miss Buffalo II.....................B-21	Nea Doxa.............................IF-2
Med Transporter...................IS-25	Miss Edna..............................K-7	Nea Elpis..............................IF-2
Mede.....................................L-11	Miss Ivy Lea II.......................I-11	Nea Tyhi...............................IF-2
Medill, Joseph {2}................C-17	Miss Ivy Lea III......................I-11	Neah Bay...............................U-4
Mekhanik Aniskin.................IA-16	Miss Midland..........................P-4	Nebraska.............................G-16
Melkki...................................IN-8	Miss Munising......................S-13	Necat A................................ID-3
Menasha {2}.........................M-21	Miss Olympia........................C-33	Nedlloyd Africa......................IP-1
Menier Consol........................T-9	Miss Shawn Simpson..........M-19	Nedlloyd America...................IP-1
Menominee..........................IG-12	Miss Superior.........................P-6	Nedlloyd Asia........................IP-1
Mervine II.............................C-22	Mississippi...........................G-16	Nedlloyd Clarence.................IP-1
Merweborg............................IW-1	Missouri {2}.........................G-16	Nedlloyd Clement..................IP-1
Mesabi Miner..........................I-6	Misty.....................................IN-4	Nedlloyd Colombo..................IP-1
Meta.....................................IO-5	Mitsa.....................................IE-8	Nedlloyd Dejima....................IP-1
Metauro................................IM-8	Mljet....................................IA-14	Nedlloyd Delft.......................IP-1
Meteor...............................MU-24	Mobile Bay............................U-4	Nedlloyd Europa....................IP-1
Metis....................................U-15	Moby Dick..............................S-7	Nedlloyd Hongkong................IP-1
Mette Clipper.........................IJ-11	Moezelborg...........................IW-1	Nedlloyd Honshu...................IP-1
Metz Beirut............................IL-3	Mohamed S...........................IS-3	Nedlloyd Hoorn......................IP-1
Metz Italia.............................IL-3	Mona S.................................IS-3	Nedlloyd Marne.....................IP-1
Michigan...............................U-3	Montana...............................G-16	Nedlloyd Musi.......................IP-1
Michigan {10}........................K-5	Montmagny............................C-5	Nedlloyd Oceania..................IP-1
Michiganborg.........................IW-1	Montrealais....................U-15/S-5	Neebish Islander..................C-25
Middle Channel.....................C-14	Moor Laker...........................IV-4	Neebish Islander II................E-2
Middletown............................O-3	Moore, Olive M.....................U-14	Nelvana...............................U-15
Midstate I...............................S-4	Morgan.................................K-6	Nelvana {1}...........................N-4
Midstate II..............................S-4	Morgenstond.........................IA-7	Nememcha...........................IS-23
Mikhail Kutuzov...................IM-12	Morillo...................................IG-3	Nenufar Atlantico..................IH-7
Mikhail Strekalovskiy...........IM-12	Morraborg.............................IW-1	Neptune...............................H-13
Milanos.................................IE-6	Morris, George.......................R-2	Neptune III...........................D-6
Milin Kamak..........................IN-6	Morton Salt 74.....................M-26	Nereis P...............................IC-16
Millenium Amethyst.............IM-10	Moscenice...........................IC-22	Neva Trader..........................IB-2
Millenium Condor................IM-10	Motovun...............................IC-22	New Jersey..........................G-16

The 1921-built Kinsman Enterprise continues in her role as a grain storage hull at Buffalo. (Bob Campbell)

Tug Lac Como, at work in the Welland Canal. (John C. Meyland)

Vessel Name / Fleet Number		
Queng #1 ....L-11	Risnes ID-9	Scan Pacific IH-7
Quo-Vadis....................IA-7	Rixta Oldendorff IE-1	Scan Partner........................IH-7
	Riza Sonay IB-8	Scan Polaris IS-7
R	Roanoke {2}.......................M-15	Scandrett, Fred T-11
R. Dedeoglu...................IS-32	Robert H. T-6	Scarab................................ID-7
R.C. L. No. 1 ....C-6	Robert John G-14	Schlaegar, Victor L.............C-17
Rab..........................IC-22	Robert W. T-7	Schwartz, H. J. U-3
Raby S.......................IS-3	Robin E.............................E-6	Sea Castle M-11
Raby S.......................IS-2	Robinson Bay S-24	Sea Eagle............................IB-13
Rachel B......................H-8	Rocket P-14	Sea Eagle II.........................B-15
Racine U-3	Rockland R-2	Sea Flower IF-1
Radisson {1}..................S-16	Rodin S-26	Sea Fox II..............................S-3
Radisson {2}..................S-25	Rollnes ID-9	Sea Lily................................IS-3
Radisson, Pierre...............C-5	Roman, Stephen B..............U-15	Sea Maid IF-1
Radnor IC-2	Rong Cheng......................IC-12	Sea Queen II A-16
Rafnes ID-9	Rong Jiang........................IC-12	Sea Rose.............................IF-1
Ragna Gorthon IG-8	Rosalee D. T-7	Sea Wolf...............................C-2
Railship I.....................IF-6	Rose Islands.......................IV-5	Seabourn Legend C-39
Randolph, Curtis D-8	Rosemary M-14	Seabourn Pride C-39
Ranger III....................U-7	Rossel Current IS-21	Seabourn Spirit C-39
Rankki IN-8	Rothnie...............................IS-4	Seaflight I..............................C-27
Rasa IL-5	Rubin Eagle........................IN-9	Seaflight II............................C-27
Raymond, Jean...............M-19	Rubin Falcon IN-9	Seaflight III...........................C-27
Rebecca Lynn A-14	Rubin Halcyon IN-9	Seaflight IV...........................C-27
Redestos.....................IM-6	Rubin Hawk........................IN-9	Seaglory...............................ID-11
Regina Oldendorff.............IE-1	Rubin Lark..........................IN-9	Seal VII................................I-8
Reinaauer, Austin..............R-2	Rubin Stork IN-9	Sealink................................IT-8
Reinauer, Bert II...............R-2	Ruder Boskovic IA-14	Sealion VII............................I-8
Reinauer, Curtis R-2	Rugia..................................IO-5	Sealuck V IT-8
Reinauer, Dace R-2	Runner B IB-5	Searanger II IT-8
Reinauer, Dean R-2	Ryerson, Edward L..............C-13	Seaway Queen U-15/S-5
Reinauer, Franklin R-2		Seba M................................IR-1
Reinauer, Janice Ann.........R-2	**S**	Sedoy..................................IG-4
Reinauer, Jill..................R-2	S. M. Spiridon IS-17	Segwun..............................M-27
Reinauer, Jo Anne III R-2	S.M.T.B. No. 7 ....G-19	Selvick, Bonnie G. S-7
Reinauer, John R-2	Sac Flix..............................IE-6	Selvick, Carla Anne..............S-7
Reinauer, Juliet R-2	Sac Huelva IE-6	Selvick, Sharon M. S-7
Reinauer, Kristy Ann R-2	Sac Malaga IE-6	Selvick, William C. S-7
Reinauer, Morgan.............R-2	Sackville MU-28	Seneca B-13
Reinauer, Stephen R-2	Sacre Bleu.........................S-12	Sentinelle II C-33
Reinauer, Zachery.............R-2	Saginaw L-14	Sentinelle III C-33
Reiss MU-21	Sagittarius IS-19	Sentinelle IV..........................C-33
Reiss, Richard E-12	Sakura ID-8	Sentinelle V C-33
Relief.........................R-7	Salty Dog No. 1 ....M-19	Sequoia U-4
Rennie, Thomas...............T-12	Salvage Monarch.................L-11	Serenade IM-11
Reserve......................O-3	Sàlvage Scow No. 1.............L-11	Serendipity Princess P-4
Resolute D-7	Sammi Aurora IP-4	Sevilla Wave.........................IT-8
Rest, William T-11	Sammi Herald......................IP-4	Shamrock {1} J-6
Retriever M-13	Samson II D-14	Shannon..............................G-1
Rhea G-6	San Juan C-4	Shannon...............................IC-2
Rhea IF-7	San Marino.........................IR-3	Shannon 66-5 ....T-5
Rhein Master.................IH-7	Sand Pebble D-5	Shark..................................C-5
Rheinstern....................IR-8	Sandpiper H-5	Shark VII..............................I-8
Rheintal IH-7	Sandy Graham.....................I-10	Sharon Jon S-15
Rhode Island.................G-16	Sapanca IS-25	Sheila P...............................P-14
Richmond R-2	Saturn {4}...........................A-7	Shelter Bay...........................U-3
Richter, C. G. W-2	Sault au Couchon M-19	Sherwin, John {2} I-6
Rickey, James W. D-11	Sauniere A-7	Shipka IN-6
Ridgeway, Benjamin..........I-3	Savard, Joseph S-16	Shirley Irene K-4
Rijeka IC-22	Scan Arctic IS-7	Shirley Joy L-3
Riot II........................U-1	Scan Atlantic IS-7	Shoreline II S-14
Risley, Samuel................C-5	Scan Bothnia IS-7	Showboat Mardi Gras H-6

The Bulgarian-registered *Malyovitza* off Port Weller piers, entering the Welland Canal. *(Jeff Cameron)*

Fleet & Vessel Listings

Canadian Transfer in the lower St. Mary's River, 30 June 1999. (Roger LeLievre)

U.S. & CANADIAN FLEETS

Listed after each vessel in order are; Type of Vessel, Year Built, Type of Engine, Cargo Capacity (at mid-summer draft in long tons) or Gross Tonnage* (tanker capacities are listed in barrels), Overall Length, Breadth and Depth (from the top of the keel to the top of the upper deck beam) or Draft*. The figures given are as accurate as possible and are given for informational purposes only. Vessels and owners are listed alphabetically as per American Bureau of Shipping and Lloyd's Register of Shipping format. Former names of vessels and years of operation under former names appear beneath the vessel's name.

For your convenience, the following abbreviations have been used.

TYPE OF VESSEL

AC ......Auto Carrier	**GA** ....Gambling Casino	**RR** ....Roll On/Roll Off
AV ......Air Cushion Vessel	**GC** ....General Cargo	**RT** ....Refueling Tanker
BB ......Bum Boat	**GL** ....Gate Lifter	**RV** ....Research Vessel
BC ......Bulk Carrier	**GU** ....Grain Self Unloader	**SB** ....Supply Boat
BK .....Bulk Carrier/Tanker	**HL** ....Heavy Lift Vessel	**SC** ....Sand Carrier
BT ......Buoy Tender	**HY** ....Hydrofoil	**SR** ....Search & Rescue
CC .....Cement Carrier	**IB** ....Ice Breaker	**SS** ....Submarine
CF ......Car Ferry	**KO** ....Corvette	**SU** ....Self Unloader
CLG ...Guided Missile Cruiser	**LS** ....Lightship	**SV** ....Survey Vessel
CS .....Crane Ship	**LT** ....Lighthouse Tender	**TB** ....Tug Boat
DB ......Deck Barge	**MB** ....Mail Boat	**TBA** ......Articulated Tug Boat
DD .....Destroyer	**MS** ....Mine Sweeper	**TF** ....Train Ferry
DR ......Dredge	**PA** ....Passenger Vessel	**TK** ....Tanker
DV .....Drilling Vessel	**PB** ....Pilot Boat	**TT** ....Tractor Tug Boat
ES .....Excursion Ship	**PC** ....Passenger Catamaran	**TV** ....Training Vessel
EV ......Env. Response Ship	**PF** ....Passenger Ferry	**WM** ....Medium Endurance Cutter
FB ......Fire Boat	**PK** ....Package Freighter	**2B** ....Brigantine
FD ......Floating Dry Dock	**PT** ....Patrol Torpedo Boat	**2S** ....2 Masted Schooner
FF......Frigate		**3S** ....3 Masted Schooner

PROPULSION

B .... Barge	**R** .... Steam - Triple Exp. Compound Engine
D .... Diesel	**S** .... Steam - Skinner "Unaflow" Engine
V .... Batteries	**T** .... Steam - Turbine
W .... Sailing Vessel	**U** .... Steam - Uniflow Engine - "Skinner" Design

Fleet #	Fleet Name Vessel Name	Type of Vessel	Year Built	Type of Engine	Cargo Cap. or Gross*	Overal Length	Breadth	Depth or Draft*
A-1	**A & L MARINE, INC., ST. JOSEPH, MI**							
	Margaret M.	TB	1956	D	167*	89' 06"	24' 00"	10' 00"
	(Shuttler '56 - '60, Margaret M. Hannah '60 - '84)							
A-2	**A .B. M. MARINE, THUNDER BAY, ON**							
	McAllister 132	DB	1954	B	7,000	343' 00"	63' 00"	19' 00"
	W. N. Twolan	TB	1962	D	299*	106' 00"	29' 05"	15' 00"
A-3	**ACME MARINE SERVICE, KNIFE RIVER, MN**							
	Dona	SB	1929	D	10*	35' 00"	9' 00"	4' 06"
	Marine Supplier	BB	1950	D	38*	57' 08"	15' 00"	7' 01"
	Marine Trader	BB	1939	D	60*	65' 00"	15' 00"	7' 06"
	Oatka	TB	1934	D	10*	40' 00"	10' 00"	4' 06"
	Trio	TB	1945	D	13*	38' 00"	11' 00"	4' 03"
A-4	**ADECON SHIPPING, INC., MISSISSAUGA, ON**							
	Canadian Challenger	GC	1976	D	15,061	462' 07"	67' 02"	38' 06"
	(Ajana '76 - '80, Calixto Garcia '80 - '95, Calix '95 - '97)							
	Canadian Pioneer	GC	1976	D	15,251	462' 07"	67' 02"	38' 06"
	(Carlos Manuel de Cespedes '76 - '89, Avon '89 - '98)							

Fleet #	Fleet Name / Vessel Name	Type of Vessel	Year Built	Type of Engine	Cargo Cap. or Gross*	Overal Length	Breadth	Depth or Draft*
A-5	**ALBERT JOHNSON, SCARBOROUGH, ON**							
	Deer Lake	ES	1925	D	104*	75' 00"		
A-6	**ALCAN ALUMINUM LTD., PORT ALFRED, QC**							
	Alexis-Simard	TT	1980	D	286*	92' 00"	34' 00"	13' 07"
	Grande Baie	TT	1972	D	194*	86' 06"	30' 00"	12' 00"
A-7	**ALGOMA CENTRAL CORP., SAULT STE. MARIE, ON**							
	ALGOMA CENTRAL MARINE GROUP - A DIVISION OF ALGOMA CENTRAL CORP.							
	Agawa Canyon	SU	1970	D	23,400	647' 00"	72' 00"	40' 00"
	Algobay	SU	1978	D	34,900	730' 00"	75' 10"	46' 06"
	(Algobay '78 - '94, Atlantic Trader '94 - '97)							
	Algocape {2}	BC	1967	D	29,950	729' 09"	75' 00"	39' 08"
	(Richelieu {3} '67 - '94)							
	Algocen {2}	BC	1968	D	28,400	730' 00"	75' 00"	39' 08"
	Algogulf {2}	BC	1961	T	26,950	730' 00"	75' 00"	39' 00"
	(J. N. McWatters {2} '61 - '91, Scott Misener {4} '91 - '94)							
	Algoisle	BC	1963	D	26,700	730' 00"	75' 00"	39' 03"
	(Silver Isle '63 - '94)							
	Algolake	SU	1977	D	32,150	730' 00"	75' 00"	46' 06"
	Algomarine	SU	1968	D	27,000	730' 00"	75' 00"	39' 08"
	(Lake Manitoba '68 - '87)							
	Algonorth	BC	1971	D	28,000	729' 09"	75' 02"	42' 11"
	(Temple Bar '71 - '76, Lake Nipigon '76 - '84, Laketon {2} '84 - '86, Lake Nipigon '86 - '87)							
	Algontario	BC	1960	D	29,100	730' 00"	75' 09"	40' 02"
	([Fore Section] Cartiercliffe Hall '76 - '88, Winnipeg {2} '88 - '94)							
	([Stern Section] Ruhr Ore '60 - '76)							
	Algoport	SU	1979	D	32,000	658' 00"	75' 10"	46' 06"
	Algorail {2}	SU	1968	D	23,750	640' 05"	72' 03"	40' 00"
	Algoriver	BC	1960	T	26,800	722' 06"	75' 00"	39' 00"
	(John A. France {2} '60 - '94)							
	Algosoo {2}	SU	1974	D	31,300	730' 00"	75' 00"	44' 06"
	Algosound	BC	1965	T	27,700	730' 00"	75' 00"	39' 00"
	(Don-De-Dieu '65 - '67, V. W. Scully '67 - '87)							
	Algosteel {2}	SU	1966	D	27,000	730' 00"	75' 00"	39' 08"
	(A. S. Glossbrenner '66 - '87, Algogulf {1} '87 - '90)							
	Algoville	SU	1967	D	31,250	730' 00"	78' 00"	39' 08"
	(Senneville '67 - '94)							
	Algoway {2}	SU	1972	D	24,000	650' 00"	72' 00"	40' 00"
	Algowest	SU	1982	D	31,700	730' 00"	75' 10"	42' 00"
	Algowood	SU	1981	D	31,750	730' 00"	75' 10"	46' 06"
	Capt. Henry Jackman	SU	1981	D	30,550	730' 00"	75' 10"	42' 00"
	(Lake Wabush '81 - '87)							
	John B. Aird	SU	1983	D	31,300	730' 00"	75' 10"	46' 06"
	SOCIETE QUEBECOISE D' EXPLORATION MINIERE - CHARTERER							
	Sauniere	SU	1970	D	23,900	642' 10"	74' 10"	42' 00"
	(Bulknes '70 - '70, Brooknes '70 - '76, Algosea '76 - '82)							
	ALGOMA TANKERS LTD. - A DIVISION OF ALGOMA CENTRAL CORP.							
	Algocatalyst	TK	1972	D	84,097	430' 05"	62' 04"	34' 05"
	(Jon Ramsoy '72 - '74, Doan Transport '74 - '86, EnerChem Catalyst '86 - '99)							
	Algoeast	TK	1977	D	77,999	431' 05"	65' 07"	35' 05"
	(Texaco Brave {2} '77 - '86, Le Brave '86 - '97, Imperial St. Lawrence {2} '97 - '97)							
	Algofax	TK	1969	D	117,602	485' 05"	70' 02"	33' 03"
	(Imperial Bedford '69 - '97)							
	Algonova	TK	1969	D	53,002	400' 06"	54' 02"	26' 05"
	(Texaco Chief {2} '69 - '87, A. G. Farquharson '87 - '98)							
	Algosar	TK	1974	D	105,645	435' 00"	74' 00"	32' 00"
	(Imperial St. Clair '74 - '97)							
	Algoscotia	TK	1966	D	82,222	440' 00"	60' 00"	31' 00"
	(Imperial Acadia '66 - '97)							
	Algotrader	TK	1961	D	64,581	430' 07"	52' 00"	28' 00"
	(J. Edouard Simard '61 - '67, Edouard Simard '67 - '82, Le Chene No. 1 '82 - '97, EnerChem Trader '97 - '99)							
	CLEVELAND TANKERS (1991) INC. - VESSELS CHARTERED BY ALGOMA TANKERS LTD.							
	Gemini	TK	1978	D	73,000	432' 06"	65' 00"	29' 04"
	Saturn {4}	TK	1974	D	45,000	384' 01"	54' 06"	25' 00"
A-8	**ALLIED SIGNAL, INC., DETROIT, MI**							
	Allied Chemical No. 12	TK	1969	B	1,545	200' 01"	35' 01"	8' 06"*
A-9	**ALLOUEZ MARINE SUPPLY, SUPERIOR, WI**							
	Allouez Marine	BB	1948	D	9*	35' 02"	11' 02"	3' 06"
	Barbara Ann {1}	BB	1948	D	5*	38' 00"	10' 00"	3' 00"
	Carroll Jean	BB		D	5*	38' 00"	10' 00"	3' 00"

49

Fleet #	Fleet Name / Vessel Name	Type of Vessel	Year Built	Type of Engine	Cargo Cap. or Gross*	Overall Length	Breadth	Depth or Draft*
A-10	**AMERICAN CANADIAN CARIBBEAN LINE, INC., WARREN, RI**							
	Grande Caribe	PA	1998	D	99*	182' 00"	39' 00"	9' 08"
	Grande Mariner	PA	1998	D	99*	182' 00"	39' 00"	9' 08"
	Grande Prince	PA	1997	D	99*	182' 00"	39' 00"	9' 08"
	Niagara Prince	PA	1994	D	687*	174' 00"	40' 00"	14' 00"
A-11	**AMERICAN DIVING & SALVAGE CO., CHICAGO, IL**							
	Eric Z.	TB		D		42' 00"	12' 07"	5' 06"
	Lauren Z.	TB		D		50' 00"	13' 07"	5' 00"
A-12	**AMERICAN MARINE CONSTRUCTION, BENTON HARBOR, MI**							
	AMC 100	DB	1979	B	2,273	200' 00"	52' 00"	14' 00"
	AMC 200	DB	1979	B	2,273	200' 00"	36' 00"	11' 08"
	AMC 300	DB	1977	B	1,048	180' 00"	54' 00"	12' 00"
	Defiance	TB	1966	D	26*	44' 08"	18' 00"	6' 00"
A-13	**AMERICAN STEAMSHIP CO., WILLIAMSVILLE, NY**							
	Adam E. Cornelius {4}	SU	1973	D	28,200	680' 00"	78' 00"	42' 00"
	(Roger M. Kyes '73 - '89)							
	American Freedom	BC	1981	B	33,700	550' 00"	78' 00"	50' 00"
	American Mariner	SU	1980	D	37,200	730' 00"	78' 00"	45' 00"
	American Republic	SU	1981	D	24,800	634' 10"	68' 00"	40' 00"
	Buffalo {3}	SU	1978	D	23,800	634' 10"	68' 00"	40' 00"
	H. Lee White {2}	SU	1974	D	35,200	704' 00"	78' 00"	45' 00"
	Indiana Harbor	SU	1979	D	78,850	1,000' 00"	105' 00"	56' 00"
	John J. Boland {4}	SU	1973	D	33,800	680' 00"	78' 00"	45' 00"
	Charles E. Wilson '73 - '99)							
	Sam Laud	SU	1975	D	23,800	634' 10"	68' 00"	40' 00"
	St. Clair {3}	SU	1976	D	44,000	770' 00"	92' 00"	52' 00"
	Walter J. McCarthy Jr.	SU	1977	D	78,850	1,000' 00"	105' 00"	56' 00"
	(Belle River '77 - '90)							
	COASTWISE BULK TRANSPORT CO. - A DIVISION OF AMERICAN STEAMSHIP CO.							
	Ocean Venture	TBA	1975	D	173*	149' 00"	40' 00"	22' 00"
	(Eliska Theriot '75 - '84, Eliska '84 - '88, Exxon Golden State '88 - '93, S/R Golden State '93 - ?)							
	STINSON, INC. - VESSEL MANAGED BY AMERICAN STEAMSHIP CO.							
	George A. Stinson	SU	1978	D	59,700	1,004' 00"	105' 00"	50' 00"
A-14	**ANDRIE, INC., MUSKEGON, MI**							
	A-390	TK	1982	B	39,000	310' 00"	60' 00"	19' 03"
	A-397	TK	1962	B	39,700	270' 00"	60' 00"	25' 00"
	A-410	TK	1955	B	41,000	335' 00"	54' 00"	26' 06"
	Barbara Andrie	TB	1940	D	298*	121' 10"	29' 06"	16' 00"
	(Edmond J. Moran '40 - '76)							
	Barbara Rita	TB	1981	D	15*	36' 00"	14' 00"	6' 00"
	Candace Andrie	CS	1958	B	1,000	150' 00"	52' 00"	10' 00"
	Clara Andrie	DR	1930	B	1,000	110' 00"	30' 00"	6' 10"
	John Joseph	TB	1993	D	15*	40' 00"	14' 00"	5' 00"
	John Purves	TB	1919	D	436*	150' 00"	27' 07"	16' 00"
	(Butterfield '19 - '42, U.S. Army Butterfield [LT-145] '42 - '45, Butterfield '45 - '57)							
	Karen Andrie {2}	TB	1965	D	433*	120' 00"	31' 06"	16' 00"
	(Sarah Hays '65 - '93)							
	Mari Beth Andrie	TB	1961	D	147*	87' 00"	24' 00"	11' 06"
	(Gladys Bea '61 - '73, American Viking '73 - '83)							
	Rebecca Lynn	TB	1964	D	433*	120' 00"	31' 08"	18' 09"
	(Kathrine Clewis '64 - '96)							
	Robert Purcell	TB	1952	D	28*	45' 00"	12' 06"	7' 09"
	LAFARGE CORP. - VESSELS MANAGED BY ANDRIE, INC.							
	Integrity	CC	1996	B	14,000	460' 00"	70' 00"	37' 00"
	Jacklyn M.	TBA	1976	D	198*	140' 02"	40' 01"	22' 03"
	(Andrew Martin '76 - '90, Robert L. Torres '90 - '94)							
	[Integrity / Jacklyn M. overall dimensions together]					543' 00"	70' 00"	37' 00"
A-15	**APEX OIL CO., GRANITE CITY, IL**							
	Apex Chicago	TK	1981	B	35,000	288' 00"	60' 00"	19' 00"
A-16	**APOSTLE ISLANDS CRUISE SERVICE, BAYFIELD, WI**							
	Eagle Island	ES	1976	D	12*	42' 00"	14' 00"	3' 06"
	Island Princess {2}	ES		D				
	Sea Queen II	ES	1971	D	12*	42' 00"	14' 00"	2' 07"
	Zeeto	3S		W		54' 00"	16' 00"	
A-17	**ARNOLD TRANSIT CO., MACKINAC ISLAND, MI**							
	Algomah	PK	1961	D	125	93' 00"	31' 00"	8' 00"
	Beaver	CF	1952	D	87*	61' 02"	30' 02"	8' 00"

Tug Missouri gives a helping hand to the George A. Stinson. (Roger LeLievre)

Fleet #	Fleet Name Vessel Name	Type of Vessel	Year Built	Type of Engine	Cargo Cap. or Gross*	Overall Length	Breadth	Depth or Draft*
	Chippewa {6}	PK	1962	D	125	93' 00"	31' 00"	8' 00"
	Corsair	CF	1955	D	98*	94' 06"	33' 00"	8' 06"
	Huron {5}	PK	1955	D	80	91' 06"	25' 00"	10' 01"
	Island Express	PC	1988	D	90*	82' 07"	28' 06"	8' 05"
	Mackinac Express	PC	1987	D	90*	82' 07"	28' 06"	8' 05"
	Ottawa {2}	PK	1959	D	125	93' 00"	31' 00"	8' 00"
	Straits Express	PC	1995	D	99*	101' 00"	29' 11"	6' 08"
	Straits of Mackinac II	PF	1969	D	89*	89' 11"	27' 00"	8' 08"

B-1 BARGE TRANSPORTATION, INC., DETROIT, MI
	Cherokee {2}	DB	1943	B	1,200	155' 00"	50' 00"	13' 06"

B-2 BASIC TOWING, INC., ESCANABA, MI
	Danicia	TB	1944	D	382*	110' 02"	27' 03"	15' 07"
	(USCG Chinook [WYT / WYTM-96] '44 - '86, Tracie B '86 - '98)							
	Erika Kobasic	TB	1939	D	226*	110' 00"	26' 05"	15' 01"
	(USCG Arundel [WYT / WYTM-90] '39 - '84, Karen Andrie {1} '84 - '90)							
	Escort II	TB	1969	D	26*	50' 00"	13' 00"	7' 00"
	L. E. Block	BC	1927	T	15,900	621' 00"	64' 00"	33' 00"
	(Last operated 31 October 1981 — Currently laid up in Escanaba, MI.)							

B-3 BAY CHALEUR MARINE LTD.,BATHURST, NB
	Eddie Mac I	TT	1992	D	120*	84' 08"	23' 07"	7' 07"

B-4 BAY CITY BOAT LINE, LLC, BAY CITY, MI
	Princess Wenonah	ES	1954	D	96*	64' 09"	32' 09"	9' 09"

B-5 BAY OCEAN MANAGEMENT, INC., ENGLEWOOD CLIFFS, NJ
	Lake Carling	BC	1992	D	26,264	591' 01"	75' 09"	45' 07"
	(Ziemia Cieszynska '92 - '93)							
	Lake Champlain	BC	1992	D	26,264	591' 01"	75' 09"	45' 07"
	(Ziemia Lodzka '92 - '92)							
	Lake Charles	BC	1990	D	26,209	591' 01"	75' 09"	45' 07"
	(Ziemia Gornoslaska '90 - '91)							

B-6 BAY SHIPBUILDING CO., STURGEON BAY, WI
	Bayship	TB	1943	D	19*	45' 00"	12' 06"	6' 00"

B-7 BAYSAIL, BAY CITY, MI
	Appledore	2S	1989	W		85' 00"	19' 00"	9' 00"*

B-8 BEAUSOLEIL FIRST NATION, CHRISTIAN ISLAND, ON
	Upper Canada	CF	1949	D	165*	143' 00"	36' 00"	11' 00"

B-9 BEAVER ISLAND BOAT CO., CHARLEVOIX, MI
	Beaver Islander	CF	1963	D	95*	96' 03"	27' 05"	9' 09"
	Emerald Isle {2}	CF	1997	D	95*	130' 00"	38' 08"	12' 00"
	South Shore	CF	1945	D	67*	64' 10"	24' 00"	9' 06"

B-10 BEST OF ALL TOURS, ERIE, PA
	Lady Kate {2}	ES	1952	D		65' 00"	16' 06"	4' 00"

B-11 BETHLEHEM STEEL CORP. - BURNS HARBOR DIVISION, CHESTERTON, IN
	Burns Harbor {2}	SU	1980	D	78,850	1,000' 00"	105' 00"	56' 00"
	Stewart J. Cort	SU	1972	D	58,000	1,000' 00"	105' 00"	49' 00"

B-12 BIGANE VESSEL FUELING CO. OF CHICAGO, CHICAGO, IL
	Jos. F. Bigane	RT	1973	D	7,500	140' 00"	40' 00"	14' 00"

B-13 BILLINGTON CONTRACTING, INC., DULUTH, MN
	Coleman	CS	1923	B	502*	153' 06"	40' 06"	10' 06"
	Duluth	DR	1962	B	401*	106' 00"	36' 00"	8' 04"
	Faith	CS	1906	B	705*	120' 00"	38' 00"	10' 02"
	Houghton	TB	1944	D	21*	45' 00"	13' 00"	6' 00"
	Seneca	TB	1939	D	152*	90' 02"	22' 00"	9' 00"
	(General {1} '39 - '39, Raymond Card '39 - '40, Keshena '40 - '47, Mary L. McAllister '47 - '81)							

B-14 BLUE CIRCLE CEMENT CO., DETROIT, MI
	Lewis G. Harriman	CC	1923	R	5,500	350' 00"	55' 00"	28' 00"
	(John W. Boardman '23 - '65)							
	(Last operated 20 April 1980 — 5 year survey expired September 1997.)							
	(Currently in use as a non-powered cement storage vessel in Green Bay, WI.)							
	St. Mary's Cement	CC	1986	B	9,400	360' 00"	60' 00"	23' 03"
	MERCE TRANSPORTATION CO. - VESSEL CHARTERED BY BLUE CIRCLE CEMENT CO.							
	Triton {2}	TB	1941	D	197*	135' 00"	30' 00"	17' 06"
	(USS Tuscarora [AT-77 / YT-341 / YTB-341 / ATA-245] '41 - '79, Challenger {1} '79 - '86)							

Fleet #	Fleet Name Vessel Name	Type of Vessel	Year Built	Type of Engine	Cargo Cap. or Gross*	Overal Length	Breadth	Depth or Draft*
B-15	**BLUE CIRCLE CEMENT CO., TORONTO, ON**							
	Sea Eagle II	TBA	1979	D	560*	132' 00"	35' 00"	19' 00"
	(Sea Eagle '79 - '81, Canmar Sea Eagle '81 - '91)							
	St. Mary's Cement II	CC	1978	B	19,513	496' 06"	76' 00"	35' 00"
	St. Mary's Cement III	CC	1980	B	4,800	335' 00"	76' 08"	17' 09"
	GREAT LAKES INT. TOWING & SALV. CO., INC. - VESSEL CHARTERED BY BLUE CIRCLE CEMENT CO.							
	Petite Forte	TB	1969	D	368*	127' 00"	32' 00"	14' 06"
	(E. Bronson Ingram '69 - '72, Jarmac 42 '720 - '73, Scotsman '73 - '81, Al Battal '81 - '86)							
B-16	**BLUE HERON CO., TOBERMORY, ON**							
	Blue Heron V	ES		D		54' 06"		
	Great Blue Heron	ES		D		79' 00"		
B-17	**BLUE WATER EXCURSIONS, INC., FORT GRATIOT, MI**							
	Huron Lady II	ES	1994	D				
B-18	**BLUE WATER FERRY LTD., SOMBRA, ON**							
	Daldean	CF	1951	D	145*	75' 00"	35' 00"	7' 00"
	Ontamich	CF	1939	D	55*	65' 00"	28' 10"	8' 06"
B-19	**BOB-LO ISLAND, AMHERSTBURG, ON**							
	Courtney-O	CF	1998	D				
	Crystal-O	CF	1946	D	65*	65' 00"	28' 10"	8' 06"
B-20	**BRIAN UTILITIES SERVICES, INC., MUSKEGON, MI**							
	Capt. Roy	TB	1987	D	27*	42' 06"	12' 08"	6' 06"
B-21	**BUFFALO CHARTERS, INC. / NIAGARA CLIPPER, INC., BUFFALO, NY**							
	Miss Buffalo	ES	1964	D	88*	64' 10"	23' 05"	7' 04"
	Miss Buffalo II	ES	1972	D	88*	86' 00"	24' 00"	6' 00"
	Niagara Clipper	ES	1983	D	65*	112' 00"	29' 00"	6' 06"*
B-22	**BUFFALO PUBLIC WORKS DEPT., BUFFALO, NY**							
	Edwin M. Cotter	FB	1900	D	208*	118' 00"	24' 00"	11' 06"
B-23	**BUSCH MARINE, INC., CARROLLTON, MI**							
	Gregory J. Busch	TB	1919	D	299*	151' 00"	28' 00"	16' 09"
	STC 2004	DB	1986	B	2,364	240' 00"	50' 00"	9' 05"
C-1	**C. A. CROSBIE SHIPPING LTD., MONTREAL, QC**							
	Arctic Viking	GC	1967	D	1,265	244' 06"	41' 03"	21' 11"
	(Baltic Viking '67 - '81)							
	Lady Franklin	GC	1970	D	3,627	339' 04"	51' 10"	27' 11"
	(Baltic Valiant '70 - '81)							
C-2	**CALUMET RIVER FLEETING, INC., WHITING, IN**							
	Des Plaines	TB	1956	D	175*	98' 00"	28' 00"	8' 04"*
	Sea Wolf	TB	1954	D	95*	72' 00"	22' 00"	7' 00"*
	Tommy B.	TB	1962	D	43*	45' 00"	11' 10"	4' 11"*
	Trinity	TB	1939	D	51*	45' 00"	12' 10"	5' 07"*
C-3	**CANADA STEAMSHIP LINES, INC., MONTREAL, QC**							
	Atlantic Erie	SU	1985	D	38,200	736' 07"	75' 10"	50' 00"
	(Hon. Paul Martin '85 - '88)							
	Atlantic Huron {2}	SU	1984	D	34,600	736' 07"	75' 10"	46' 06"
	(Prairie Harvest '84 - '89, Atlantic Huron {2} '89 - '94, Melvin H. Baker II {2} '94 - '97)							
	CSL Niagara	SU	1972	D	35,300	740' 00"	78' 00"	48' 00"
	(J. W. McGiffin '72 - '99)							
	Ferbec	BC	1966	D	56,887	732' 06"	104' 02"	57' 09"
	(Fugaku Maru '65 - '77)							
	Frontenac {5}	SU	1968	D	27,500	729' 07"	75' 03"	39' 08"
	Halifax	SU	1963	T	30,100	730' 02"	75' 00"	39' 03"
	(Frankcliffe Hall {2} '63 - '88)							
	Hon Paul J. Martin {2}	SU	1973	D	35,300	740' 00"	78' 00"	48' 00"
	(H.M. Griffith '73-'00)							
	Jean Parisien	SU	1977	D	33,000	730' 00"	75' 00"	46' 06"
	Louis R. Desmarais	SU	1977	D	33,000	730' 00"	75' 00"	46' 06"
	Manitoulin {5}	SU	1966	D	28,100	729' 09"	75' 00"	41' 00"
	Nanticoke	SU	1980	D	35,100	729' 10"	75' 08"	46' 06"
	Tadoussac {2}	SU	1969	D	29,700	730' 00"	75' 03"	42' 00"
	LAFARGE CANADA, INC. - VESSEL MANAGED BY CANADA STEAMSHIP LINES, INC.							
	English River	CC	1961	D	7,450	404' 03"	60' 00"	36' 06"
C-4	**CANADA WEST INDIES MOLASSES CO. LTD., MISSISSAUGA, ON**							
	San Juan	TK	1962	B	913*	195' 00"	35' 00"	12' 06"

Fleet #	Fleet Name / Vessel Name	Type of Vessel	Year Built	Type of Engine	Cargo Cap. or Gross*	Overal Length	Breadth	Depth or Draft*
C-5	**CANADIAN COAST GUARD, OTTAWA, ON**							
	CENTRAL AND ARCTIC REGION - SARNIA, ON							
	Advent	RV	1972	D	72*	77' 01"	18' 05"	5' 03"*
	Bittern	SR	1982	D	21*	40' 08"	13' 06"	4' 04"
	Cape Hurd	SR	1982	D	55*	70' 10"	18' 00"	8' 09"
	Caribou Isle	BT	1985	D	92*	75' 06"	19' 08"	7' 04"
	CG 119	SR	1973	D	20*	40' 03"	13' 01"	5' 11"
	CGR-100	SR	1986	D	21*	45' 11"	15' 09"	5' 07"
	Cove Isle	BT	1980	D	92*	65' 07"	19' 08"	7' 04"
	Griffon	IB	1970	D	2,212*	234' 00"	49' 00"	21' 06"
	Gull Isle	BT	1980	D	80*	65' 07"	19' 08"	7' 04"
	Limnos	RV	1968	D	460*	147' 00"	32' 00"	12' 00"
	Louis M. Lauzier	RV	1976	D	322*	125' 00"	27' 01"	11' 06"
	Samuel Risley	IB	1985	D	1,988*	228' 09"	47' 01"	21' 09"
	Shark	RV	1971	D	30*	52' 06"	14' 09"	7' 03"
	Simcoe	BT	1962	D	961*	179' 01"	38' 00"	15' 06"
	Sora	SR	1982	D	21*	41' 00"	14' 01"	4' 04"
	Spray	SR	1994	D	42*	51' 09"	17' 00"	8' 02"
	Spume	SR	1994	D	42*	51' 09"	17' 00"	8' 02"
	Tobermory	SR	1973	D	17*	44' 01"	12' 06"	6' 07"
	Westfort	SR	1973	D	22*	44' 01"	12' 08"	5' 11"
	LAURENTIAN REGION - QUEBEC, QC							
	Calanus II	RV	1991	D	160*	65' 04"	22' 07"	12' 02"
	Cap Goelands	SR	1985	D	20*	44' 01"	12' 08"	3' 04"*
	Cap Aux Meules	SR	1982	D	32*	51' 09"	17' 00"	4' 01"
	Des Groseilliers	IB	1983	D	5,910*	322' 07"	64' 00"	35' 06"
	E. P. Le Quebecois	RV	1968	D	186*	93' 00"	23' 10"	12' 03"
	F. C. G. Smith	SV	1985	D	439*	114' 02"	45' 11"	11' 02"
	Frederick G. Creed	SV	1988	D	151*	66' 11"	32' 00"	11' 10"
	GC-03	SV	1973	D	57*	60' 08"	21' 00"	5' 11"*
	George R. Pearkes	IB	1986	D	3,809	272' 04"	53' 02"	25' 02"
	Ile Des Barques	BT	1985	D	92*	75' 06"	19' 08"	7' 04"
	Ile Saint-Ours	BT	1986	D	92*	75' 06"	19' 08"	7' 04"
	Isle Rouge	SR	1980	D	57*	70' 10"	18' 01"	8' 09"
	Louisbourg	RV	1977	D	295*	124' 00"	26' 11"	11' 06"
	Martha L. Black	IB	1986	D	3,818*	272' 04"	53' 02"	25' 02"
	Montmagny	BT	1963	D	497*	147' 07"	29' 11"	11' 06"
	Pierre Radisson	IB	1978	D	5,910*	322' 00"	62' 10"	35' 06"
	Sterne	SR	1987	D	20*	40' 08"	13' 06"	6' 11"
	Tracy	BT	1968	D	963*	181' 01"	38' 00"	16' 00"
	Waban-Aki	AV	1987	D	48*	80' 05"	36' 09"	26' 10"
C-6	**CANADIAN DREDGE & DOCK, INC., NORTH YORK, ON**							
	Bagotville	TB	1964	D	65*	65' 00"	18' 06"	10' 00"
	Flo Cooper	TB	1962	D	97*	80' 00"	21' 00"	10' 09"
	Halton	TB	1942	D	15*	42' 09"	14' 00"	7' 06"
	Paula M.	TB	1959	D	12*	46' 06"	16' 01"	4' 10"
	R.C. L. No. 1	TB	1958	D	20*	42' 09"	14' 03"	5' 09"
C-7	**CANADIAN FOREST NAVIGATION CO. LTD., MONTREAL, QC**							
	Kakawi	BC	1981	D	29,514	590' 01"	76' 00"	47' 07"
	(Yannis C. '81 - '86, Pindos '86 - '87, Ikan Selayang '87 - '98)							
	Pintail	BC	1983	D	28,035	647' 08"	75' 10"	46' 11"
	(Puncia '83 - '95)							
C-8	**CAPT. JOE BOAT SERVICE, CHICAGO, IL**							
	Eleanor R.	ES	1988	D	75*	90' 00"	22' 00"	4' 06"*
C-9	**CAPTAIN NORMAC'S RIVERBOAT INN LTD., TORONTO, ON**							
	Jadran	GC	1957	D	2,520*	295' 06"	42' 08"	24' 08"
	(Former Jadranska Plovidba vessel which last operated in 1975.)							
	(Currently in use as a floating restaurant in Toronto, ON.)							
C-10	**CAROL N. BAKER, PENETANGUISHENE, ON**							
	Dawnlight	TB	1891	D	64*	75' 00"	24' 00"	12' 00"
	(Le Roy Brooks 1891 - '25, Henry Stokes '25 - '54, Aburg '54 - '81)							
C-11	**CARTIER CONSTRUCTION, INC., BELLEVILLE, ON**							
	Canadian	DR	1954	B	1,088*	174' 00"	50' 00"	14' 00"
	Carl M.	TB	1957	D	21*	47' 00"	14' 06"	6' 00"
	Oshawa	TB	1971	D	24*	45' 00"	14' 00"	5' 00"
	Whitby	TB	1978	D	24*	45' 00"	14' 00"	5' 00"

Fleet #	Fleet Name / Vessel Name	Type of Vessel	Year Built	Type of Engine	Cargo Cap. or Gross*	Overal Length	Breadth	Depth or Draft*
C-12	**CELEST BAY TIMBER & MARINE, DULUTH, MN**							
	Essayons	TB	1908	R	117*	85' 06"	21' 02"	11' 09"
C-13	**CENTRAL MARINE LOGISTICS, HIGHLAND, IN**							
	Edward L. Ryerson	BC	1960	T	27,500	730' 00"	75' 00"	39' 00"
	(Last operated 12 December 1998 — 5 year survey expires December 2001.)							
	(Currently laid up in Sturgeon Bay, WI.)							
	Joseph L. Block	SU	1976	D	37,200	728' 00"	78' 00"	45' 00"
	Wilfred Sykes	SU	1949	T	21,500	678' 00"	70' 00"	37' 00"
C-14	**CHAMPION'S AUTO FERRY, INC., ALGONAC, MI**							
	Champion {1}	CF	1941	D	65*	65' 00"	29' 00"	8' 06"
	Middle Channel	CF	1997	D	97*	79' 00"	31' 00"	8' 03"
	North Channel	CF	1967	D	67*	75' 00"	30' 00"	8' 00"
	South Channel	CF	1973	D	94*	79' 00"	31' 00"	8' 03"
C-15	**CHARLEVOIX COUNTY ROAD COMMISSION, BOYNE CITY, MI**							
	Charlevoix {1}	CF	1926	D	43*	50' 00"	32' 00"	3' 09"
C-16	**CHICAGO CRUISES, INC., CHICAGO, IL**							
	Chicago II	ES	1983	D	42*	123' 03"	28' 06"	7' 00"
C-17	**CHICAGO FIRE DEPT., CHICAGO, IL**							
	Joseph Medill {2}	FB	1949	D	350*	92' 06"	24' 00"	11' 00"
	Victor L. Schlaegar	FB	1949	D	350*	92' 06"	24' 00"	11' 00"
C-18	**CHICAGO FIREBOAT CRUISE CO., CHICAGO, IL**							
	Fred A. Busse	FB	1937	D	209*	92' 00"	23' 00"	8' 00"
	Islander {1}	ES	1946	D	39*	53' 04"	21' 00"	5' 05"
C-19	**CHICAGO FROM THE LAKE LTD., CHICAGO, IL**							
	Fort Dearborn	ES	1985	D	72*	64' 10"	22' 00"	7' 04"
	Innisfree	ES	1953	D	34*	61' 08"	16' 00"	4' 06"
	Marquette {6}	ES	1957	D	29*	50' 07"	15' 00"	4' 00"
C-20	**CHICAGO WATER PUMPING STATION, CHICAGO, IL**							
	James J. Versluis	TB	1957	D	126*	83' 00"	22' 00"	11' 02"
C-21	**CHRISTENSEN CANADIAN AFRICAN LINES, MONTREAL, QC**							
	Thorscape	GC	1977	D	20,075	541' 08"	75' 02"	48' 03"
	Thorshope	GC	1990	D	17,565	569' 02"	75' 09"	45' 01"
	(Yevgeniy Mravinskiy '90 - '96, Marcela R '96 - '96, Alioth Star '96 - '97, Global Hawk '97 - '98, Nordana Kampala '98 - '99, Cobra '99 - '99)							
	Thorslake	GC	1990	D	17,565	569' 03"	75' 11"	45' 01"
	(Krasnodon '90 - '96, Elena K '96 - '98, Res Cogitans '98 - '99)							
C-22	**CHRISTOPHER LADD, PUT-IN-BAY, OH**							
	Ladler	DB	1950	B	100	100' 00"	26' 00"	5' 06"*
	Mervine II	TB	1942	D	22*	46' 08"	14' 00"	5' 01"*
C-23	**CLARKE TRANSPORT CANADA, MONTREAL, QC**							
	Cabot	RR	1979	D	7,132	564' 09"	73' 11"	45' 09"
	(Cavallo '79 - '88)							
	Cicero	RR	1978	D	6,985	482' 10"	73' 11"	45' 09"
	Trans-St-Laurent	RR	1963	D	645	261' 11"	62' 04"	18' 00"
C-24	**CLEVELAND FIRE DEPT., CLEVELAND, OH**							
	Anthony J. Celebrezze	FB	1961	D		66' 00"	17' 00"	5' 00"
C-25	**CLIFFORD TYNER, BARBEAU, MI**							
	Neebish Islander	CF	1950	D	49*	55' 00"	20' 07"	6' 00"
	(Last operated in 1995 — Currently laid up iat Neebish Island, MI.)							
C-26	**CLINTON RIVER CRUISE CO., CLINTON TOWNSHIP, MI**							
	Clinton	ES	1949	D	12*	44' 00"	11' 01"	4' 00"*
	Gibraltar	ES	1984	D	47*	64' 11"	22' 00"	3' 00"*
C-27	**CLUB CANAMAC CRUISES, TORONTO, ON**							
	Aurora Borealis	ES	1983	D	277*	101' 00"	24' 00"	6' 00"*
	Jaguar II	ES	1968	D	142*	95' 03"	20' 00"	9' 00"
	Stella Borealis	ES	1989	D	356*	118' 00"	26' 00"	7' 00"
	HYDROFOIL LAKE JET LINES, INC. - VESSELS MANAGED BY CLUB CANAMAC CRUISES							
	Seaflight I	HY	1994	D	135*	113' 02"	33' 10"	5' 11"
	Seaflight II	HY	1996	D	135*	113' 02"	33' 10"	5' 11"
	Seaflight III	HY	1996	D	135*	113' 02"	33' 10"	5' 11"
	Seaflight IV	HY	1995	D	135*	113' 02"	33' 10"	5' 11"

Fueling vessel Jos. F. Bigane at Indiana Harbor. Ispat-Inland and the LTV steel docks are in the background. (Roger LeLievre)

Bumboat Marine Trader alongside John G. Munson. Sailors shop for newspapers, cigarettes and other necessities carried by this floating store.
(Franz VonRiedel)

Barge Pere Marquette 41, pushed by the tug Undaunted, with a load of scrap iron at Sault Ste. Marie. (John Vournakis)

Fleet #	Fleet Name Vessel Name	Type of Vessel	Year Built	Type of Engine	Cargo Cap. or Gross*	Overal Length	Breadth	Depth or Draft*
C-28	**COLUMBIA YACHT CLUB, CHICAGO, IL**							
	Abegweit {1}	CF	1947	D	6,694*	372' 06"	61' 00"	24' 09"
	(Former CN Marine, Inc. vessel which last operated in 1981 .)							
	(Currently in use as a floating club house in Chicago, IL.)							
C-29	**CONSTANTINOS MAKAYDAKIS, ATHENS, GREECE**							
	The Straits of Mackinac	CF	1928	R	736*	202' 11"	48' 00"	16' 07"
	(Last operated in 1968 — 5 year survey expired September 1971.)							
	(Currently laid up in Sturgeon Bay, WI.)							
C-30	**CONTESSA CRUISE LINES, L.L.C., LAFAYETTE, LA**							
	Arthur K. Atkinson	PA	1917	D	3,241*	384' 00"	56' 00"	20' 06"
	(Ann Arbor No. 6 '17 - '59)							
	(Last operated in 1984 — 5 year survey expired August 1985 — Currently laid up in Ludington, MI.)							
	Viking {2}	PA	1925	D	2,713*	360' 00"	56' 03"	21' 06"
	(Ann Arbor No. 7 '25 - '64)							
	(Last operated 11 April 1982 — 5 year survey expires May 2001 — Currently laid up in Erie, PA.)							
C-31	**CONTINENTAL MARINE, INC., LEMONT, IL**							
	Brandon E.	TB	1945	D	19*	42' 01"	12' 10"	5' 02"*
C-32	**CORP. OF PROFESSIONAL GREAT LAKES PILOTS, ST. CATHARINES, ON**							
	J. W. Cooper	PB		D				
	Juleen I	PB		D				
	Mrs. C.	PB		D				
C-33	**CROISIERES AML, INC., QUEBEC, QC**							
	Cavalier des Mers	ES	1974	D	128*	105' 00"	21' 00"	4' 08"
	Cavalier Grand Fleuve	ES	1987	D	499*	145' 00"	30' 00"	5' 06"
	Cavalier Maxim	ES	1962	D	752*	191' 02"	42' 00"	11' 07"
	Cavalier Royal	ES	1971	D	283*	125' 00"	24' 00"	5' 00"
	Louis-Jolliet	ES	1938	R	2,436*	170' 01"	70' 00"	17' 00"
	M/V Montreal	ES	1975	D	281*	106' 00"	24' 00"	
	Miss Olympia	ES	1972	D	29*	62' 08"	14' 00"	4' 08"
	Nouvelle-Orleans	ES	1989	D	234*	90' 00"	25' 00"	5' 03"
	Sentinelle II	ES	1993	D	9*	29' 09"	8' 00"	2' 00"
	Sentinelle III	ES	1993	D	9*	29' 09"	8' 00"	2' 00"
	Sentinelle IV	ES	1993	D	9*	29' 09"	8' 00"	2' 00"
	Sentinelle V	ES	1993	D	9*	29' 09"	8' 00"	2' 00"
	Tandem	ES	1991	D	102*	66' 00"	22' 00"	2' 02"
	Transit	ES	1992	D	102*	66' 00"	22' 00"	2' 08"
	Ville Marie II	ES	1947	R	887*	176' 00"	66' 00"	13' 06"
C-34	**CROISIERES DES ILES DE SOREL, INC., SAINTE-ANNE-DE-SOREL, QC**							
	Le Survenant III	ES	1974	D	105*	65' 00"	13' 00"	5' 00"
C-35	**CROISIERES M/S JACQUES-CARTIER, TROIS-RIVIERES, QC**							
	Jacques Cartier	ES	1924	D	441*	135' 00"	35' 00"	10' 00"
	Le Draveur	ES	1992	D	79*			
C-36	**CROISIERES MARJOLAINE, INC., CHICOUTIMI, QC**							
	Marjolaine II	ES	1904	D		92' 00"	27' 00"	9' 00"
C-37	**CROISIERES RICHELIEU, INC., SAINT-JEAN-SUR-RICHELIEU, QC**							
	Fort Saint-Jean II	ES	1967	D	109*	62' 09"	19' 10"	
	Suroit IV	ES	1973	D	64*	58' 00"	16' 00"	10' 04"
C-38	**CSL INTERNATIONAL, INC., BEVERLY, MA**							
	CSL Atlas	SU	1990	D	67,308	746' 01"	105' 02"	63' 00"
	CSL Cabo	SU	1971	D	31,364	596' 02"	84' 04"	49' 10"
	(Bockenheim '71 - '80, Cabo San Lucas '80 - '95)							
	CSL Trailblazer	SU	1978	D	26,608	583' 11"	85' 02"	46' 03"
	([Main Cargo Section] Colon Brown '74 - '75, Gold Bond Conveyor '75 - '78)							
	([Completed Vessel] Gold Bond Trailblazer '78 - '98)							
	M. H. Baker III	SU	1982	D	38,900	730' 00"	75' 10"	50' 00"
	(Atlantic Superior '82 - '97)							
	EGON OLDENDORFF LTD. - PARTNERSHIP WITH CSL INTERNATIONAL, INC.							
	Bernhard Oldendorff	SU	1991	D	77,548	803' 10"	105' 08"	60' 00"
	(Yeoman Burn '91 - '94)							
	Christopher Oldendorff	SU	1982	D	62,732	747' 02"	106' 00"	63' 00"
	(Pacific Peace '82 - '86, Atlantic Huron {1} '86 - '88, CSL Innovator '88 - '93)							
	Hai Wang Xing	SU	1995	D	37,532	612' 02"	95' 02"	43' 04"

Fleet #	Fleet Name / Vessel Name	Type of Vessel	Year Built	Type of Engine	Cargo Cap. or Gross*	Overal Length	Breadth	Depth or Draft*
C-39	**CUNARD LINE LTD., MIAMI, FL**							
	SEABOURN MARITIME MANAGEMENT A/S - A DIVISION OF CUNARD LINE LTD.							
	Seabourn Legend	PA	1992	D	9,961*	442' 11"	67' 03"	40' 08"
	Seabourn Pride	PA	1988	D	9,975*	439' 00"	67' 03"	40' 08"
	Seabourn Spirit	PA	1989	D	9,975*	439' 00"	67' 03"	40' 08"
D-1	**DALE T. DEAN — WALPOLE - ALGONAC FERRY LINE, PORT LAMBTON, ON**							
	City of Algonac	CF	1990	D	92*	80' 04"	26' 01"	6' 09"
	Walpole Islander	CF	1986	D	71*	74' 00"	33' 00"	7' 00"
D-2	**DALMIG MARINE, INC., QUEBEC, QC**							
	Dalmig	CF	1957	D	538*	175' 10"	40' 01"	11' 10"
D-3	**DAN MINOR & SONS, INC., PORT COLBORNE, ON**							
	Andrea Marie I	TB	1963	D	87*	75' 02"	24' 07"	7' 03"
	Susan Michelle	TB	1995	D	89*	79' 10"	20' 11"	6' 02"
	Welland	TB	1954	D	94*	86' 00"	20' 00"	8' 00"
D-4	**DAVID MALLOCH, SCUDDER, ON**							
	Cemba	TK	1960	D	151	50' 00"	15' 06"	7' 06"
D-5	**DAWES MARINE TUG & BARGE, INC., NORTH TONAWANDA, NY**							
	Apache	TB	1954	D	119*	71' 00"	19' 06"	9' 06"
	(Lewis Castle '54 - '97)							
	Fourth Coast	TB	1957	D	17*	40' 00"	12' 06"	4' 00"
	Sand Pebble	TB	1969	D	30*	48' 00"	15' 00"	8' 00"
	Tommy Ray	TB	1954	D	19*	45' 00"	12' 05"	6' 00"
D-6	**DEAN CONSTRUCTION CO. LTD., BELLE RIVER, ON**							
	Americo Dean	TB	1956	D	15*	45' 00"	15' 00"	5' 00"
	Annie M. Dean	TB	1981	D	58*	50' 00"	19' 00"	5' 00"
	Neptune III	TB	1939	D	23*	53' 10"	15' 06"	5' 00"
	Wayne Dean	TB	1946	D	10*	45' 00"	13' 00"	5' 00"
D-7	**DETOUR MARINE, INC., DETOUR, MI**							
	Resolute	TB	1935	D	17*	36' 10"	12' 05"	4' 00"*
D-8	**DETROIT CITY FIRE DEPT., DETROIT, MI**							
	Curtis Randolph	FB	1979	D	85*	77' 10"	21' 06"	9' 03"
D-9	**DIAMOND JACK'S RIVER TOURS, GROSSE ILE, MI**							
	Diamond Belle	ES	1958	D	93*	93' 06"	25' 10"	10' 01"
	Diamond Jack	ES	1955	D	82*	72' 00"	25' 00"	8' 00"
	Diamond Queen	ES	1956	D	94*	92' 00"	25' 00"	10' 00"
D-10	**DIRK SPILLMAKER, EAST LANSING, MI**							
	Verendrye	RV	1958	D	297*	167' 06"	34' 00"	16' 07"
	(Currently laid up in Toronto, ON.)							
D-11	**DISSEN & JUHN CORP., MACEDON, NY**							
	Constructor	TB	1950	D	14*	39' 00"	11' 00"	5' 00"
	James W. Rickey	TB	1935	D	24*	46' 00"	14' 00"	7' 00"
	Portside Belle	TB	1953	D	13*	35' 00"	10' 06"	6' 00"
D-12	**DOW CHEMICAL CO., LUDINGTON, MI**							
	DC 710	TK	1969	B	25,500	260' 00"	50' 00"	9' 00"
	E-63	TK	1980	B	60,000	407' 00"	60' 00"	20' 00"
D-13	**DUC d' ORLEANS CRUISE BOAT, CORUNNA, ON**							
	Duc d' Orleans	ES	1943	D	112*	112' 00"	17' 10"	6' 03"
D-14	**DUROCHER DOCK & DREDGE, INC., CHEBOYGAN, MI**							
	Betty D.	TB	1953	D	14*	40' 00"	13' 00"	6' 00"
	Champion {3}	TB	1974	D	125*	75' 00"	24' 00"	9' 06"
	General {2}	TB	1954	D	119*	71' 00"	19' 06"	9' 06"
	(U.S. Army ST-1999 '54 - '61, USCOE Au Sable '61 - '84, Challenger {3} '84 - '87)							
	Joe Van	TB	1955	D	32*	57' 09"	16' 06"	9' 00"
	Meagan Beth	TB	1982	D	94*	60' 00"	22' 00"	9' 00"
	Nancy Anne	TB	1969	D	73*	60' 00"	20' 00"	6' 00"
	Ray Durocher	TB	1943	D	20*	45' 06"	12' 05"	7' 06"
	Samson II	CS	1959	B	700	90' 00"	50' 00"	7' 02"
	Witch	TB	1950	D	14*	30' 08"	9' 05"	6' 00"
E-1	**EASTERN CANADA TOWING LTD., HALIFAX, NS**							
	Point Carroll	TB	1973	D	366*	127' 00"	30' 05"	14' 05"

Fleet #	Fleet Name Vessel Name	Type of Vessel	Year Built	Type of Engine	Cargo Cap. or Gross*	Overall Length	Breadth	Depth or Draft*
	Point Chebucto	TT	1993	D	412*	110' 00"	33' 00"	17' 00"
	Pointe Aux Basques	TB	1972	D	396*	105' 00"	33' 06"	19' 06"
	Pointe Comeau	TT	1976	D	391*	104' 00"	40' 00"	19' 00"
	Pointe Sept-Iles	TB	1980	D	424*	105' 00"	34' 06"	19' 06"
	Point Halifax	TT	1986	D	417*	110' 00"	36' 00"	19' 00"
	Point Valiant {2}	TT	1998	D	302*	80' 00"	30' 01"	14' 09"
	Point Vibert	TB	1961	D	236*	96' 03"	28' 00"	14' 06"
	(Foundation Vibert '61 - '73)							
	Point Vigour	TB	1962	D	207*	98' 05"	26' 10"	13' 05"
	(Foundation Vigour '62 - '74)							
	Point Vim	TB	1962	D	207*	98' 05"	26' 10"	13' 05"
	(Foundation Vim '62 - '74)							
E-2	**EASTERN UPPER PENINSULA TRANSIT AUTHORITY, SAULT STE. MARIE, MI**					84' 00"	30' 00"	8' 03"
	Drummond Islander	CF	1947	D	99*	84' 00"	30' 00"	8' 03"
	Drummond Islander III	CF	1989	D	96*	108' 00"	37' 00"	12' 03"
	Drummond Islander IV	CF	2000	D		140' 00"	40' 00"	12' 00"
	Neebish Islander II	CF	1946	D	90*	89' 00"	29' 06"	6' 09"
	Sugar Islander II	CF	1995	D	223*	114' 00"	40' 00"	10' 00"
	Thunder Bay	TB	1953	D	15*	45' 00"	13' 00"	7' 00"
E-3	**EDELWEISS CRUISE DINING, MILWAUKEE, WI**							
	Edelweiss I	ES	1988	D	87*	64' 08"	18' 00"	6' 00"
	Edelweiss II	ES	1989	D	89*	73' 08"	20' 00"	7' 00"
E-4	**EDWARD E. GILLEN CO., MILWAUKEE, WI**							
	Andrew J.	TB	1950	D	25*	47' 00"	15' 07"	8' 00"
	Edith J.	TB	1962	D	19*	45' 03"	13' 00"	8' 00"
	Edward E. Gillen III	TB	1988	D	95*	75' 00"	26' 00"	9' 06"
	Harbor Builder	DB	1930	B	662*	150' 00"	42' 05"	12' 05"
E-5	**EDWIN M. ERICKSON, BAYFIELD, WI**							
	Outer Island	PK	1942	D	300	112' 00"	32' 00"	8' 06"
	(USS LSM-? '42 - '46, Pluswood '46 - '53)							
E-6	**EGAN MARINE CORP., LEMONT, IL**							
	Alice E.	TB	1950	D	183*	100' 00"	26' 00"	9' 00"
	(L. L. Wright '50 - '55, Martin '55 - '74, Mary Ann '74 - '77, Judi C. '77 - '94)							
	Becky E.	TB	1943	D	146*	81' 01"	24' 00"	9' 10"
	(DPC 51 '43 - '44, WSA 6 '44 - '46, Chas E. Trout '46 - '78, Naomi Marie '78 - '80, South Haven '80 - '90)							
	Crow	TB	1963	D	152*	84' 06"	25' 00"	11' 06"
	Daniel E.	TB	1967	D	70*	70' 00"	18' 06"	6' 08"
	(Foster M. Ford '67 - '84)							
	Denise E.	TB	1912	D	138*	80' 07"	21' 06"	10' 03"
	(Caspian '12 - '48, Trojan '48 - '81, Cherokee {1} '81 - '93)							
	Derek E.	TB	1907	D	85*	72' 06"	20' 01"	10' 06"
	(John Kelderhouse '07 - '25, Sachem '25 - '90)							
	Ethel E.	TB	1913	D	96*	81' 00"	20' 00"	12' 06"
	(Michigan {4} '13 - '78, Ste. Marie II '78 - '81, Dakota '81 - '92)							
	Lisa E.	TB	1963	D	75*	65' 06"	20' 00"	8' 06"
	(Dixie Scout '63 - '90)							
	Robin E.	TB	1889	D	123*	84' 09"	19' 00"	9' 00"
	(Asa W. Hughes 1889 - '13, Triton {1} '13 - '81, Navajo {2} '81 - '92)							
	Susan E.	TB	1921	D	96*	81' 00"	20' 00"	12' 06"
	(Oregon {1} '21 - '78, Ste. Marie I '78 - '81, Sioux {2} '81 - '91)							
E-7	**EMPIRE CRUISE LINES, U. S. A., ST. THOMAS, ON**							
	Marine Star	PA	1945	T	12,773*	520' 00"	71' 06"	43' 06"
	(USNS Marine Star '45 - '55, Aquarama '55 - '94)							
	(Last operated in 1962 — 5 year survey expired May 1965 — Currently laid up in Lackawanna, NY.)							
E-8	**EMPIRE SANDY, INC., TORONTO, ON**							
	Empire Sandy	3S	1943	W	434*	140' 00"	32' 08"	14' 00"
	Wayward Princess	ES	1976	D	325*	92' 00"	26' 00"	10' 00"
E-9	**EMPRESS OF CANADA ENTERPRISES LTD., TORONTO, ON**							
	Empress of Canada	ES	1980	D	399*	116' 00"	28' 00"	6' 06"*
E-10	**EMPRESS RIVER CASINO, JOLIET, IL**							
	Empress	GA	1992	D	1,136*	214' 00"	66' 00"	6' 07"*
	Empress II	GA	1993	D	1,248*	230' 00"	67' 00"	6' 08"*
	Empress III	GA	1994	D	1,126*	288' 00"	76' 00"	10' 07"*

Listings continued on Page 70

Colors of the Great Lakes & Seaway Smokestacks

A.B.M. Marine
Thunder Bay, ON

ACME Marine Sevices
Knife River, MN

Algoma Central Marine Group
Div. of Algoma Central Corp.
St. Catharines, ON

Algoma Tankers Ltd.
Div. of Algoma Central Corp.
Dartmouth, NS

American Canadian Caribbean Line, Inc.
Warren, RI

American Marine Construction
Benton Harbor, MI

American Steamship Co.
Williamsville, NY

Andrie, Inc.
Muskegon, MI

Arnold Transit Co.
Mackinac Island, MI

Atlantic Towing Ltd.
Div. of Irvingdale Shipping Ltd.
St. John, NB

Basic Towing, Inc.
Escanaba, MI

Beaver Island Boat Co.
Charlevoix, MI

Bethlehem Steel Corp.
Chesterton, IN

Bigane Vessel Fueling Co.
Chicago, IL

Billington Contracting Inc.
Duluth, MN

Blue Circle Cement Co.
Detroit, MI
Toronto, ON

Buffalo Public Works Dept.
Buffalo, NY

Busch Marine
Carrollton, MI

Canada Steamship Lines, Inc.
Montreal, QC

Canadian Coast Guard
Ottawa, ON

Canadian Dredge & Dock Inc.
North York, ON

Central Marine Logistics, Inc.
Highland, IN

Chicago Fire Department
Chicago, IL

Christensen Canadian African Lines
Montreal, QC

Cleveland Fire Department
Cleveland, OH

Cleveland Tankers (1991), Inc.
Algoma Tankers, Ltd. Mgr.
Cleveland, OH

Clipper Cruise Lines
Subsidiary of Intrav
St. Louis, MO

Croisieres AML Inc.
Quebec, QC

Croisieres Nordik, Inc.
Div. of Transport Desgagnes, Inc.
Quebec, QC

C.A. Crosbie Shipping Ltd.
Montreal, QC

Dan Minor & Sons, Inc.
Port Colborne, ON

Dean Construction Co.
Belle River, ON

City of Detroit Fire Department
Detroit, MI

Diamond Jack's River Tours
Detroit, MI

Durocher Dock & Dredge, Inc.
Cheboygan, MI

Eastern Canada Towing Ltd.
Halifax, NS

Eastern Upper Peninsula Transportation Authority
Sault Ste. Marie, MI

Erie Sand & Gravel Co. Erie Sand Steamship Co.
Erie, PA

Essroc Canada, Inc. Upper Lakes Group, Mgr
Downsville, ON

Fednav International Ltd.
Montreal, QC

Fraser Shipyards, Inc.
Superior, WI

Gaelic Tug Boat Co.
Grosse Ile, MI

Gananoque Boat Line
Gananoque, ON

Edward E. Gillen Co.
Milwaukee, WI

Goodtime Transit Boats, Inc.
Cleveland, OH

Gravel & Lake Services, Ltd.
Thunder Bay, ON

Great Lakes Clipper Preservation Association
Muskegon, MI

Great Lakes Associates, Inc.
Rocky River, OH

Great Lakes International Towing & Salvage Ltd.
Burlington, ON

Great Lakes Maritime Academy
Northwestern Michigan College
Traverse City, MI

Great Lakes Towing Co.
Cleveland, OH

Hamilton Marine & Engineering Ltd.
Div. of ULS Corp.
Port Colborne, ON

Hannah Marine Corp.
Lemont, IL

Holly Marine Towing
Chicago, IL

Inland Bulk Transfer
Cleveland, OH

Inland Lakes Management, Inc.
Alpena, MI

The Interlake Steamship Co.
Lakes Shipping Co.
Richfield, OH

Kadinger Marine Service, Inc.
Milwaukee, WI

Kent Line International Ltd
Div. of Irvingdale Shipping Ltd.
St. John, NB

Keystone Great Lakes, Inc.
Bala Cynwyd, PA

King Construction Co.
Holland, MI

Lafarge Cement Corp.
Toronto, ON
Alpena, MI

Lake Michigan Carferry Service, Inc.
Ludington, MI

Lake Michigan Contractors, Inc.
Holland, MI

Le Groupe Ocean
Quebec, QC

Lee Marine, Ltd.
Port Lambton, ON

Lock Tours Canada
Sault Ste. Marie, ON

Logistec Navigation, Inc.
Transport Igloolik - Mgr.
Montreal, QC

Lower Lakes Towing, Ltd.
Port Dover, ON

Luedtke Engineering Co.
Frankfort, MI

M.C.M. Marine Inc.
Sault Ste Marie, MI

MacDonald Marine Ltd.
Goderich, ON

Madeline Island Ferry Line, Inc.
LaPointe, WI

Maid of the Mist Steamboat Co., Ltd.
Niagara Falls, ON

Marine Atlantic, Inc.
Moncton, NB

Mariposa Cruise Line
Toronto, ON

McAllister Towing & Salvage, Inc.
Subsidiary of Le Groupe Ocean, Inc.
Montreal, QC

McKeil Marine Ltd.
Hamilton, ON

Miller Boat Line, Inc.
Put-In-Bay, OH

**Museum Ship
CCGC Alexander Henry**
Kingston, ON

**Museum Ship
HMCS Haida**
Toronto, ON

**Museum Ship
Keewatin**
Douglas, MI

**Museum Ships
USS Little Rock
USS The Sullivans**
Buffalo, NY

**Museum Ship
Meteor**
Superior, WI

**Museum Ship
City of Milwaukee**
Frankfort, MI

**Museum Ships
Norgoma** (Sault Ste. Marie,ON)
Norisle (Manitowaning,ON)

**Museum Ship
Valley Camp**
Sault Ste. Marie, MI

**Museum Ship
William A. Irvin**
Duluth, MN

**Museum Ships
Willis B. Boyer** (Toledo,OH)
William G. Mather (Cleveland,OH)

**Muskoka Lakes Navigation
& Hotel Co.**
Gravenhurst, ON

Nadro Marine Services
Port Dover, ON

**Neuman Cruise & Ferry
Line, Inc.**
Sandusky, OH

**Oglebay Norton Marine
Services Co.**
Cleveland, OH

**Ontario Ministry of Transportation
& Communication**
Kingston, ON

Osborne Materials Co.
Mentor, OH

**Owen Sound
Transportation Co. Ltd.**
Owen Sound, ON

**P & H Shipping
Div. of Parrish & Heimbecker Ltd.**
Mississauga, ON

N.M. Paterson & Sons Ltd.
Thunder Bay, ON

**Pelee Island
Transportation Services**
Pelee Island, ON

Pere Marquette Shipping Co.
Ludington, MI

**Provmar Fuels, Inc.
Div. of ULS Corporation**
Toronto, ON

Purvis Marine Ltd.
Sault Ste. Marie, ON

**Purvis Marine Ltd.
M/V Yankcanuck**
Sault Ste. Marie, ON

**Reinauer Transportation
Companies, Inc.**
Staten Island, NY

**Rigel Shipping Canada, Inc.
Rigel Shipping Co., Inc**
Shediac, NB

Roen Salvage Co.
Sturgeon Bay, WI

**Sea Fox Thousand
Islands Tours**
Kingston, ON

Selvick Marine Towing Corp.
Sturgeon Bay, WI

Shell Canadian Tankers Ltd.
Montreal, QC

**Societe des Traversiers
du Quebec**
Quebec, QC

**Society Quebecoise
D'Exploration Miniere
Algoma Central Corp.-Mgr.**
Sault Ste. Marie, ON

Soo Locks Boat Tours
Sault Ste. Marie, MI

Southdown, Inc.
Cleveland, OH

**St. Lawrence
Cruise Lines, Inc.**
Kingston, ON

**St. Lawrence Seaway
Management Corp.**
Cornwall, ON

St. Lawrence Seaway Development Corp.
Massena, NY

Three Rivers Boatmen, Inc.
Trois Rivieres, QC

Toronto Metropolitan Park Dept.
Toronto, ON

Transport Desgagnes, Inc.
Quebec, QC

Transport Iglooik, Inc.
Montreal, QC

Trump Indiana, Inc.
Gary, IN

Upper Lakes Group Jackes Shipping, Inc. ULS Marbulk, Inc.
Ottawa, ON

United States Army Corps of Engineers Great Lakes and Ohio River Division
Chicago, IL

United States Coast Guard 9th Coast Guard District
Cleveland, OH

United States Environmental Protection Agency
Bay City, MI

USS Great Lakes Fleet, Inc.
Duluth, MN

U.S.S. Great Lakes Fleet, Inc. M/V Presque Isle
Duluth, MN

University of Michigan Center for Great Lakes & Aquatic Sciences
Ann Arbor, MI

Upper Lakes Towing Company, Inc.
Escanaba, MI

Vista Fleet
Duluth, MN

Colors of Major International Seaway Fleets

Alba Shipping Ltd. A/S
Aalborg, Denmark

Anglo-Georgian Shipping Co. Ltd.
London, England

Atlantska Plovidba
Dubrovnik, Croatia

Aurora Shipping, Inc.
Manila, Philippines

Azov Sea Shipping Co.
Mariupol, Ukraine

B&N Bylok & Nordsjofraktas
Oslo, Norway

Bay Ocean Management, Inc
Englewood Cliffs, NJ

Bergen Bulk Carriers A/S
Bergen, Norway

Bison Shipmanagement & Chartering Co. Pte. Ltd.
Singapore

Canadian Forest Navigation Co. Ltd. Fednav Ltd. Mgr.
Montreal, QC

Canada Maritime Ltd.
Hamilton, Bermuda

Cape Shipping S.A.
Piraeus, Greece

Ceres Hellenic Shipping Enterprises
Piraeus, Greece

Chellaram Shipping Ltd.
Hong Kong, PRC

China Ocean Shipping Group
Bejing, PRC

Commercial Trading & Discount Co., Ltd.
Athens, Greece

Compagnie des Iles du Ponant M/V LeLevant
Nantes, France

Densan Shipping Co. Ltd.
Istanbul, Turkey

Det Nordenfjeldske D/S AS
Trondheim, Norway

Diana Shipping Agencies S.A.
Piraeus, Greece

Donnelly Shipmanagment Ltd.
Limassol, Cyprus

ER Denizcilik Sanayi Nakliyat ve Ticaret A.S.
Istanbul, Turkey

Egon Oldendorff Ltd.
Luebeck, Germany

Eidsiva Rederi ASA Fednav Ltd. Mgr.
Oslo, Norway

Fafalios Shipping S.A.
Piraeus, Greece

Fednav International Ltd.
Montreal, QC

Gourdomichalis Maritime S.A.
Piraeus, Greece

Great Lakes European Shipping AS
Ornskoldsvik, Sweden

Hapag Lloyd Cruises M/V c. Columbus
Hamburg, Germany

Hilal Shipping, Trading & Industry Co.
Istanbul, Turkey

H.S.S. Holland Ship Service B.V.
Rotterdam, Netherlands

Jugoslavenska Oceanska Plovidba
Kotor, Yugoslavia

Knutsen O.A.S. Shipping
Haugesund, Norway

Laurin Maritime, Inc
Houston, TX

Lithuanian Shipping Co.
Klaipeda, Lithuania

Lynx Shipping Co.
Athens, Greece

M.T.M. Ship Management Pte. Ltd.
Singapore

Mammoet Shipping Ltd.
Roosendaahl, Netherlands

Marine Managers, Ltd.
Piraeus, Greece

Millenium Maritime Services Ltd.
Piraeus, Greece

Metron Shipping & Agencies, Ltd.
Piraeus, Greece

Murmansk Shipping Co.
Murmansk, Russia

Navigation Maritime Bulgare Ltd.
Varna, Bulgaria

Neste OYJ
Espoo, Finland

Oceanbulk Maritime S.A.
Athens, Greece

Olympic Shipping and Management S.A.
Athens, Greece

Orion Schiffahrts-Gesellschaft
Hamburg, Germany

PACC Ship Managers Pte. Ltd.
Singapore, Malaysia

Pacific Basin Agencies Ltd. Fednav Ltd. Mgr.
Hong Kong

Pegasus Denizeilik
Istanbul, Turkey

Polclip (Luxembourg) S.A.
Luxembourg, Luxembourg

Polish Steamship Co.
Szczecin, Poland

Prime Orient Shipping S.A.
Panama City, Panama

Prisco (UK) Ltd.
London, England

Scanscot Shipping Services GmbH
Hamburg, Germany

Seastar Navigation Co. Ltd.
Athens, Greece

Sherimar Management Co. Ltd.
Athens, Greece

Shipping Corp. of India Ltd.
Bombay, India

Shunzan Kaiun Co., Ltd.
Ehime, Japan

Sidemar Servizi Accessori S.p.A.
Genoa, Italy

**Societe Anonyme Monegasque d'
Administration Maritime et Aerienne**
Monte Carlo, Monaco

Sohtorik Denizcilik ve Ticaret A.S.
Istanbul, Turkey

Spar Shipping A.S.
Bergen, Norway

**Spliethoff's
Bevrachtingskantoor Ltd.**
Amsterdam, Netherlands

Split Ship Management, Ltd.
Split, Croatia

Stolt Parcel Tankers
Greenwich, CT

Team Ship Management
Bergen, Norway

Teo Shipping Corp.
Piraeus, Greece

**Thenamaris Ships
Management, Inc.**
Athens, Greece

Thoresen & Co. Ltd.
Bangkok, Thailand

**Transman Shipping
Enterprises S.A.**
Athens, Greece

Univan Ship Management Ltd.
Hong Kong

V. Ships (Cyprus) Ltd.
Limassol, Cyprus

Wagenborg Shipping B.V.
Delfzijl, Netherlands

**Zirkel Verwaltungsges,
MBH**
Brake, Germany

International Code Flags & Pennants

ALFA
Have Diver Down
Keep Clear

BRAVO
Dangerous Cargo/Refueling

CHARLIE
Yes

DELTA
Keep Clear,
Maneuvering With Difficulty

ECHO
Altering Course Starboard

FOXTROT
Disabled, Communicate
With Me

GOLF
Require A Pilot

HOTEL
Pilot On Board

INDIA
Altering Course To Port

JULIETT
On Fire, Have Dangerous
Cargo, Keep Clear

KILO
Wish To Communicate

LIMA
Stop Instantly

MIKE
Vessel Stopped,
Making No Way

NOVEMBER
No

OSCAR
Man Overboard

PAPA
In Harbor-All Persons
Report On Board

QUEBEC
Request Free Pratique

ROMEO

SIERRA
Engines Going Astern

TANGO

UNIFORM
You Are Running
Into Danger

VICTOR
Require Assistance

WHISKEY
Require Medical Assistance

X-RAY
Stop your intentions,
watch for signals

YANKEE
Dragging My Anchor

ZULU
Require A Tug

0

1

2

3

4

5

6

7

8

9

House Flags of Great Lakes & Seaway Fleets

Algoma Central Marine Group

American Steamship Co.

Atlantic Towing Ltd. Kent Line Ltd.

Bethlehem Steel Corp.

Canada Steamship Lines, Inc.

Cleveland Tankers, (1991) Inc.

Erie Navigation Co. Erie Sand & Gravel

Gaelic Tug Boat Co.

Great Lakes Associates Inc.

Great Lakes Towing Co.

Inland Lakes Management, Inc.

Interlake Steamship Co. Lakes Shipping Co.

LaFarge Cement Corp.

Lake Michigan Carferry Service, Inc.

Lower Lakes Towing Co.

McKeil Marine Ltd.

Oglebay Norton Marine Services Co.

Owen Sound Transportation Co. Ltd.

P. & H. Shipping

N.M. Paterson & Sons Ltd.

Purvis Marine Ltd.

Seaway Bulk Carriers

Seaway Self Unloaders

Southdown Inc.

Transport Desgagnes, Inc.

Upper Lakes Group, Inc.

USS Great Lakes Fleet, Inc.

U.S. Army Corps of Engineers

Flags of Major Nations in the Marine Trade

Antigua & Barbuda

Bahamas

Barbados

Belgium

Bosnia & Herzegovinia

Brazil

Canada

Chile

China

Cote D'Ivoire

Croatia

Cyprus

Czech Republic

Denmark

Egypt

Finland

France

Germany

Ghana

Greece

Hong Kong

Hungary

India

Ireland

Isle of Man

Israel

Italy

Japan

Liberia

Lithuania

Luxembourg

Malta

Mexico

Morocco

Netherlands

Norway

Panama

Philippines

Poland

Romania

Russia

Singapore

Spain

St. Vincent & The Grenadines

Sweden

Switzerland

Turkey

United Kingdom

United States

Yugoslavia

Sykes' wheelhouse: '50 Years of Smooth Sailing'. *(Rod Burdick)*

WILFRED SYKES – NIFTY 50

Vessel Spotlight

WILFRED SYKES

Length	678'
Beam	70'
Depth	37"
Built	1949
Tonnage	21,500

When the **Wilfred Sykes** turned 50 in 1999, there were no cake and candles, just business as usual for this veteran of the Lake Michigan aggregates trade. But to mark the milestone, she carried a "50 Years of Smooth Sailing" banner painted across her pilothouse, a fitting tribute to a spotless record.

Although she was biggest and fastest on the lakes when launched, the Sykes' real claim to fame lies in her pacesetting design, which set the style for most Great Lakes vessels built from the 1950s until the era of the 1,000-footer in the 1970s. Alas, much of what her original architects created was marred in 1975 with the addition of aft-mounted, self-unloading machinery; however, without such modifications, the vessel would probably not have survived to celebrate her milestone birthday.

Besides her sense of style, the Sykes has two other claims to fame, both involving shipwrecks. A Citation for Bravery from the Lake Carriers' Association, in the form of a plaque still aboard the vessel, commends the ship and crew for their efforts in rescuing survivors from the steamer **Henry Steinbrenner**, which sank in Lake Superior off Isle Royale 11 May, 1953. The Sykes was called into action, with less happy results, on 10 November 1975 to search for survivors of the ill-fated **Edmund Fitzgerald**.

— Roger LeLievre

Looking toward the bow of the Wilfred Sykes, upbound on Lake Michigan. (Roger LeLievre)

Fleet #	Fleet Name / Vessel Name	Type of Vessel	Year Built	Type of Engine	Cargo Cap. or Gross*	Overal Length	Breadth	Depth or Draft*
E-11	**ERIE ISLANDS PETROLEUM, INC., PUT-IN-BAY, OH**							
	Cantankerous	TK	1955	D	323	53' 00"	14' 00"	5' 00"*
E-12	**ERIE SAND & GRAVEL CO., ERIE, PA**							
	J. S. St. John	SC	1945	D	680	174' 00"	32' 02"	15' 00"
	(USS YO-178 '45 - '51, Lake Edward '51 - '67)							
	ERIE NAVIGATION CO. - VESSELS MANAGED BY ERIE SAND & GRAVEL CO.							
	Day Peckinpaugh	CC	1921	D	1,490	254' 00"	36' 00"	14' 00"
	(Interwaterways Line Incorporated 101 '21 - '32, I.L.I. 101 '32 - '36, Richard J. Barnes '36 - '58)							
	(Last operated 9 September, 1994 — 5 year survey expired August 1995 — Currently laid up in Erie, PA.)							
	John R. Emery	SC	1905	D	490	140' 00"	33' 00"	14' 00"
	(Trenton {1} '05 - '25)							
	ERIE SAND STEAMSHIP CO. - VESSEL MANAGED BY ERIE SAND & GRAVEL CO.							
	Richard Reiss	SU	1943	D	14,900	620' 06"	60' 03"	35' 00"
	(Launched as Adirondack, Richard J. Reiss {2} '43 - '86)							
F-1	**FAIRMONT SHIPPING (CANADA) LTD., VANCOUVER, BC**							
	Eurasian Charm	BC	1982	D	22,558	539' 02"	75' 02"	44' 06"
	(Sunstars '82 - '85, Castano '85 - '94)							
	Ophelia	GC	1986	D	12,359	399' 07"	65' 08"	36' 02"
	(Super Vision '86 - '96)							
F-2	**FAMILLE DUFOUR CROISIERES, SAINTE-ANNE-DE-BEAUPRE, QC**							
	Famille DuFour	ES	1992	D	451*	132' 00"	29' 00"	11' 00"
	Famille DuFour II	PC	1995	D	465*	127' 06"	34' 09"	10' 06"
	Marie-Clarisse	2S		W	126*	130' 00"	21' 04"	11' 05"*
F-3	**FAUST CORP., DETROIT, MI**							
	Comorant	TB	1991	D	10*	25' 02"	14' 00"	4' 06"
	Linnhurst	TB	1930	D	11*	37' 06"	10' 06"	4' 08"
F-4	**FEDNAV LTD., MONTREAL, QC**							
	CANARCTIC SHIPPING CO. LTD. - A DIVISION OF FEDNAV LTD.							
	Arctic	BC	1978	D	26,440	692' 04"	75' 05"	49' 05"
	Arctic Kalvik	SB	1983	D	4,391	288' 09"	57' 05"	32' 10"
	(Kalvik '83 - '97)							
	FEDERAL TERMINALS LTD. - A DIVISION OF FEDNAV LTD.							
	Brochu	TT	1973	D	390*	100' 00"	36' 00"	14' 06"
	Vachon	TT	1973	D	390*	100' 00"	36' 00"	14' 06"
	FEDNAV INTERNATIONAL LTD. - A DIVISION OF FEDNAV LTD.							
	Federal Asahi {2}	BC	2000	D	35,700	629' 08"	77' 01"	48' 09"
	Federal Baffin	BC	1995	D	43,732	623' 04"	100' 00"	54' 06"
	Federal Franklin	BC	1995	D	43,706	623' 04"	100' 00"	54' 06"
	Federal Kivalina	BC	2000	D	35,700	629' 08"	77' 01"	48' 09"
	Federal Maas {2}	BC	1997	D	34,372	656' 02"	77' 01"	48' 11"
	Federal Oshima	BC	1999	D	35,700	629' 08"	77' 01"	48' 09"
	Federal Rhine {2}	BC	1997	D	34,372	656' 02"	77' 01"	48' 11"
	Federal Rideau	BC	2000	D	35,700	629' 08"	77' 01"	48' 09"
	Federal Saguenay {2}	BC	1996	D	34,372	656' 02"	77' 01"	48' 11"
	Federal Schelde {2}	BC	1997	D	34,372	656' 02"	77' 01"	48' 11"
	Federal St. Laurent {2}	BC	1996	D	34,372	656' 02"	77' 01"	48' 11"
	Federal Sumida {2}	BC	1998	D	72,493	738' 02"	105' 08"	61' 04"
	Federal Yukon	BC	2000	D	35,700	629' 08"	77' 01"	48' 09"
	BAY OCEAN MANAGEMENT, INC. - VESSELS CHARTERED BY FEDNAV INTERNATIONAL LTD.							
	Lake Erie	BC	1980	D	35,630	737' 06"	76' 02"	47' 01"
	(Federal Ottawa '80 - '95)							
	Lake Michigan	BC	1981	D	38,294	729' 11"	76' 03"	47' 01"
	(Federal Maas {1} '81 - '95)							
	Lake Ontario	BC	1980	D	35,630	729' 11"	76' 03"	47' 01"
	(Federal Danube '80 - '95)							
	Lake Superior	BC	1981	D	35,630	729' 11"	76' 03"	47' 01"
	(Federal Thames '81 - '95)							
	EIDSIVA REDERI ASA - VESSELS CHARTERED BY FEDNAV INTERNATIONAL LTD.							
	Federal Oslo	BC	1985	D	29,462	601' 00"	76' 00"	48' 11"
	(Paolo Pittaluga '85 - '91)							
	Federal Vibeke	BC	1981	D	30,900	617' 06"	76' 00"	47' 07"
	(Nosira Lin '81 - '89, Dan Bauta '89 - '89, Kristianiafjord '89 - '93)							
	PACIFIC BASIN AGENCIES LTD. - VESSEL CHARTERED BY FEDNAV INTERNATIONAL LTD.							
	Federal Bergen	BC	1984	D	29,159	593' 00"	76' 00"	47' 00"
	(High Peak '84 - '90, Federal Bergen '90 - '92, Thunder Bay '92 - '93)							
	TEAM SHIP MANAGEMENT AS - VESSELS CHARTERED BY FEDNAV INTERNATIONAL LTD.							
	Federal Fuji	BC	1986	D	29,536	599' 09"	75' 11"	48' 07"
	Federal Polaris	BC	1985	D	29,536	599' 09"	75' 11"	48' 07"

Tanker Algosar in
the Welland Canal
Flight Locks.

(David T. Catlin)

Fleet #	Fleet Name / Vessel Name	Type of Vessel	Year Built	Type of Engine	Cargo Cap. or Gross*	Overal Length	Breadth	Depth or Draft*
	M & N SHIPPING CORP. - VESSELS CHARTERED BY FEDNAV INTERNATIONAL LTD.							
	Federal Fraser {2}	BC	1983	D	35,315	730' 01"	75' 09"	48' 00"
	(Selkirk Settler '83 - '91, Federal St. Louis '91 - '91)							
	Federal MacKenzie	BC	1983	D	35,315	730' 01"	75' 09"	48' 00"
	(Canada Marquis '83 - '91, Federal Richelieu '91 - '91)							
	Lady Hamilton {2}	BC	1983	D	34,500	730' 01"	75' 09"	48' 00"
	(Saskatchewan Pioneer '83 - '95)							
	VANGUARD ENTERPRISE CO. LTD. - VESSEL CHARTERED BY FEDNAV INTERNATIONAL LTD.							
	Federal Agno	BC	1985	D	29,643	599' 09"	75' 11"	48' 07"
	(Federal Asahi '85 - '89)							
F-5	**FERRISS MARINE CONTRACTING CORP., DETROIT, MI**							
	Magnetic	TB	1925	D	30*	55' 00"	14' 00"	6' 06"
	Norma B.	TB	1940	D	14*	43' 00"	15' 00"	4' 00"
F-6	**FRASER SHIPYARDS, INC., SUPERIOR, WI**							
	Brenda L.	TB	1941	D	11*	36' 00"	10' 00"	3' 08"
	(Harbour I '41 - '58, Su-Joy III '58 -'78)							
	Maxine Thompson	TB	1959	D	30*	47' 04"	13' 00"	6' 06"
	(Susan A. Fraser '59 - '78)							
	Murray R.	TB	1946	D	17*	42' 10"	12' 00"	4' 07"
	Phil Milroy	TB	1957	D	41*	47' 11"	16' 08"	8' 04"
	(Barney B. Barstow '57 - '78)							
	Reuben Johnson	TB	1912	D	71*	78' 00"	17' 00"	11' 00"
	(Buffalo {1} '12 - '28, USCOE Churchill '28 - '46, USCOE Buffalo {1} '46 - '74, Todd Fraser '74 - '78)							
	Todd L.	TB	1965	D	22*	42' 10"	12' 00"	5' 06"
	(Robert W. Fraser '65 - '78)							
	Troy L. Johnson	TB	1959	D	24*	42' 08"	12' 00"	5' 05"
	Wally Kendzora	TB	1956	D	24*	43' 00"	12' 00"	5' 06"
	(Byron S. Nelson '56 - '65)							
	Wells Larson	TB	1953	D	22*	42' 10"	12' 00"	5' 06"
	(E. C. Knudsen '53 - '74)							
F-7	**FREDERICK PAINE, SUPERIOR, WI**							
	Spanky Paine	TB	1894	D	124*	94' 06"	22' 00"	11' 00"
	(Tioga 1894 - ?, Calumet ? - ?, John F. Drews ? - '67, Wiiliam J. Dugan '67 - '91)							
F-8	**FROST ENGINEERING CO., FRANKFORT, MI**							
	Captain George	TB	1929	D	61*	63' 00"	17' 00"	7' 08"
	(USCOE Captain George '29 - '68, Captain George '68 - '73, Kurt R. Luetdke '73 - '91)							
G-1	**GAELIC TUG BOAT CO., GROSSE ILE, MI**							
	Blackie B.	TB	1952	D	146*	85' 00"	25' 00"	11' 00"
	(Bonita {2} '52 - '85, Susan Hoey {2} '85 - '95)							
	Carolyn Hoey	TB	1951	D	146*	90' 00"	25' 00"	11' 00"
	(Atlas '51 - '84 Susan Hoey {1} '84 - '85, Atlas '85 - '87)							
	G.T.B. No. 1	DB	1956	B	2,500	248' 00"	43' 00"	12' 00"
	L.S.C. 236	TK	1946	B	10,000	195' 00"	35' 00"	10' 06"
	Marysville	TK	1973	B	16,000	200' 00"	50' 00"	12' 06"
	Patricia Hoey {2}	TB	1949	D	146*	88' 06"	25' 00"	11' 00"
	(Propeller '49 - '82, Bantry Bay '82 - '91)							
	Roger Stahl	TB	1944	D	148*	110' 00"	26' 05"	15' 05"
	(USCG Kennebec [WYT-61] '44 - '44, USCG Kaw [WYT-61] '44 - '80, Kaw '80 - '97)							
	Shannon	TB	1944	D	145*	101' 00"	28' 00"	13' 00"
	(USS Connewango [YTB-338] '44 - '77)							
	Susan Hoey	TB	1950	D	146*	82' 00"	25' 00"	10' 07"
	(Navajo {1} '50 - '53, Seaval '53 - '64, Mary T. Tracy '64 - '69, Yankee '69 - '70, Minn '70 - '74, William S. Bell '74 - '83, Newcastle '83 - '93, Laura Lynn '93-'99)							
	William Hoey	TB	1924	D	99*	85' 00"	21' 06"	10' 09"
	(Martha C. '24 - '52, Langdon C. Hardwicke '52 - '82, Wabash {2} '82 - '93, Katie Ann '93 - '99)							
G-2	**GALACTICA 001 ENTERPRISE LTD., TORONTO, ON**							
	Enterprise 2000	ES	1998	D				
	Galactica 001	ES	1957	D	67*	50' 00"	16' 00"	6' 03"
G-3	**GALLAGHER MARINE CONSTRUCTION CO., INC., ESCANABA, MI**							
	Bee Jay	TB	1939	D	19*	45' 00"	13' 00"	7' 00"
G-4	**GANANOQUE BOAT LINE LTD., GANANOQUE, ON**							
	Thousand Islander	ES	1972	D	200*	96' 11"	22' 01"	5' 05"
	Thousand Islander II	ES	1973	D	200*	99' 00"	22' 01"	5' 00"
	Thousand Islander III	ES	1975	D	376*	118' 00"	28' 00"	6' 00"
	Thousand Islander IV	ES	1976	D	347*	110' 09"	28' 04"	10' 08"
	Thousand Islander V	ES	1979	D	246*	88' 00"	24' 00"	5' 00"

Fleet #	Fleet Name / Vessel Name	Type of Vessel	Year Built	Type of Engine	Cargo Cap. or Gross*	Overall Length	Breadth	Depth or Draft*
G-5	**GANNON UNIVERSITY, ERIE, PA**							
	Environaut	RV	1950	D	17*	55' 00"	13' 06"	3' 10"*
G-6	**GARY ZULAUF, OSHAWA, ON**							
	Rhea	MS	1943	D	245*	136' 00"	24' 06"	10' 00"
	(USS YMS-299 '43 - '47, USS Rhea [AMS-52 / MSCO-52] '47 - '60)							
	(The Rhea earned 3 Battle Stars during World War II as the USS YMS-299.)							
G-7	**GENESEE MARINE, INC.**							
	Spirit of Rochester	ES	1975	D	80*	124' 03"	28' 06"	7' 03"
G-8	**GEORGIAN BAY CRUISE CO., PARRY SOUND, ON**							
	Chippewa {5}	PA	1954	D		65' 00"	16' 00"	6' 06"
G-9	**GILLESPIE OIL & TRANSIT, INC., ST. JAMES, MI**							
	American Girl	PK	1922	D	40	64' 00"	14' 00"	8' 03"
	Oil Queen	TK	1949	B	620	65' 00"	16' 00"	6' 00"
G-10	**GODERICH ELEVATORS LTD., GODERICH, ON**							
	Willowglen	BC	1943	R	16,300	620' 06"	60' 00"	35' 00"
	(Launched as Mesabi, Lehigh {3} '43 - '81, Joseph X. Robert '81 - '82)							
	(Last operated 21 December 1992 — 5 year survey expired October 1997.)							
	(Currently in use as a stationary grain storage vessel in Goderich, ON.)							
G-11	**GOODTIME ISLAND CRUISES, INC., SANDUSKY, OH**							
	Goodtime I	ES	1960	D	81*	111' 00"	29' 08"	9' 05"
G-12	**GOODTIME TRANSIT BOATS, INC., CLEVELAND, OH**							
	Goodtime III	ES	1990	D	95*	161' 00"	40' 00"	11' 00"
G-13	**GRAND VALLEY STATE UNIVERSITY, ALLENDALE, MI**							
	ROBERT B. ANNIS WATER RESOURCES INSTITUTE							
	D. J. Angus	RV	1986	D	14*	45' 00"	14' 00"	4' 00"*
	W. G. Jackson	RV	1996	D	80*	64' 10"	20' 00"	5' 00"*
G-14	**GRAVEL & LAKE SERVICES LTD., THUNDER BAY, ON**							
	Donald Mac	TB	1914	D	69*	71' 00"	17' 00"	10' 00"
	F. A. Johnson	TB	1953	B	439*	150' 00"	32' 00"	10' 00"
	(Capt. Charles T. Parker '52 - '54, Rapid Cities '54 - '69, S. P. Renolds '69 - '70)							
	George N. Carleton	TB	1943	D	97*	82' 00"	21' 00"	11' 00"
	(Bansaga '43 - '64)							
	Peninsula	TB	1944	D	261*	111' 00"	27' 00"	13' 00"
	(HMCS Norton [W-31] '44 - '45, W.A.C. 1 '45 - '46)							
	Robert John	TB	1945	D	98*	82' 00"	20' 01"	11' 00"
	(Bansturdy '45 - '66)							
	Wolf River	BC	1956	D	5,880	349' 02"	43' 07"	25' 04"
	(Tecumseh {2} '56 - '67, New York News {3} '67 - '86, Stella Desgagnes '86 - '93, Beam Beginner '94 - '95)							
G-15	**GREAT LAKES ASSOCIATES, INC., ROCKY RIVER, OH**							
	Kinsman Enterprise {2}	BC	1927	T	16,000	631' 00"	65' 00"	33' 00"
	(Harry Coulby {2} '27 - '89)							
	(Last operated 13 December 1995 — 5 year survey expired May 1998 — Currently laid up in Buffalo, NY.)							
	Kinsman Independent {3}	BC	1952	T	18,800	642' 03"	67' 00"	35' 00"
	(Charles L. Hutchinson {3} '52 - '62, Ernest R. Breech '62 - '88)							
G-16	**THE GREAT LAKES GROUP, CLEVELAND, OH**							
	THE GREAT LAKES TOWING CO. - A DIVISION OF THE GREAT LAKES GROUP							
	Alabama {2}	TB	1916	D	98*	81' 00"	21' 03"	12' 05"
	Arizona	TB	1931	D	98*	84' 04"	20' 00"	12' 06"
	Arkansas {2}	TB	1909	D	98*	81' 00"	21' 03"	12' 05"
	(Yale '09 - '48)							
	California	TB	1926	D	98*	81' 00"	20' 00"	12' 06"
	Colorado	TB	1928	D	98*	84' 04"	20' 00"	12' 06"
	Delaware {4}	TB	1924	D	98*	81' 00"	20' 00"	12' 06"
	Favorite	FD		B	250	90' 00"	50' 00"	5' 00"
	Florida	TB	1926	D	99*	81' 00"	20' 00"	12' 06"
	Idaho	TB	1931	D	98*	84' 00"	20' 00"	12' 06"
	Illinois {2}	TB	1914	D	99*	81' 00"	20' 00"	12' 06"
	Indiana	TB	1911	D	97*	81' 00"	20' 00"	12' 06"
	Iowa	TB	1915	D	98*	81' 00"	20' 00"	12' 06"
	Kansas	TB	1927	D	98*	81' 00"	20' 00"	12' 06"
	Kentucky {2}	TB	1929	D	98*	84' 04"	20' 00"	12' 06"
	Louisiana	TB	1917	D	98*	81' 00"	20' 00"	12' 06"
	Maine {1}	TB	1921	D	96*	81' 00"	20' 00"	12' 06"
	(Maine {1} '21 - '82, Saipan '82 - '83, Hillsboro '83 - '84)							

Fleet #	Fleet Name Vessel Name	Type of Vessel	Year Built	Type of Engine	Cargo Cap. or Gross*	Overal Length	Breadth	Depth or Draft*
	Maryland {2}	TB	1925	D	98*	81' 00"	21' 03"	12' 05"
	(Maryland {2} '25 - '82, Tarawa '82 - '83, Pasco '83 - '84)							
	Massachusetts	TB	1928	D	98*	84' 04"	20' 00"	12' 06"
	Minnesota {1}	TB	1911	D	98*	81' 00"	20' 00"	12' 06"
	Mississippi	TB	1916	D	98*	81' 00"	20' 00"	12' 06"
	Missouri {2}	TB	1927	D	149*	88' 04"	24' 06"	12' 03"
	(Rogers City {1} '27 - '56, Dolomite {1} '56 - '81, Chippewa {7} '81 - '90)							
	Montana	TB	1929	D	98*	84' 04"	20' 00"	12' 06"
	Nebraska	TB	1929	D	98*	84' 04"	20' 00"	12' 06"
	New Jersey	TB	1924	D	98*	81' 00"	20' 00"	12' 06"
	(New Jersey '24 - '52, Petco-21 '52 - '53)							
	New York	TB	1913	D	98*	81' 00"	20' 00"	12' 06"
	North Carolina {2}	TB	1952	D	145*	87' 09"	24' 01"	10' 07"
	(Limestone '52 - '83, Wicklow '83 - '90)							
	North Dakota	TB	1910	D	97*	81' 00"	20' 00"	12' 06"
	(John M. Truby '10 - '38)							
	Ohio {3}	TB	1903	D	194*	118' 00"	24' 00"	13' 06"
	(M.F.D. No. 15 '03 - '52, Laurence C. Turner '52 - '73)							
	Oklahoma	TB	1913	D	97*	81' 00"	20' 00"	12' 06"
	(T. C. Lutz {2} '13 - '34)							
	Oregon {2}	TB	1952	D	149*	88' 07"	24' 10"	10' 09"
	(Jennifer George '52 - '82, Galway Bay '82 - '90)							
	Pennsylvania {3}	TB	1911	D	98*	81' 00"	20' 00"	12' 06"
	Rhode Island	TB	1930	D	98*	84' 04"	20' 00"	12' 06"
	South Carolina	TB	1925	D	102*	86' 00"	21' 00"	11' 00"
	(Welcome {2} '25 - '53, Joseph H. Callan '53 - '72 South Carolina '72 - '82, Tulagi '82 - '83)							
	Superior {3}	TB	1912	D	147*	97' 00"	22' 00"	12' 00"
	(Richard Fitzgerald '12 - '46)							
	Tennessee	TB	1917	D	98*	81' 00"	20' 00"	12' 06"
	Texas	TB	1916	D	97*	81' 00"	20' 00"	12' 06"
	Vermont	TB	1914	D	98*	81' 00"	20' 00"	12' 06"
	Virginia {2}	TB	1914	D	97*	81' 00"	20' 00"	12' 06"
	Washington {1}	TB	1925	D	97*	81' 00"	20' 00"	12' 06"
	Wisconsin {4}	TB	1897	D	105*	90' 03"	21' 00"	12' 03"
	(America {3} 1897 - '82, Midway '82 - '83)							
	Wyoming	TB	1929	D	104	84' 04"	20' 00"	12' 06"
G-17	**GREAT LAKES MARINE ENGINEERING & SALVAGE, INC., ALPENA, MI**							
	Atlas	RV	1941	D	157*	90' 07"	21' 04"	11' 00"
G-18	**GREAT LAKES MARITIME ACADEMY, TRAVERSE CITY, MI**							
	Anchor Bay	TV	1953	D	23*	45' 00"	13' 00"	7' 00"*
	GLMA Barge	TV	1960	B	25	80' 00"	20' 00"	7' 00"
	Northwestern {2}	TV	1969	D	12*	55' 00"	15' 00"	6' 06"
G-19	**GREAT LAKES RESPONSE CORP.**							
	Dover Light	EV	1968	B	7,870	146' 05"	50' 00"	13' 07"
	Sillery	EV	1963	D	9,415	175' 00"	36' 00"	14' 00"
	S.M.T.B. No. 7	EV	1969	B	7,502	150' 00"	33' 00"	14' 00"
G-20	**GREAT LAKES SCHOONER CO., TORONTO, ON**							
	Challenge	3S	1980	W	76*	96' 00"	16' 06"	8' 00"
	True North of Toronto	2S	1947	W	95*	115' 00"	20' 00"	10' 06"
G-21	**GREAT LAKES SHIPWRECK HISTORICAL SOCIETY, SAULT STE. MARIE, MI**							
	Antiquarian	RV		D		40' 00"	12' 00"	4' 00"
	David Boyd	RV	1982	D	23*	47' 00"	17' 00"	3' 00"*
G-22	**GREAT LAKES TRANSPORT LTD., HALIFAX, NS**							
	Sarah Spencer	SU	1959	B	23,200	611" 03"	72' 00"	40' 00"
	(Adam E. Cornelius {3} '59 - '89, Capt. Edward V. Smith '89 - '91, Sea Barge One '91 - '96)							
	ATLANTIC TOWING LTD. - VESSEL CHARTERED BY GREAT LAKES TRANSPORT LTD.							
	Atlantic Hickory	TB	1973	D	886*	153' 06"	38' 10"	22' 00"
	(Irving Miami '73 - '95)							
G-23	**GREEN BAY ACQUISITION CO., INC., MENOMINEE, MI**							
	William H. Donner	CS	1914	R	9,400	524' 00"	54' 00"	30' 00"
	(Last operated in 1969 — Currently in use as a cargo transfer vessel in Menominee, MI.)							
H-1	**HALRON OIL CO., INC., GREEN BAY, WI**							
	Mr. Micky	TK	1940	B	10,500	195' 00"	35' 00"	10' 00"
H-2	**HAMILTON HARBOUR COMMISSIONERS, HAMILTON, ON**							
	Judge McCombs	TB	1948	D	10*	36' 00"	10' 03"	4' 00"

Melissa Desgagnes, upbound for Lake Superior. (Roger LeLievre)

Great Lakes-built, keeper-class U.S. Coast Guard cutter Barbara Mabrity 8 August 1999, bound for service on saltwater. (Roger LeLievre)

Fleet #	Fleet Name Vessel Name	Type of Vessel	Year Built	Type of Engine	Cargo Cap. or Gross*	Overal Length	Breadth	Depth or Draft*
H-3	**HANK VAN ASPERT, WINDSOR, ON**							
	Queen City {2}	PA	1911	D	248*	116' 00"	23' 00"	12' 07"
	(Last operated in 1982 — Currently laid up in LaSalle, ON.)							
H-4	**HANNAH MARINE CORP., LEMONT, IL**							
	Daryl C. Hannah {2}	TB	1956	D	268*	102' 00"	28' 00"	8' 00"
	(Cindy Jo '56 - '66, Katherine L. '66 - '93)							
	Donald C. Hannah	TB	1962	D	191*	91' 00"	29' 00"	11' 06"
	Hannah D. Hannah	TB	1955	D	134*	86' 00"	24' 00"	10' 00"
	(Harbor Ace '55 - '61, Gopher State '61 - '71, Betty Gale '71 - '93)							
	Hannah 1801	TK	1967	B	18,550	240' 00"	50' 00"	12' 00"
	Hannah 1802	TK	1967	B	18,550	240' 00"	50' 00"	12' 00"
	Hannah 2801	TK	1980	B	28,665	275' 00"	54' 00"	17' 06"
	Hannah 2901	TK	1962	B	17,400	264' 00"	52' 06"	.12' 06"
	Hannah 2902	TK	1962	B	17,360	264' 00"	52' 06"	12' 06"
	Hannah 2903	TK	1962	B	17,350	264' 00"	52' 06"	12' 06"
	(2903 '62 - '90)							
	Hannah 3601	TK	1972	B	35,360	290' 00"	60' 00"	18' 03"
	Hannah 5101	TK	1978	B	49,660	360' 00"	60' 00"	22' 06"
	James A. Hannah	TB	1945	D	593*	149' 00"	33' 00"	16' 00"
	(U.S. Army LT-280 '45 - '65, Muskegon {1} '65 - '71)							
	Kristin Lee Hannah	TB	1945	D	602*	149' 00"	33' 00"	16' 00"
	(U.S. Army LT-815 '45 - '64, Henry Foss '64 - '84, Kristin Lee '84 - '93)							
	Mark Hannah	TBA	1969	D	191*	127' 05"	32' 01"	14' 03"
	(Lead Horse '69 - '73, Gulf Challenger '73 - '80, Challenger {2} '80 - '93)							
	Mary E. Hannah	TB	1945	D	612*	149' 00"	33' 00"	16' 00"
	(U.S. Army LT-821 '45 - '47, Brooklyn '47 - '66, Lee Reuben '66 - '75)							
	Mary Page Hannah {2}	TB	1972	D	99*	59' 08"	24' 01"	10' 03"
	(Kings Squire '72 - '78, Juanita D. '78 - '79 Katherine L. '79 - '93)							
	No. 25	TK	1949	B	19,500	254' 00"	54' 00"	11' 00"
	No. 26	TK	1949	B	19,500	254' 00"	54' 00"	11' 00"
	No. 28	TK	1957	B	20,725	240' 00"	50' 00"	12' 06"
	No. 29 {2}	TK	1952	B	22,000	254' 00"	54' 00"	11' 06"
	Peggy D. Hannah	TB	1920	D	145*	108' 00"	25' 00"	14' 00"
	(William A. Whitney '20 - '92)							
H-5	**HARBOR LIGHT CRUISE LINES, INC., TOLEDO, OH**							
	Sandpiper	ES	1984	D	19*	65' 00"	16' 00"	4' 00"
H-6	**HARRAH'S CASINO, EAST CHICAGO, IN**							
	Showboat Mardi Gras	GA	1996	D	12,182*	340' 00"	74' 00"	17' 06"
H-7	**HARRY GAMBLE SHIPYARDS, PORT DOVER, ON**							
	H. A. Smith	TB	1944	D	24*	55' 00"	16' 00"	5' 06"
	J. A. Cornett	TB	1937	D	60*	65' 00"	17' 00"	9' 00"
H-8	**HILTVEIT ASSOCIATES INC., NEW YORK, NY**							
	Martha A	TK	1986	D	103,130	433' 01"	67' 00"	36' 09"
	Rachel B	TK	1987	D	103,520	433' 01"	67' 00"	36' 09"
H-9	**HOLLY MARINE TOWING, CHICAGO, IL**							
	Chris Ann	TB	1981	D	45*	51' 09"	17' 00"	6' 01"
	(Captain Robbie '81 - '90, Philip M. Pearse '90 - '97)							
	Holly Ann	TB	1926	D	220*	108' 00"	26' 06"	15' 00"
	(Wm. A. Lydon '26 - '92)							
	Margaret Ann	TB	1954	D	131*	82' 00"	24' 06"	11' 06"
	(John A. McGuire '54 - '87, William Hoey '87 - '94)							
	New Mexico {2}	TB	1961	D	96*	65' 06"	24' 00"	9' 00"
H-10	**HORNE TRANSPORTATION, WOLFE ISLAND, ON**							
	William Darrell	CF	1952	D	66*	66' 00"	28' 00"	6' 00"
H-11	**HOWE ISLAND TOWNSHIP, KINGSTON, ON**							
	The Howe Islander	CF	1946	D	13*	53' 00"	12' 00"	3' 00"
H-12	**HULLFORMS (CANADA), INC., WIARTON, ON**							
	Cloud Chaser	ES	1979	D	62*	67' 00"	17' 00"	11' 00"
H-13	**HYDROGRAPHIC SURVEY CO., CHICAGO, IL**							
	Neptune	RV	1970	D		67' 00"	18' 05"	5' 00"
I-1	**ILLINOIS MARINE TOWING, INC., LEMONT, IL**							
	Aggie C	TB	1977	D	89*	81' 00"	26' 00"	6' 10"*
	Albert C	TB	1971	D	47*	61' 02"	18' 00"	5' 08"*
	Chicago Peace	TB	1979	D	101*	61' 04"	26' 00"	8' 00"*

Fleet #	Fleet Name / Vessel Name	Type of Vessel	Year Built	Type of Engine	Cargo Cap. or Gross*	Overall Length	Breadth	Depth or Draft*
	Eileen C	TB	1982	D	122*	75' 00"	26' 00"	8' 00"*
	Hennepin I	TB	1957	D	35*	48' 04"	16' 00"	4' 00"*
	Mary C	TB	1946	D	34*	56' 02"	18' 00"	5' 00"*
	William C	TB	1968	D	105*	76' 06"	24' 00"	6' 06"*
I-2	**IMPERIAL OIL LTD. - ESSO PETROLEUM CANADA DIVISION, DARTMOUTH, NS**							
	Imperial Dartmouth	RT	1970	D	15,265	205' 06"	40' 00"	16' 00"
	Imperial Lachine {2}	RT	1963	D	9,415	175' 00"	36' 00"	14' 00"
I-3	**INLAND BULK TRANSFER, CLEVELAND, OH**							
	Benjamin Ridgeway	TB	1969	D	51*	53' 00"	18' 05"	7' 05"
	Frank Palladino Jr.	TB	1980	D	89*	100' 00"	32' 00"	13' 00"
	(Lady Ida '80 - '92)							
	Inland 2401	DB	1968	B	2,589	240' 00"	72' 00"	14' 00"
	James Palladino	TB	1999	D	392*	109' 11"	34' 01"	16' 01"
	Kellstone 1	SU	1957	B	9,000	396' 00"	71' 00"	22' 06"
I-4	**INLAND LAKES MANAGEMENT, INC., ALPENA, MI**							
	Alpena {2}	CC	1942	T	15,550	519' 06"	67' 00"	35' 00"
	(Leon Fraser '42 - '91)							
	E. M. Ford	CC	1898	Q	7,100	428' 00"	50' 00"	28' 00"
	(Presque Isle {1} 1898 - '56)							
	(Last operated 16 September 1996 — 5 year survey expires July 2001.)							
	(Currently in use as a stationary cement storage/transfer vessel in Saginaw, MI.)							
	J. A. W. Iglehart	CC	1936	T	12,500	501' 06"	68' 03"	37' 00"
	(Pan Amoco '36 - '55, Amoco '55 - '60, H. R. Schemn '60 - '65)							
	Paul H. Townsend	CC	1945	D	8,400	447' 00"	50' 00"	29' 00"
	(USNS Hickory Coll '45 - '46, USNS Coastal Delegate '46 - '52)							
	S. T. Crapo	CC	1927	R	8,900	402' 06"	60' 03"	29' 00"
	(Last operated 4 September 1996 — 5 year survey expired October 1997.)							
	(Currently in use as a stationary cement storage/transfer vessel in Green Bay, WI.)							
I-5	**INLAND SEAS EDUCATION ASSOCIATION, SUTTONS BAY, MI**							
	Inland Seas	RV	1994	W	41*	61' 06"	17' 00"	7' 00"
I-6	**THE INTERLAKE STEAMSHIP CO., RICHFIELD, OH**							
	Charles M. Beeghly	SU	1959	T	31,000	806' 00"	75' 00"	37' 06"
	(Shenango II '59 - '67)							
	Elton Hoyt 2nd {2}	SU	1952	T	22,300	698' 00"	70' 00"	37' 00"
	Herbert C. Jackson	SU	1959	T	24,800	690' 00"	75' 00"	37' 06"
	James R. Barker	SU	1976	D	63,300	1,004' 00"	105' 00"	50' 00"
	Mesabi Miner	SU	1977	D	63,300	1,004' 00"	105' 00"	50' 00"
	Paul R. Tregurtha	SU	1981	D	68,000	1,013' 06"	105' 00"	56' 00"
	(William J. DeLancey '81 - '90)							
	INTERLAKE TRANSPORTATION, INC. - A DIVISION OF THE INTERLAKE STEAMSHIP CO.							
	Dorothy Ann	TBA	1999	D	1,600*	124' 03"	44' 00"	24' 00"
	Pathfinder {3}	SU	1953	B	21,260	606' 02"	70' 00"	36' 00"
	(J. L. Mauthe '53 - '97)							
	[Dorothy Ann / Pathfinder {3} overall dimensions together]					700' 00"	70' 00"	36' 00"
	LAKES SHIPPING CO., INC. - A DIVISION OF THE INTERLAKE STEAMSHIP CO.							
	John Sherwin {2}	BC	1958	T	31,500	806' 00"	75' 00"	37' 06"
	(Last operated 16 November 1981 — 5 year survey expired May 1984.)							
	(Currently laid up in Superior, WI.)							
	Kaye E. Barker	SU	1952	T	25,900	767' 00"	70' 00"	36' 00"
	(Edward B. Greene '52 - '85, Benson Ford {3} '85 - '89)							
	Lee A. Tregurtha	SU	1942	T	29,300	826' 00"	75' 00"	39' 00"
	(Laid down as Mobiloil, Launched as Samoset, USS Chiwawa [AO-68] '42 - '46,							
	Chiwawa '46 - '61, Walter A. Sterling '61 - '85, William Clay Ford {2} '85 - '89)							
	(The Lee A. Tregurtha earned 2 Battle Stars during World War II as the USS Chiwawa.)							
I-7	**INTERNATIONAL MARINE SYSTEMS LTD., MILWAUKEE, WI**							
	Iroquois {1}	ES	1946	D	57*	61' 09"	21' 00"	6' 04"
I-8	**IRVINGDALE SHIPPING LTD., SAINT JOHN, NB**							
	ATLANTIC TOWING LTD. - A DIVISION OF IRVINGDALE SHIPPING LTD.							
	ATL 2301	DB	1977	B	3,500	230' 00"	60' 00"	14' 00"
	ATL 2302	DB	1977	B	3,500	230' 00"	60' 00"	14' 00"
	ATL 2401	DB	1981	B	4,310	240' 00"	70' 00"	15' 00"
	ATL 2402	DB	1981	B	4,310	240' 00"	70' 00"	15' 00"
	Atlantic Adler	TB	1982	D	149*	59' 09"	28' 00"	11' 00"
	(Gordon Gill '82 - '97)							
	Atlantic Beech	TB	1983	D	294*	104' 02"	30' 03"	13' 02"
	(Irving Beech '83 - '98)							

J.A.W. Iglehart in the Welland Canal,
13 July 1999. (Roger LeLievre)

Fleet # Fleet Name Vessel Name	Type of Vessel	Year Built	Type of Engine	Cargo Cap. or Gross*	Overall Length	Breadth	Depth or Draft*
Atlantic Birch	TT	1967	D	827*	162' 03"	38' 02"	19' 08"
(Irving Birch '67 - '99)							
Atlantic Cedar	TB	1974	D	708*	148' 04"	35' 07"	21' 06"
(Sinni '74 - '81, Irving Cedar '81 - '96)							
Atlantic Elm	TB	1980	D	427*	116' 01"	31' 06"	18' 08"
(Irving Elm '80 - '98)							
Atlantic Hemlock	TT	1996	D	290*	101' 00"	36' 06"	12' 06"
Atlantic Maple	TB	1966	D	487*	125' 08"	32' 04"	17' 06"
(Irving Maple '66 - '98)							
Atlantic Oak	TB	1981	D	464*	160' 00"	34' 00"	15' 08"
(Canmar Tugger '81 - '93)							
Atlantic Poplar	TB	1965	D	195*	96' 06"	30' 00"	14' 00"
(Amherstburg '66 - '75, Irving Poplar '75 - '96)							
Atlantic Spruce {2}	TT	1998	D	290*	101' 00"	36' 06"	17' 00"
Atlantic Teak	TB	1976	D	265*	104' 00"	30' 00"	14' 03"
(Essar '76 - '79, Irving Teak '79 - '96)							
Atlantic Willow	TT	1998	D	383*	101' 00"	36' 06"	17' 00"
Irving Dolphin	TK	1964	B	1,441	200' 00"	50' 00"	13' 00"
Irving Juniper	TB	1961	D	247*	110' 00"	27' 02"	13' 03"
(Thorness '61 - '84)							
Irving Pine	TB	1976	D	159*	70' 00"	24' 00"	7' 08"
(Grampa Shorty '76 - '76)							
Irving Tamarack	TB	1969	D	86*	70' 00"	20' 00"	12' 00"
Seal VII	TK	1974	B	3,390	223' 06"	51' 03"	14' 00"
Sealion VII	TK	1969	B	1,548	359' 00"	74' 01"	27' 00"
Shark VII	TK	1964	B	1,441	200' 00"	50' 00"	13' 00"
KENT LINE INTERNATIONAL LTD. - A DIVISION OF IRVINGDALE SHIPPING LTD.							
Irving Arctic	TK	1974	D	292,960	629' 00"	90' 03"	48' 03"
Irving Canada	TK	1981	D	297,407	628' 06"	90' 02"	48' 03"
Irving Eskimo	TK	1980	D	292,960	629' 00"	90' 03"	48' 03"
Irving Timber	RR	1978	D	9,265	415' 00"	66' 03"	38' 05"
(Uta-Sabine '78 - '78, Merzario Lombardia '78 - '79, Uta-Sabine '79 - '82, Camino '82 - '85, Uta-Sabine '85 - '86)							
Kent Carrier	GC	1971	B	8,128	363' 00"	82' 02"	22' 03"
Kent Express	GC	1999	D	13,020*			
Kent Voyageur	GC	1982	D	15,912	488' 10"	78' 01"	42' 00"
(Reed Voyageur '82 - '88, Daishowa Voyageur '88 - '96)							
Kent Transport	GC	1971	D	7,366	362' 10"	82' 02"	22' 03"
(Rothesay Carrier '71 - '97)							
Wellington Kent {2}	TK	1980	D	120,790	433' 11"	67' 04"	30' 04"
(Irving Nordic '80 - '93)							
I-9 ISLAND ROCKET BOAT LINES, SANDUSKY, OH							
Island Rocket	PF		D				
Island Rocket II	PF	1999	D				
I-10 ISLAND FERRY SERVICES CORP., CHEBOYGAN, MI							
Bob Lo Islander	PF	1957	D	31*	68' 00"	21' 00"	5' 00"*
Sandy Graham	CF	1957	D	194*			
I-11 IVY LEA 1,000 ISLANDS BOAT TOURS, IVY LEA, ON							
Miss Ivy Lea II	ES		D		66' 00"	15' 00"	5' 00"
Miss Ivy Lea III	ES		D		48' 00"	12' 00"	5' 00"
J-1 J. M. MARINE TOWING CORP., SYRACUSE, NY							
Ariel	TB	1945	D	27*	56' 00"	15' 10"	7' 00"*
Dynamic	TB	1958	D	19*	34' 11"	12' 00"	4' 08"*
J-2 J. W. WESTCOTT CO., DETROIT, MI							
J. W. Westcott II	MB	1949	D	11*	46' 01"	13' 04"	4' 06"
Joseph J. Hogan	MB	1957	D	16*	40' 00"	12' 06"	5' 00"
(Ottawa '57 - '95)							
J-3 JACOBS INVESTMENTS - JRM, INC., CLEVELAND, OH							
Nautica Queen	ES	1981	D	95*	124' 00"	31' 02"	8' 10"
J-4 JAMES MAZUREK, HARRISON TWP., MI							
West Wind	TB	1941	D	54*	60' 04"	17' 01"	7' 07"
J-5 JOSEPH G. GAYTON, HARROW, ON							
Jenny T. II	TB	1915	D	66*	68' 07"	17' 00"	11' 00"
(Ashtabula '15 - '55, Tiffin '55 - '69)							
Princess No. 1	TB	1903	D	87*	77' 00"	20' 04"	7' 11"
(Radiant '03 - '33, Anna Sheridan '33 - '62, Princess '62 - '77)							

Fleet #	Fleet Name Vessel Name	Type of Vessel	Year Built	Type of Engine	Cargo Cap. or Gross*	Overal Length	Breadth	Depth or Draft*
J-6	JOSEPH MARTIN, BEAVER ISLAND, MI							
	Shamrock {1}	TB	1933	D	60*	64' 00"	18' 00"	7' 04"
J-7	JUBILEE QUEEN CRUISES, TORONTO, ON							
	Jubilee Queen	ES	1986	D	269*	122' 00"		
	Pioneer Princess	ES	1984	D	74*	56' 00"		
	Pioneer Queen	ES	1968	D	110*	85' 00"	30' 06"	7' 03"
J-8	JULIO CONTRACTING CO., HANCOCK, MI							
	Winnebago	TB	1945	D	14*	40' 00"	10' 02"	4' 06"
K-1	KEMMA JO WALSH, ZEELAND, MI							
	Captain Barnaby	TB	1956	D	146*	94' 00"	27' 00"	11' 09"
	(William C. Gaynor '56 - '88)							
K-2	KADINGER MARINE SERVICE, INC., MILWAUKEE, WI							
	David J. Kadinger Jr.	TB	1969	D	98*	65' 06"	22' 00"	8' 06"
	Jason A. Kadinger	TB	1963	D	60*	52' 06"	19' 01"	7' 04"
	Ruffy J. Kadinger	TB	1981	D	74*	55' 00"	23' 00"	7' 02"
K-3	KCBX TERMINALS CO., CHICAGO, IL							
	Matador VI	TB	1971	D	31*	42' 00"	18' 00"	6' 00"*
K-4	KELLEY'S ISLAND FERRY BOAT LINES, MARBLEHEAD, OH							
	Erie Isle	CF	1951	D	59*	72' 00"	24' 00"	8' 03"
	Kayla Marie	CF	1975	D		122' 00"	40' 00"	
	Shirley Irene	CF	1991	D	68*	160' 00"	46' 00"	9' 00"
K-5	KEYSTONE GREAT LAKES, INC., BALA CYNWYD, PA							
	Great Lakes {2}	TK	1982	B	75,000	414' 00"	60' 00"	30' 00"
	(Amoco Great Lakes '82 - '85)							
	Michigan {10}	TB	1982	D	293*	107' 08"	34' 00"	16' 00"
	(Amoco Michigan '82 - '85)							
	[Great Lakes {2} / Michigan {10} overall dimensions together]					454' 00"	60' 00"	30' 00"
K-6	KINDRA LAKE TOWING LP., DOWNERS GROVE, IL							
	Buckley	TB	1958	D	94*	95' 00"	26' 00"	11' 00"
	(Linda Brooks '58 - '67, Eddie B. {2} '67 - '95)							
	Morgan	TB	1974	D	134*	90' 00"	30' 00"	10' 06"
	(Donald O' Toole '74 - '86, Bonesey B. '86 - '95)							
	Old Mission	TB	1945	D	94*	85' 00"	23' 00"	10' 04"
	(U.S. Army ST-880 '45 - '47, USCOE Avondale '47 - '64, Adrienne B. '64 - '95)							
K-7	KING COMPANY, INC., HOLLAND, MI							
	Barry J	TB	1943	D	42*	46' 00"	13' 00"	7' 00"
	Carol Ann	TB	1981	D	115*	68' 00"	24' 00"	8' 08"
	Julie Dee	TB	1903	D	59*	63' 03"	17' 05"	9' 00"
	(Bonita {1} '03 - '16, Chicago Harbor No. 4 '16 - '60, Eddie B. {1} '60 - '69, Seneca Queen '69 - '70, Ludington '70 -?)							
	Miss Edna	TB	1935	D	29*	36' 08"	11' 02"	4' 08"
	Muskegon {2}	TB	1973	D	138*	75' 00"	24' 00"	11' 06"
K-8	KINGSTON 1,000 ISLANDS CRUISES, KINGSTON, ON							
	Island Belle I	ES	1988	D	150*	65' 00"	22' 00"	8' 00"
	Island Queen III	ES	1975	D	300*	96' 00"	26' 00"	11' 00"
	Island Star	ES	1994	D	220*	97' 00"	30' 00"	10' 00"
L-1	LAFARGE CORP., SOUTHFIELD, MI							
	J. B. Ford	CC	1904	R	8,000	440' 00"	50' 00"	28' 00"
	(Edwin F. Holmes '04 - '16, E. C. Collins '16 - '59)							
	(Last operated 15 November 1985 — 5 year survey expired November 1989.)							
	(Currently in use as a stationary cement storage/transfer vessel in South Chicago, IL.)							
L-2	LAKE MICHIGAN CARFERRY SERVICE, INC., LUDINGTON, MI							
	Badger [43] {2}	CF	1953	S	4,244*	410' 06"	59' 06"	24' 00"
	Spartan [42] {2}	CF	1952	S	4,244*	410' 06"	59' 06"	24' 00"
	(Last operated 20 January 1979 — 5 year survey expired January 1981.)							
	(Currently laid up in Ludington, MI.)							
	Wynken, Blynken and Nod	CF	1957	D	73*	61' 01"	28' 10"	8' 06"
L-3	LAKE MICHIGAN CONTRACTORS, INC., HOLLAND, MI							
	Art Lapish	TB	1954	D	15*	44' 03"	12' 08"	5' 04"
	Cherokee {3}	DB	1943	B	1,500	155' 00"	50' 00"	13' 00"
	CMT-2	DB	1979	B	504*	100' 00"	40' 00"	7' 00"
	Curly B.	TB	1956	D	131*	84' 00"	26' 00"	9' 02"
	(Waverly '56 - '74, Bother Collins '74 - '80)							

Fleet #	Fleet Name / Vessel Name	Type of Vessel	Year Built	Type of Engine	Cargo Cap. or Gross*	Overal Length	Breadth	Depth or Draft*
	G. W. Falcon	TB	1936	D	22*	49' 07"	13' 08"	6' 02"
	Illinois {3}	DB	1971	B	521*	140' 00"	50' 00"	9' 00"
	Iroquois {2}	DB	1950	B	495*	120' 00"	30' 00"	7' 00"
	James Harris	TB	1943	D	18*	41' 09"	12' 05"	5' 07"
	John Henry	TB	1954	D	66*	70' 00"	20' 06"	9' 07"
	(U.S. Army ST-2013 '54 - '80)							
	Ojibway {2}	DB	1954	B	517*	120' 00"	50' 00"	10' 00"
	Shirley Joy	TB	1978	D	98*	72' 00"	26' 00"	7' 06"
	(Douglas B. Mackie '78 - '97)							
	Sioux {1}	DB	1954	B	518*	120' 00"	50' 00"	10' 00"
L-4	**LAKE MICHIGAN HARDWOOD CO., LELAND, MI**							
	Glen Shore	PK	1957	D	105	68' 00"	21' 00"	6' 00"
L-5	**LAKE SUPERIOR EXCURSIONS, BEAVER BAY, MN**							
	Grampa Woo III	ES	1978	D		115' 00"	22' 00"	5' 00"*
L-6	**LAKE TOWING, INC., AVON, OH**							
	Jiggs	TB	1911	D	45*	61' 00"	16' 00"	8' 00"
	Johnson	TB	1976	D	287*	140' 06"	40' 00"	15' 06"
	Johnson II	TB	1975	D	311*	194' 00"	40' 00"	17' 00"
L-7	**LAKES PILOTS ASSOCIATION, PORT HURON, MI**							
	Huron Belle	PB	1979	D	21*	50' 00"	16' 00"	7' 09"
	Huron Maid	PB	1976	D		46' 00"	16' 00"	
L-8	**LAURIN MARITIME (AMERICA), INC., HOUSTON, TX**							
	Mountain Blossom	TK	1986	D	70,020	527' 07"	74' 11"	39' 04"
	Nordic Blossom	TK	1981	D	152,216	505' 03"	74' 07"	45' 04"
	(Nordic Sun '81 - '89, Nordic '89 - '94)							
	Sunny Blossom	TK	1986	D	92,326	527' 07"	74' 11"	39' 05"
L-9	**LE BATEAU-MOUCHE AU VIEUX, MONTREAL, QC**							
	Le Bateau-Mouche	ES	1992	D	190*	108' 00"	22' 00"	3' 00"
L-10	**LE BRUN NORTHERN CONTRACTING, THUNDER BAY, ON**							
	Henry T.	DB	1932	B	1,000	120' 00"	44' 00"	11' 00"
L-11	**LE GROUPE OCEAN, INC., QUEBEC, QC**							
	Betsiamites	SU	1969	B	11,600	402' 00"	75' 00"	24' 00"
	Elmglen {2}	BC	1952	B	21,425	678' 00"	68' 03"	36' 03"
	(John O. McKellar {2} '52 - '84)							
	(Last operated in 24 June 1990 — Currently laid up in Quebec, QC.)							
	La Prairie	TB	1975	D	110*	73' 09"	25' 09"	11' 08"
	Lac St-Francois	BC	1979	B	1,200	195' 00"	35' 00"	12' 00"
	McAllister No. 3	DB	1956	B	1,000	165' 00"	38' 00"	9' 00"
	Mede	DB	1991	B		30' 00"	16' 00"	4' 00"
	Nanook	GC	1946	B	736	225' 00"	38' 00"	12' 06"
	Ocean Abys	DB	1948	B	1,000	140' 00"	40' 00"	9' 00"
	Ocean Bravo	TB	1970	D	320*	110' 00"	28' 06"	17' 00"
	(Takis V. '70 - '80, Donald P '80 - '80, Nimue '80 - '83, Donald P. '83 - '98)							
	Ocean Charlie	TB	1973	D	448*	123' 02"	31' 06"	18' 09"
	(Leonard W. '73 - '98)							
	Ocean Delta	TB	1973	D	722*	136' 08"	35' 08"	22' 00"
	(Sistella '73 - '78, Sandy Cape '78 - '80, Captain Ioannis S. '80 - '99)							
	Ocean Echo II	TBA	1969	D	438*	104' 08"	35' 05"	18' 00"
	(Atlantic '69 - '75, Laval '75 - '96)							
	Ocean Foxtrot	TB	1971	D	700*	184' 05"	38' 05"	16' 07"
	(Polor Shore '71 - '77, Canmar Supplier VII '77 - '95)							
	Salvage Scow No. 1	DB	1964	B	650	160' 00"	50' 00"	7' 00"
	McALLISTER TOWING & SALVAGE, INC. - A SUBSIDIARY OF LE GROUPE OCEAN, INC.							
	Basse-Cote	DB	1932	B	400	201' 00"	40' 00"	12' 00"
	Cathy McAllister	TB	1954	D	225*	101' 10"	26' 00"	13' 08"
	(Charlie S. '54 - '75)							
	Gercon #1	CS	1940	B	500	110' 00"	30' 00"	9' 00"
	Gercon #2	DB	1968	B		35' 00"	12' 00"	4' 00"
	McAllister No. 50	CS	1931	B		100' 00"	45' 00"	10' 00"
	Navcomar #1	DB	1955	B	500	135' 00"	35' 00"	9' 00"
	Ocean Alpha	TB	1960	D	202*	91' 06"	27' 03"	12' 06"
	(Jerry G. '60 - '98)							
	Ocean Golf	TB	1959	D	152*	103' 00"	25' 10"	11' 09"
	(Launched as Scranton, Helen M. McAllister '59 - '97)							
	Ocean Hercule	TB	1976	D	448*	120' 00"	32' 00"	19' 00"
	(Stril Pilot '76 - '81, Spirit Sky '81 - '86, Ierland '86 - '89, Ierlandia '89 - '95, Charles Antoine '95 - '97)							

Oakglen departs the Harvest States Elevator No. 1 in Superior, WI, with a load of canola. Tug Minnesota assists. *(Terry Sechen)*

OAKGLEN

Vessel Spotlight

OAKGLEN	
Length	714'06"
Beam	70'03"
Depth	37'03"
Built	1954
Tonnage	22,950

This traditionally-styled straight-decker entered service in 1954 as **T.R. McLagan** for Canada Steamship Lines, Montreal, QC. She was the last laker built by Midland Shipbuilding Co. Her power is derived from an 8,500 horsepower, Westinghouse steam-turbine engine, and she is equipped with a bowthruster. The vessel's 21 hatches feed into 6 holds; she can carry 22,950 tons at her maximum mid-summer draft of 26 feet, 7 inches.

Sailing on behalf of Canada Steamship Lines, the T.R. McLagan set several cargo records in her time. These include 22,257 tons of coal from Ashtabula, OH, to Hamilton, ON, on 1 August 1954, and a corn record of 22,256 tons from Duluth to Montreal, set early in the Seaway era. The T.R. McLagan was retired by CSL on 3 November 1984, and laid up at Kingston, ON. She was towed to Toronto in October 1987 to store soybeans.

After a refit at Port Weller Dry Docks, St. Catharines, ON in 1988, the T.R. McLagan returned to service under charter to P. & H.Shipping Ltd., Mississauga, ON. P. & H. purchased the vessel, renaming her **Oakglen**, while she was laid up at Goderich, ON, during the winter of 1989-90. The Oakglen continues to sail for P. & H., serving the parent company's (Parrish & Heimbecker) grain elevators at Owen Sound and Goderich, with occasional voyages to St. Lawrence River ports. The odd iron ore load rounds out the Oakglen's schedule.

— George Wharton

Fleet #	Fleet Name Vessel Name	Type of Vessel	Year Built	Type of Engine	Cargo Cap. or Gross*	Overal Length	Breadth	Depth or Draft*
	Ocean Intrepide	TT	1998	D	302*	80' 00"	30' 01"	14' 09"
	OKA No. 12	CS	1956	B	1,000	165' 00"	38' 00"	9' 00"
	P. S. Barge No. 1	BC	1923	B	3,000	258' 06"	43' 01"	20' 00"
	(Edwin T. Douglas '23 - '60)							
	Queng #1	DB	1924	B	500	100' 00"	38' 00"	9' 00"
	Salvage Monarch	TB	1959	D	219*	97' 09"	28' 00"	14' 06"
	SOREL TUGBOATS, INC. - A SUBSIDIARY OF McALLISTER TOWING & SALVAGE, INC.							
	Omni-Atlas	CS	1913	B	479*	133' 00"	42' 00"	10' 00"
	Omni-Richelieu	TB	1969	D	144*	83' 00"	24' 06"	13' 06"
	(Port Alfred II '69 - '82)							
	Omni Sorel	TB	1962	D	71*	72' 00"	19' 00"	12' 00"
	(Angus M. '62 - '92)							
	Omni St-Laurent	TB	1957	D	161*	99' 02"	24' 09"	12' 06"
	(Diligent '57 - '89)							
L-12	**LEE MARINE LTD., SOMBRA, ON**							
	Hammond Bay	ES	1992	D	43*	54' 00"	16' 00"	3' 00"
	Nancy A. Lee	TB	1939	D	9*	40' 00"	12' 00"	3' 00"
L-13	**LOCK TOURS CANADA BOAT CRUISES, SAULT STE. MARIE, ON**							
	Chief Shingwauk	ES	1965	D	109*	70' 00"	24' 00"	4' 06"
L-14	**LOWER LAKES TOWING LTD., PORT DOVER, ON**							
	Cuyahoga	SU	1943	D	15,675	620' 00"	60' 00"	35' 00"
	(J. Burton Ayers '43 - '95)							
	Saginaw	SU	1953	T	20,200	639' 03"	72' 00"	36' 00"
	(John J. Boland {3} '53 - '99)							
L-15	**LUEDTKE ENGINEERING CO., FRANKFORT, MI**							
	Alan K. Luedtke	TB	1944	D	149*	86' 04"	23' 00"	10' 03"
	(U.S. Army ST-527 '44 - '55, USCOE Two Rivers '55 - '90)							
	Chris E. Luedtke	TB	1936	D	18*	45' 00"	12' 03"	6' 00"
	Erich R. Luedtke	TB	1939	D	18*	45' 00"	12' 03"	6' 00"
	Gretchen B.	TB	1943	D	18*	45' 00"	12' 03"	6' 00"
	Karl E. Luedtke	TB	1928	D	32*	59' 03"	14' 09"	8' 00"
	Kurt Luedtke	TB	1956	D	96*	72' 00"	22' 06"	7' 06"
	(Jere C. '56 - '90)							
	Paul L. Luedtke	TB	1935	D	18*	42' 06"	11' 09"	6' 09"
M-1	**M. C. M. MARINE, INC., SAULT STE. MARIE, MI**							
	Drummond Islander II	CF	1961	D	97*	65' 00"	36' 00"	9' 00"
	Mackinaw City	TB	1943	D	23*	38' 00"	11' 05"	4' 07"
	Wolverine	TB	1952	D		42' 05"	12' 05"	5' 00"
M-2	**MacDONALD MARINE LTD., GODERICH, ON**							
	Debbie Lyn	TB	1950	D	10*	45' 00"	14' 00"	10' 00"
	(Skipper '50 - '60)							
	Donald Bert	TB	1953	D	11*	45' 00"	14' 00"	10' 00"
	Dover	TB	1931	D	70*	84' 00"	17' 00"	6' 00"
	Ian Mac	TB	1955	D	12*	45' 00"	14' 00"	10' 00"
M-3	**MADELINE ISLAND FERRY LINE, INC., LaPOINTE, WI**							
	Bayfield	CF		D		120'00"	43'00"	
	Island Queen {2}	CF	1966	D	90*	75' 00"	34' 09"	10' 00"
	Madeline	CF	1984	D	97*	90' 00"	35' 00"	8' 00"
	Nichevo II	CF	1962	D	89*	65' 00"	32' 00"	8' 09"
M-4	**MAID OF THE MIST STEAMBOAT CO. LTD., NIAGARA FALLS, ON**							
	Maid of the Mist	ES	1987	D	54*	65' 00"	16' 00"	7' 00"
	Maid of the Mist III	ES	1972	D	54*	65' 00"	16' 00"	7' 00"
	Maid of the Mist IV	ES	1976	D	74*	72' 00"	16' 00"	7' 00"
	Maid of the Mist V	ES	1983	D	74*	72' 00"	16' 00"	7' 00"
	Maid of the Mist VI	ES	1990	D	155*	78' 09"	29' 06"	7' 00"
	Maid of the Mist VII	ES	1997	D	160*	80' 00"	30' 00"	7' 00"
M-5	**MALCOLM MARINE, ST. CLAIR, MI**							
	Manitou {2}	TB	1943	D	491*	110' 00"	26' 05"	11' 06"
	(USCG Manitou [WYT-60] '43 - '84)							
M-6	**MANITOU ISLAND TRANSIT, LELAND, MI**							
	Manitou Isle	PK	1946	D	10	52' 00"	14' 00"	8' 00"
	(Namaycush '46 - '59)							
	Mishe-Mokwa	CF	1966	D	49*	65' 00"	17' 06"	8' 00"

Fleet # / Fleet Name / Vessel Name	Type of Vessel	Year Built	Type of Engine	Cargo Cap. or Gross*	Overal Length	Breadth	Depth or Draft*
M-7 **MANSON CONSTRUCTION CO., INC., BUFFALO, NY**							
Burro	TB	1965	D	19*	36' 00"	13' 03"	5' 01"
J. G. II	TB	1944	D	16*	42' 03"	13' 00"	5' 06"
Marcey	TB	1966	D	22*	42' 00"	12' 06"	6' 10"
M-8 **MARINE ATLANTIC, INC., MONCTON, NB**							
Atlantic Freighter	RR	1978	D	8,661	495' 05"	71' 01"	48' 01"
Caribou	CF	1986	D	27,213*	587' 04"	84' 01"	27' 06"
Joseph & Clara Smallwood	CF	1989	D	27,614*	587' 03"	84' 01"	22' 02"
M-9 **MARINE CONTRACTING CORP., PORT CLINTON, OH**							
Ambridge 528	DB	1937	B	409	114' 10"	26' 10"	7' 10"*
Ambridge 529	DB	1937	B	409	114' 10"	26' 10"	7' 10"*
Clyde	DB	1922	B	727	150' 00"	40' 00"	9' 06"*
Pioneerland	TB	1943	D	45*	59' 06"	17' 00"	7' 06"*
Prairieland	TB	1955	D	29*	50' 00"	15' 07"	6' 05"*
Timberland	TB	1946	D	19*	44' 00"	13' 05"	6' 11"*
M-10 **MARINE MANAGEMENT, INC., BRUSSELS, WI**							
Nathan S.	TB	1954	D	76*	66' 00"	19' 00"	9' 00"
(Sanita '54 - '77, Soo Chief '77 - '81, Susan M. Selvick '81 - '91)							
Nicole S.	TB	1949	D	146*	88' 07"	24' 10"	10' 09"
(Evening Star '49 - '86, Protector '86 - '94)							
M-11 **MARINE SALVAGE CO. LTD., PORT COLBORNE, ON**							
Sea Castle	CC	1909	B	2,600	260' 00"	43' 00"	25' 03"
(Kaministiquia {2} '09 - '16, Westoil '16 - '23, J. B. John {1} '23 - '51, John L. A. Galster '51 - '69)							
(5 year survey expired November 1983 — Currently laid up in Muskegon, MI.)							
M-12 **MARINE TECH OF DULUTH, INC., DULUTH, MN**							
B. Yetter	DR	1986	B	338*	120' 00"	48' 00"	7' 00"
Jason	TB	1945	D	21*	48' 00"	12' 01"	7' 00"
(Ashland {2} '44 - '72, Charles F. Liscomb '72 - '94)							
Nancy Ann	TB	1910	D	51*	64' 03"	16' 09"	8' 06"
(Chattanooga '10 - '79, Howard T. Hagen '79 - '94)							
M-13 **MARINE TOWING, INC., PORT CLINTON, OH**							
Retriever	TB	1960	D	13*	38' 00"	12' 01"	5' 04"*
M-14 **MARIPOSA CRUISE LINE, TORONTO, ON**							
Captain Matthew Flinders	ES	1982	D	696*	144' 00"	40' 00"	8' 06"
Mariposa Belle	ES	1970	D	195*	93' 00"	23' 00"	8' 00"
Northern Spirit I	ES	1983	D	489*	136' 00"	31' 00"	9' 00"
Oriole	ES	1987	D	200*	75' 00"	23' 00"	9' 00"
Rosemary	ES	1960	D	52*	68' 00"	15' 06"	6' 08"
Showboat Royal Grace	ES	1988	D	135*	58' 00"	18' 00"	4' 00"
Torontonian	ES	1962	D	68*	68' 00"	18' 06"	6' 08"
M-15 **MARITIME INVESTING LLC., GLADSTONE, MI**							
Manitowoc	TF	1926	B	27 rail cars	371' 03"	67' 03"	22' 06"
Roanoke {2}	TF	1930	B	30 rail cars	381' 06"	58' 03"	22' 06"
(City of Flint 32 '30 - '70)							
Windsor {2}	TF	1930	B	28 rail cars	370' 05"	65' 00"	21' 06"
(Above three last operated 1 May 1994 — Currently laid up in Toledo, OH.)							
Pere Marquette 10	TF	1945	B	27 rail cars	400' 00"	53' 00"	22' 00"
(Last operated 7 October 1994 — Currently laid up in Port Huron, MI.)							
M-16 **MARTIN GAS & OIL, BEAVER ISLAND, MI**							
West Shore {2}	CF	1947	D	94*	64' 10"	30' 00"	9' 03"
M-17 **McASPHALT INDUSTRIES LTD., SCARBOROUGH, ON**							
McAsphalt 401	TK	1966	B	48,000	300' 00"	60' 00"	23' 00"
(Pittson 200 '66 - '73, Pointe Levy '73 - '87)							
M-18 **McCUE & OTHERS, CEDAR POINT, ON**							
Indian Maiden	PF	1987	D	128*	74' 00"	23' 00"	8' 00"
M-19 **McKEIL MARINE LTD., HAMILTON, ON**							
Albert B.	DB		B	475	120' 00"	32' 00"	8' 00"
Alice A.	TB	1970	D	564*	135' 00"	34' 09"	19' 04"
(Warrawee '70 - '76, Seaspan Raider '76 - '87, Raider '87 - '87, Raider IV '87 - '88)							
Argue Martin	TB	1895	D	71*	69' 00"	19' 06"	9' 00"
(Ethel 1895 - '38, R. C. Co. Tug No.1 '38 - '58, R. C. L. Tug No. 1 '58 - '62)							
Atomic	TB	1945	D	96*	82' 00"	20' 00"	10' 00"
Beaver D.	TB	1955	D	15*	36' 02"	14' 09"	4' 04"

Fleet #	Fleet Name / Vessel Name	Type of Vessel	Year Built	Type of Engine	Cargo Cap. or Gross*	Overall Length	Breadth	Depth or Draft*
	Billie M.	TB	1897	D	35*	58' 00"	16' 00"	7' 00"
	Black Carrier	DB	1908	B	1,200	200' 06"	43' 01"	10' 00"
	Cargo Carrier #1	DB		B	500	90' 00"	30' 00"	10' 00"
	Cargo Carrier #2	DB		B	1,000	90' 00"	60' 00"	10' 00"
	Cargo Master	CS		B	600	136' 00"	50' 00"	9' 00"
	Colinette	TB	1943	D	64*	65' 00"	16' 00"	7' 00"
	(Ottawa {1} '43 - '57, Lac Ottawa '57 - '66)							
	CSL Trillium	BC	1966	B	18,064	489' 10"	75' 00"	37' 05"
	Doug McKeil {2}	TB	1943	D	196*	130' 00"	30' 00"	15' 01"
	(U.S. Army LT-643 '44 - '77, Taurus '77 - '90, Gaelic Challenge '90 - '95, Frankie D. '95 - '97, Dawson B. '97 - '98)							
	Duchess V	TB	1955	D	18*	55' 00"	16' 00"	6' 08"
	Erie West	DB	1951	B	1,800	290' 00"	50' 00"	12' 00"
	Escort Protector	TB	1972	D	719*	171' 00"	38' 00"	16' 00"
	(Nordic VI '72 - '73, Federal 6 '73 - '81, Seafed Avalon '81 - '83, Artic Mallik '83 - '90)							
	Evans McKeil	TB	1936	D	284*	110' 07"	25' 06"	11' 06"
	(Alhajuela '36 - '70, Barbara Ann {2} '70 - '89)							
	Florence McKeil	TB	1962	D	207*	98' 05"	26' 00"	9' 07"
	(T. 4 '62 - ?, Foundation Viceroy ? - '72, Feuille D' Erable '72 - '97)							
	Glenbrook	TB	1944	D	91*	81' 00"	20' 00"	9' 07"
	Glenevis	TB	1944	D	91*	80' 06"	20' 00"	9' 07"
	Handy Andy	DB		B	700	100' 00"	44' 00"	11' 00"
	Handy Boy	DB		B	350			
	Jarrett McKeil	TB	1956	D	197*	91' 08"	27' 04"	13' 06"
	(Robert B. No. 1 '56 - '97)							
	Jean Raymond	DB	1941	B	6,800	409' 00"	57' 00"	18' 00"
	Jerry Newberry	TB	1956	D	244*	98' 00"	28' 02"	14' 04"
	(Foundation Victor '56 - '73, Point Victor '73 - '77, Kay Cole '77 - '95)							
	John Spence	TB	1972	D	719*	171' 00"	38' 00"	15' 01"
	(Mary B. VI '72 - '81, Mary B. '81 - '82, Mary B. VI '82 - '83, Artic Tuktu '83 - '94)							
	Kate B.	TB	1950	D	12*	46' 00"	12' 10"	3' 00"
	Konigsberg	TB	1960	D	91*	41' 07"	13' 02"	7' 07"
	Lac Como	TB	1944	D	63*	65' 00"	16' 10"	7' 10"
	(Tanac 74 '44 - '64)							
	Lac Erie	TB	1944	D	65*	65' 00"	16' 10"	7' 07"
	(Tanmac '44 - '74)							
	Lac Manitoba	TB	1944	D	65*	65' 00"	16' 10"	7' 07"
	(Tanac 75 '44 - '52, Manitoba '52 - '57)							
	Le Vent	DB	1969	B	13,920	379' 09"	63' 03"	33' 08"
	Lorena 1	GC	1961	D	5,039	404' 01"	60' 05"	36' 06"
	(French River '61 - '81, Jensen Star '81 - '86, Woodland '86 - '91, Woodlands '91 - '98)							
	Macassa Bay	ES	1986	D	200*	93' 07"	29' 07"	10' 04"
	(Currently laid up in Hamilton, ON.)							
	McAllister 252	DB	1969	B	2,636*	250' 00"	76' 01"	16' 01"
	Miss Shawn Simpson	ES		D	30*	55' 02"	13' 02"	5' 00"
	(Currently laid up in Hamilton, ON.)							
	Ocean Hauler	BK	1943	B	8,500/88,735	382' 07"	69' 07"	25' 07"
	Offshore Supplier	TB	1979	D	127*	92' 00"	25' 00"	11' 06"
	(Elmore M. Misener '79 - '94)							
	Paul E. No. 1	TB	1945	D	97*	80' 00"	20' 00"	9' 07"
	(W.A.C. 4 '45 - '46, E. A. Rockett '46 - '76)							
	Peter Kamingoak	DB	1975	B	12,000	351' 03"	91' 00"	20' 08"
	St. Clair {2}	TF	1927	B	27 rail cars	400' 00"	54' 00"	22' 00"
	(Pere Marquette 12 '27 - '70)							
	Stormont	TB	1953	D	108*	80' 00"	20' 00"	9' 07"
	Salty Dog No. 1	TB	1945	B	88,735	313' 00"	68' 03"	26' 07"
	Sault au Couchon	DB	1969	B	10,000	422' 11"	74' 10"	25' 07"
	Toledo	TK	1962	B	6,388	135' 00"	34' 00"	9' 00"
	Toni D.	TB	1959	D	15*	50' 00"	16' 00"	5' 00"
	Wyatt McKeil	TB	1950	D	237*	102' 06"	26' 00"	13' 06"
	(Otis Wack '50 - '97)							
	MONTREAL BOATMAN - A SUBSIDARY OF McKEIL MARINE LTD.							
	Aldo H.	TB	1979	D	37*	56' 04"	15' 04"	6' 02"
	Boatman No. 3	TB	1965	D	13*	33' 08"	11' 00"	6' 00"
	Boatman No. 4	TB	1967	D	15*	43' 03"	14' 01"	5' 09"
	Boatman No. 6	TB	1979	D	39*	56' 07"	18' 07"	6' 03"
	Pilot 1	TB	1994	D	14*	32' 01"	5' 08"	2' 06"
	REMORQUEURS & BARGES MONTREAL LTEE - A SUBSIDARY OF McKEIL MARINE LTD.							
	Cavalier	TB	1944	D	18*	40' 00"	10' 05"	4' 08"
	Connie E.	TB	1974	D	9*	30' 00"	11' 00"	6' 00"

Fleet #	Fleet Name / Vessel Name	Type of Vessel	Year Built	Type of Engine	Cargo Cap. or Gross*	Overal Length	Breadth	Depth or Draft*
	D. C. Everest	CS	1953	D	3,017	259' 00"	43' 06"	21' 00"
	(D. C. Everest '53 - '81, Condarrell '82 - '89)							
	Dufresne M-58	TB	1944	D	40*	58' 08"	14' 08"	6' 02"
	Flo-Mac	TB	1960	D	15*	40' 00"	13' 00"	6' 00"
	Greta V	TB	1951	D	14*	44' 00"	12' 00"	5' 00"
	Lac Vancouver	TB	1943	D	65*	65' 00"	16' 10"	7' 07"
	Pacific Standard	TB	1967	D	451*	127' 08"	31' 00"	15' 06"
	(Irishman '67 - '76, Kwakwani '76 - '78, Lorna B. '78 - '81)							
	Techno Venture	TB	1939	D	470*	138' 03"	30' 07"	15' 01"
	(Dragonet '39 - '61, Foundation Venture '61 - '73, M.I.L. Venture '73 - '79)							
	Wilmac	TB	1959	D	16*	40' 00"	13' 00"	3' 07"
	Wyn Cooper	TB	1973	D	25*	48' 00"	13' 00"	4' 00"
M-20	**McMULLEN & PITZ CONSTRUCTION CO., MANITOWOC, WI**							
	Dauntless	TB	1937	D	25*	52' 06"	15' 06"	5' 03"
M-21	**MENASHA TUGBOAT CO., SARNIA, ON**							
	Menasha {2}	TB	1949	D	147*	78' 00"	24' 00"	9' 08"
	(W. C. Harms '49 - '54, Hamilton '54 - '86, Ruby Casho '86 - '88, W. C. Harms '88 - '97)							
M-22	**MERCURY CRUISE LINES, PALATINE, IL**							
	Chicago's First Lady	ES	1991	D	62*	96' 00"	22' 00"	9' 00"
	Chicago's Little Lady	ES	1999	D		68' 00"	23' 00"	8' 06"*
	Skyline Princess	ES	1956	D	56*	59' 04"	16' 00"	4' 08"
	Skyline Queen	ES	1959	D	45*	61' 05"	16' 10"	6' 00"
M-23	**MILLER BOAT LINE, INC., PUT-IN-BAY, OH**							
	Islander {3}	CF	1983	D	92*	90' 03"	38' 00"	8' 03"
	Put-In-Bay {3}	CF	1997	D	95*	96' 00"	38' 06"	9' 06"
	South Bass	CF	1989	D	95*	96' 00"	38' 06"	9' 06"
	Wm. Market	CF	1993	D	95*	96' 00"	38' 06"	8' 09"
M-24	**MILWAUKEE BULK TERMINALS, INC., MILWAUKEE, WI**							
	MBT 10	DB	1994	B	1,960	200' 00"	35' 00"	13' 00"
	MBT 20	DB	1994	B	1,960	200' 00"	35' 00"	13' 00"
	MBT 33	DB	1976	B	3,793	240' 00"	52' 06"	14' 06"*
M-25	**MONTREAL SHIPPING, INC., STEPHENVILLE, NF**							
	Point Viking	TT	1962	D	207*	98' 05"	27' 10"	13' 05"
	(Foundation Viking '62 - '75)							
M-26	**MORTON SALT CO., CHICAGO, IL**							
	Morton Salt 74	DB	1974	B	2,101	195' 00"	35' 00"	12' 00"
M-27	**MUSKOKA LAKES NAVIGATION & HOTEL CO., GRAVENHURST, ON**							
	Segwun	PA	1887	R	168*	128' 00"	24' 00"	7' 06"
	Wanda III	ES	1915	R	60*	94' 00"	12' 00"	5' 00"
N-1	**N. M. PATERSON & SONS LTD. - MARINE DIVISION, THUNDER BAY, ON**							
	Cartierdoc {2}	BC	1959	D	29,100	730' 00"	75' 09"	40' 02"
	(Ems Ore '59 - '76, Montcliffe Hall '76 - '88)							
	Comeaudoc	BC	1960	D	26,750	730' 00"	75' 06"	37' 09"
	(Murray Bay {2} '60 - '63)							
	(Last operated 4 December 1996 — 5 year survey expires July 2001.)							
	(Currently laid up in Montreal, QC.)							
	Mantadoc {2}	BC	1967	D	17,650	607' 10"	62' 00"	36' 00"
	Paterson {2}	BC	1985	D	32,600	736' 07"	75' 10"	42' 00"
	Quedoc {3}	BC	1965	D	28,050	730' 00"	75' 00"	39' 02"
	(Beavercliffe Hall '65 - '88)							
	(Last operated 20 December 1991 — 5 year survey expired June 1993.)							
	(Currently laid up in Thunder Bay, ON.)							
	Vandoc {2}	BC	1964	D	16,000	605' 00"	62' 00"	33' 10"
	(Sir Denys Lowson '64 - '79)							
	(Last operated 21 December 1991 — Currently laid up in Thunder Bay, ON.)							
	Windoc {2}	BC	1959	D	29,100	730' 00"	75' 09"	40' 02"
	(Rhine Ore '59 - '76, Steelcliffe Hall '76 - '88)							
N-2	**NADRO MARINE SERVICES LTD.,PORT DOVER, ON**							
	Bert Verge	TB	1959	D	22*	43' 07"	14' 00"	4' 06"
	C. West Pete	TB	1956	D	29*	63' 00"	17' 03"	7' 00"
	Carolyn Jo	TB	1941	D	60*	65' 06"	17' 00"	7' 00"
	([Unnamed] '41 - '56, Sea Hound '56 - '80)							
	Intreped	TB	1976	D	39*	66' 00"	17' 00"	7' 06"
	Lois T.	TB	1943	D	32*	63' 00"	16' 06"	7' 06"
	(Kolbe '43 - '86)							

Carferry Badger enters port at Ludington, MI. (Courtesy Lake Michigan Carferry Service)

Fleet #	Fleet Name / Vessel Name	Type of Vessel	Year Built	Type of Engine	Cargo Cap. or Gross*	Overal Length	Breadth	Depth or Draft*
	Miseford	TB	1915	D	116*	85' 00"	20' 00"	10' 06"
	Nadro Clipper	TB	1939	D	64*	70' 00"	23' 00"	6' 06"
	(Stanley Clipper '39 - '94)							
	Progress	TB	1948	D	123*	86' 00"	21' 00"	10' 00"
	(P. J. Murer '48 - '81, Michael D. Misner '81 - '93, Thomas A. Payette '93 - '96)							
	Terry S.	TB	1958	D	16*	52' 00"	17' 00"	6' 00"
	Vac	TB	1942	D	37*	65' 00"	21' 00"	6' 06"
N-3	**NELSON CONSTRUCTION CO., LaPOINTE, WI**							
	Eclipse	TB	1937	D	23*	47' 00"	13' 00"	6' 00"
N-4	**NELVANA YACHT CHARTERS, TORONTO, ON**							
	Nelvana {1}	ES	1963	D	61*	55' 10"	16' 00"	5' 00"
N-5	**NEUMAN CRUISE & FERRY LINE, SANDUSKY, OH**							
	Commuter	CF	1960	D	81*	64' 06"	33' 00"	9' 00"
	Emerald Empress	ES	1994	D	94*	151' 00"	33' 00"	10' 06"
	Endeavor	CF	1987	D	98*	101' 00"	34' 06"	10' 00"
	Kelley Islander	CF	1969	D	95*	100' 00"	34' 03"	8' 00"
N-6	**NEWFOUNDLAND TRANSSHIPMENT LTD., ST. JOHN, NF**							
	Placentia Hope	TT	1998	D	925*	125' 00"	42' 08"	17' 05"
	Placentia Pride	TT	1998	D	925*	125' 00"	42' 08"	17' 05"
N-7	**NEW WORLD SHIP MANAGEMENT LLC, ST. LOUIS, MO**							
	Clipper Adventurer	PA	1975	D	4,364*	328' 01"	53' 03"	23' 00"
	Clipper Odyssey	PA	1989	D	5,200*	341' 00"	50' 06"	14' 00"*
	Nantucket Clipper	PA	1984	D	96*	207' 00"	37' 00"	11' 06"
	Yorktown Clipper	PA	1988	D	97*	257' 00"	43' 00"	12' 05"
N-8	**NICHOLSON TERMINAL & DOCK CO., RIVER ROUGE, MI**							
	Charles E. Jackson	TB	1956	D	12*	35' 00"	10' 06"	5' 01"
	Detroit {1}	TF	1904	B	22 rail cars	308' 00"	76' 09"	19' 06"
N-9	**NORTHUMBERLAND FERRIES LTD. / BAY FERRIES LTD., CHARLOTTETOWN, PEI**							
	Confederation {2}	CF	1993	D	8,060*	374' 08"	61' 07"	17' 09"
	Holiday Island	CF	1971	D	3,037*	325' 00"	67' 06"	16' 06"
	Incat 046	CF	1997	D	5,060*	300' 00"	85' 03"	12' 01"
	Princess of Acadia	CF	1971	D	10,051*	480' 01"	66' 00"	12' 06"
O-1	**OAK GROVE MARINE AND TRANSPORTATION, INC., CLAYTON, NY**							
	Maple Grove	PK	1954	D	55	75' 00"	21' 00"	5' 06"*
	Oak Grove	PK	1953	D	18	53' 02"	14' 00"	4' 00"*
O-2	**ODYSSEY CRUISES, CHICAGO, IL**							
	Odyssey II	ES	1993	D	101*	200' 00"	41' 00"	9' 00"*
O-3	**OGLEBAY NORTON MARINE SERVICES CO., CLEVELAND, OH**							
	Armco	SU	1953	T	25,500	767' 00"	70' 00"	36' 00"
	Buckeye {3}	SU	1952	T	22,300	698' 00"	70' 00"	37' 00"
	(Sparrows Point '52 - '90)							
	Columbia Star	SU	1981	D	78,850	1,000' 00"	105' 00"	56' 00"
	Courtney Burton	SU	1953	T	22,300	690' 00"	70' 00"	37' 00"
	(Ernest T. Weir {2} '53 - '78)							
	David Z. Norton {3}	SU	1973	D	19,650	630' 00"	68' 00"	36' 11"
	(William R. Roesch '73 - '95)							
	Earl W. Oglebay	SU	1973	D	19,650	630' 00"	68' 00"	36' 11"
	(Paul Thayer '73 - '95)							
	Fred R. White Jr.	SU	1979	D	23,800	636' 00"	68' 00"	40' 00"
	Joseph H. Frantz	SU	1925	D	13,600	618' 00"	62' 00"	32' 00"
	Middletown	SU	1942	T	26,300	730' 00"	75' 00"	39' 03"
	(Marquette '42 - '42, USS Neshanic [AO-71] '43 - '47, Gulfoil '47 - '61, Pioneer Challenger '61 - '62)							
	Oglebay Norton	SU	1978	D	78,850	1,000' 00"	105' 00"	56' 00"
	(Launched as Burns Harbor {1}, Lewis Wilson Foy '78 - '90)							
	Reserve	SU	1953	T	25,500	767' 00"	70' 00"	36' 00"
	Wolverine {4}	SU	1974	D	19,650	630' 00"	68' 00"	36' 11"
O-4	**ONTARIO MINISTRY OF TRANSPORTATION & COMMUNICATION, KINGSTON, ON**							
	Amherst Islander {2}	CF	1955	D	184*	106' 00"	38' 00"	10' 00"
	(Currently laid up in Kingston, ON.)							
	Frontenac II	CF	1962	D	666*	181' 00"	45' 00"	10' 00"
	Glenora	CF	1952	D	209*	127' 00"	33' 00"	9' 00"
	The Quinte Loyalist	CF	1954	D	209*	127' 00"	32' 00"	8' 00"
	Wolfe Islander III	CF	1975	D	985*	205' 00"	68' 00"	6' 00"

Fleet #	Fleet Name Vessel Name	Type of Vessel	Year Built	Type of Engine	Cargo Cap. or Gross*	Overall Length	Breadth	Depth or Draft*
O-5	**ONTARIO WATERWAY CRUISES, INC., ORILLIA, ON**							
	Kawartha Voyager	PA	1983	D	264*	108' 00"	22' 00"	5' 00"
O-6	**ORILLIA BOAT CRUISES LTD., ORILLIA, ON**							
	Lady Belle II	ES	1967	D	89*	65' 00"	19' 00"	5' 00"
	Island Princess {1}	ES	1989	D	194*	65' 00"	27' 00"	5' 00"
O-7	**OSBORNE MATERIALS CO., MENTOR, OH**							
	Emmet J. Carey	SC	1948	D	900	114' 00"	23' 00"	11' 00"
	(Beatrice Ottinger '48 - '63, James B. Lyons '63 - '88)							
	F. M. Osborne {2}	SC	1910	D	500	150' 00"	29' 00"	11' 03"
	(Grand Island {1} '10 - '58, Lesco '58 - '75)							
O-8	**OWEN SOUND TRANSPORTATION CO. LTD., OWEN SOUND, ON**							
	Chi-Cheemaun	CF	1974	D	6,991*	365' 05"	61' 00"	21' 00"
	Nindawayma	CF	1976	D	6,197*	333' 06"	55' 00"	36' 06"
	(Last operated in 1992 — 5 year survey expired January 1996 — Currently laid up in Owen Sound, ON.)							
	PELEE ISLAND TRANS. SERVICES - A DIVISION OF OWEN SOUND TRANS. CO. LTD.							
	Jiimaan	CF	1992	D	2,830*	176' 09"	42' 03"	13' 06"
	Pelee Islander	CF	1960	D	334*	145' 00"	32' 00"	10' 00"
P-1	**P.& H. SHIPPING - A DIVISION OF PARRISH & HEIMBECKER LTD., MISSISSAUGA, ON**							
	Mapleglen {2}	BC	1960	T	26,100	714' 11"	75' 00"	37' 09"
	(Carol Lake '60 - '87, Algocape {1} '87 - '94)							
	Oakglen {2}	BC	1954	T	22,950	714' 06"	70' 03"	37' 03"
	(T. R. McLagan '54 - '90)							
P-2	**PEMBINA EXPLORATION LTD., PORT COLBORNE, ON**							
	Louis J. Coulet	DV	1957	B	2,099*	259' 00"	43' 11"	22' 06"
	(5 year survey expired November 1995 — Currently laid up in Port Dover, ON.)							
P-3	**PENETANGUISHENE 30,000 ISLAND CRUISES, PENETANGUISHENE, ON**							
	Georgian Queen	ES	1918	D	249*	119' 00"	36' 00"	16' 06"
P-4	**PENETANGUISHENE MIDLAND COACH LINE 30,000 ISLAND BOAT CRUISES, MIDLAND, ON**							
	Miss Midland	ES	1974	D	119*	68' 07"	19' 04"	6' 04"
	Serendipity Princess	ES	1982	D	93*	69' 00"	23' 00"	4' 03"*
P-5	**PERE MARQUETTE SHIPPING CO., LUDINGTON, MI**							
	Pere Marquette 41	SU	1941	B	4,545	400' 00"	58' 00"	23' 06"
	(City of Midland 41 '41 - '97)							
	Undaunted	TBA	1944	D	860*	143' 00"	33' 01"	17' 00"
	(USS Undaunted [ATR-126 / ATA-199] '44 - '63, USMA Kings Pointer '63 - '93, Krystal K. '93 - '97)							
	[Pere Marquette 41 / Undaunted overall dimensions together]					494' 00"	58' 00"	23' 06"
P-6	**PICTURED ROCKS CRUISES, INC., MUNISING, MI**							
	Grand Island {2}	ES	1989	D	51*	68' 00"	16' 01"	5' 01"
	Miners Castle	ES	1974	D	72*	68' 00"	17' 00"	5' 00"
	Miss Superior	ES	1984	D	76*	68' 00"	17' 00"	5' 00"
	Pictured Rocks	ES	1972	D	47*	60' 00"	14' 00"	4' 04"
P-7	**PIERRE GAGNE CONTRACTING LTD., THUNDER BAY, ON**							
	M A C Gagne	BC	1964	B	30,500	730' 00"	75' 02"	44' 08"
	(Saguenay {2} '64 - '98)							
	(Last operated 30 November 1992 — Currently laid up in Thunder Bay, ON.)							
P-8	**PLAUNT TRANSPORTATION CO., INC., CHEBOYGAN, MI**							
	Kristen D.	CF	1988	D	83*	64' 11"	36' 00"	6' 05"
P-9	**PORT CITY PRINCESS CRUISES, INC., MUSKEGON, MI**							
	Port City Princess	ES	1966	D	79*	64' 09"	30' 00"	5' 06"
P-10	**PORT DALHOUSIE PIERS, INC., ST. CATHARINES, ON**							
	Normac	PA	1902	D	462*	124' 06"	25' 00"	18' 00"
	(Former Owen Sound Transportation Commision vessel which last operated in 1968.)							
	(Currently in use as a floating restaurant in Port Dalhousie, ON.)							
P-11	**PORTOFINO ON THE RIVER, WYANDOTTE, MI**							
	Friendship	ES	1968	D	78*	69' 06"	23' 05"	7' 04"
P-12	**PRESIDENT RIVERBOAT CASINO, INC., ST. LOUIS, MO**							
	Majestic Star {2}	GA	1997	D	12,805*	330' 00"	76' 00"	20' 00"
P-13	**PROJECT LIBERTY SHIP, BALTIMORE, MD**							
	John W. Brown	GC	1942	R	13,799	417' 09"	56' 11"	37' 04"
	(World War II Liberty Ship is visiting the Great Lakes during the summer of 2000.)							

Fleet # Fleet Name Vessel Name	Type of Vessel	Year Built	Type of Engine	Cargo Cap. or Gross*	Overal Length	Breadth	Depth or Draft*
P-14 **PURVIS MARINE LTD., SAULT STE. MARIE, ON**							
Adanac	TB	1913	D	108*	80' 03"	19' 02"	10' 06"
(Edward C. Whalen '13 - '66, John McLean '66 - '95)							
Anglian Lady	TB	1953	D	398*	136' 06"	30' 00"	14' 01"
(Hamtun '53 - '72, Nathalie Letzer '72 - '88)							
Avenger IV	TB	1962	D	293*	120' 00"	30' 05"	17' 05"
(Avenger '62 - '85)							
Charles W. Johnson	DB	1916	B	1,685	245' 00"	43' 00"	14' 00"
Chief Wawatam	DB	1911	B	4,500	347' 00"	62' 03"	15' 00"
Goki	TB	1940	D	24*	57' 00"	12' 08"	7' 00"
Malden	DB	1946	B	1,075	150' 00"	41' 09"	10' 03"
Martin E. Johnson	TB	1959	D	26*	46' 00"	16' 00"	5' 09"
McKeller	CS	1935	B	200	90' 00"	33' 00"	8' 00"
Osprey	TB	1944	D	36*	45' 00"	13' 06"	7' 00"
P.M.L. Alton	DB	1951	B	150	93' 00"	30' 00"	8' 00"
P.M.L. Salvager	DB	1945	B	5,200	341' 00"	54' 00"	27' 00"
P.M.L. 357	DB	1944	B	600	138' 00"	38' 00"	11' 00"
P.M.L. 2501	TK	1980	B	25,000	302' 00"	52' 00"	17' 00"
Rocket	TB	1901	D	39*	70' 00"	15' 00"	8' 00"
Sheila P.	TB	1940	D	15*	40' 00"	14' 00"	
Tecumseh II	DB	1976	B	2,500	180' 00"	54' 00"	12' 00"
Wilfred M. Cohen	TB	1948	D	284*	104' 00"	28' 00"	14' 06"
(A. T. Lowmaster '48 - '75)							
W. I. Scott Purvis	TB	1938	D	206*	96' 06"	26' 04"	10' 04"
(Orient Bay '38 - '75, Guy M. No. 1 '75 - '90)							
W. J. Ivan Purvis	TB	1938	D	191*	100' 06"	25' 06"	9' 00"
(Magpie '38 - '66, Dana T. Bowen '66 - '75)							
Yankcanuck {2}	CS	1963	D	4,760	324' 03"	49' 00"	26' 00"
P-15 **PUT-IN-BAY BOAT LINE CO., PUT-IN-BAY, OH**							
Express Shuttle	PF		D				
Jet Express	PC	1989	D	93*	92' 08"	28' 06"	8' 04"
Jet Express II	PC	1992	D	85*	92' 06"	28' 06"	8' 04"
R-1 **RAYMOND BURTON BERKSHIRE, PLACENTIA, NF**							
Paradise Sound	GC	1969	D	430	137' 04"	25' 00"	11' 01"
Placentia Sound	GC	1969	D	713	173' 11"	29' 00"	12' 01"
R-2 **REINAUER TRANSPORTATION COMPANIES, INC., STATEN ISLAND, NY**							
Austin Reinauer	TB	1978	D	183*	116' 00"	32' 00"	16' 07"
(Morania No. 20 '78 - '88, Mobil 5 '88 - '93, Tamarac '93 - '95, Morania No. 1 '95 - ?)							
Bert Reinauer II	TK	1938	D	13,442	293' 07"	43' 01"	17' 04"
(Paratex '38 - '75)							
Curtis Reinauer	TB		D	94*	82' 00"	26' 00"	
Dace Reinauer	TB	1968	D	84*	130' 00"	31' 00"	14' 06"
Dean Reinauer	TB		D	88*	79' 00"	26' 00"	
Franklin Reinauer	TB	1983	D	99*	86' 00"	28' 00"	12' 00"
Fulton	TK	1969	B	21,000	242' 07"	43' 05"	14' 10"
George Morris	TK	1982	B	56,000	325' 00"	60' 00"	22' 00"
Janice Ann Reinauer	TB		D	149*			
Jill Reinauer	TB	1967	D	195*	91' 06"	26' 10"	9' 08"
(Ranger '67 - '97)							
Jo Anne Reinauer III	TB	1970	D	160*	100' 00"	28' 00"	13' 09"
John Reinauer	TB	1969	D	144*	96' 00"	27' 08"	12' 03"
(launched as Crystal River, Enco Crystal River '69 - '73, Exxon Crystal River '73 - '93)							
Juliet Reinauer	TB	1972	D	242*	86' 00"	30' 00"	9' 06"
Kristy Ann Reinauer	TB		D	207*			
May McGuirl	TB	1973	D	296*	109' 02"	32' 00"	17' 00"
(Texaco Diesel Chief '73 - '90, Star Diesel Chief '90 - '91, Morania No. 5 '91 - ?)							
Morgan Reinauer	TB	1981	D	184*	134' 00"	34' 00"	16' 00"
(Elise M '81 - '88, Exxon Garden State '88 - '93)							
New London	TK		B	25,200	295' 00"	42' 00"	12' 06"*
Peter R. Hearne	TK	1971	B	20,000	227' 00"	43' 00"	14' 09"
Putnam	TK	1974	B	42,000	300' 00"	60' 00"	27' 00"
Richmond	TK	1975	B	42,000	300' 00"	60' 00"	17' 00"
Rockland	TK	1975	B	67,000	316' 06"	59' 05"	26' 02"
Stephen Reinauer	TB	1970	D	151*	109' 00"	31' 06"	16' 00"
(Esso Bay State '70 - '73, Exxon Bay State '73 - '93)							
Stephen-Scott	TB	1967	D	188*	100' 06"	28' 00"	13' 10"
Westchester	TK	1975	B	67,000	316' 00"	60' 00"	26' 02"
Zachery Reinauer	TB	1971	D	271*	100' 00"	28' 00"	14' 11"
(Mobil 1 '71 - '91, Tioga '91 - '93)							

Fleet # Fleet Name Vessel Name	Type of Vessel	Year Built	Type of Engine	Cargo Cap. or Gross*	Overal Length	Breadth	Depth or Draft*
R-3	**RIGEL SHIPPING CANADA, INC., SHEDIAC, NB**						
Diamond Star	TK	1992	D	68,019	405' 11"	58' 01"	34' 09"
(Elbestern '92 - '93)							
Emerald Star	TK	1992	D	68,019	405' 11"	58' 01"	34' 09"
(Emsstern '92 - '92)							
Jade Star	TK	1993	D	68,019	405' 11"	58' 01"	34' 09"
(Jadestern '93 - '94)							
R-4	**ROCKPORT BOAT LINE (1994) LTD., ROCKPORT, ON**						
Ida M.	ES	1970	D	29*	55' 00"	14' 00"	3' 00"
Ida M. II	ES	1973	D	116*	63' 02"	22' 02"	5' 00"
R-5	**ROEN SALVAGE CO., STURGEON BAY, WI**						
Chas Asher	TB	1967	D	10*	50' 00"	18' 00"	8' 00"
John R. Asher	TB	1943	D	93*	70' 00"	20' 00"	8' 06"
(U.S. Army ST-71 '43 - '46, Russell 8 '46 - '64, Reid McAllister '64 - '67, Donegal '67 - '85)							
Louie S.	TB	1956	D	43*	37' 00"	12' 00"	5' 00"
Spuds	TB	1944	D	19*	42' 00"	12' 06"	6' 00"
Stephen M. Asher	TB	1954	D	60*	65' 00"	19' 01"	5' 04"
(Captain Bennie '54 - '82, Dumar Scout '82 - '87)							
Timmy A.	TB	1953	D	12*	33' 00"	10' 08"	5' 02"
R-6	**RUSSELL ISLAND TRANSIT CO., ALGONAC, MI**						
Islander {2}	CF	1982	D		41' 00"	15' 00"	3' 06"
R-7	**RYBA MARINE CONSTRUCTION CO., CHEBOYGAN, MI**						
Alcona	TB	1957	D	18*	40' 00"	12' 06"	5' 06"
Amber Mae	TB	1922	D	67*	65' 00"	14' 01"	10' 00"
(E. W. Sutton '22 - '52, Venture '52 - ?)							
Derrick No. 4	CS	1956	B		122' 06"	41' 02"	8' 08"
Harbor Master	CS	1979	B	100*	70' 00"	27' 00"	4' 00"
Kathy Lynn	TB	1944	D	140*	85' 00"	24' 00"	9' 06"
(U.S. Army ST-693 '44 - '79, Sea Islander '79 - '91)							
Jarco 1402	CS	1981	B	473*	140' 00"	39' 00"	9' 00"
Relief	CS	1924	B	1,000	160' 00"	40' 00"	9' 00"
Rochelle Kaye	TB	1963	D	52*	51' 06"	19' 04"	7' 00"
(Jaye Anne '63 - ?, Katanni ? - '97)							
Tonawanda	CS	1935	B	600	120' 00"	45' 00"	8' 00"
S-1	**SANKORE MARINE IMMERSION HIGH SCHOOL, DETROIT, MI**						
Huron Lady	ES	1961	D	55*	65' 00"	17' 00"	5' 00"
S-2	**SCIO SHIPPING, INC., NEW YORK, NY**						
Island Gem	BC	1984	D	28,005	584' 08"	76' 02"	48' 05"
Island Skipper	BC	1984	D	28,031	584' 08"	76' 02"	48' 05"
S-3	**SEA FOX THOUSAND ISLANDS BOAT TOURS, KINGSTON, ON**						
Sea Fox II	ES	1988	D	55*	39' 08"	20' 00"	2' 00"*
Limestone Clipper	ES	1968	D	110*	85' 00"	30' 06"	7' 03"
S-4	**SEARS OIL CO., ROME, NY**						
Midstate I	TB	1942	D	106*	86' 00"	24' 00"	12' 00"
Midstate II	TB	1945	D	137*	89' 00"	24' 00"	12' 06"
S-5	**SEAWAY MARINE TRANSPORT, ST. CATHARINES, ON**						
	*PARTNERSHIP BETWEEN ALGOMA CENTRAL CORP. AND UPPER LAKES GROUP, INC.**						

ALGOMA CENTRAL CORP.		UPPER LAKES GROUP, INC.	
Algobay	Algoriver	Canadian Century	Canadian Trader
Algocape	Algosound	Canadian Enterprise	Canadian Transfer
Algocen	Algosoo	Canadian Leader	Canadian Transport
Algogulf	Algosteel	Canadian Mariner	Canadian Venture
Algoisle	Algoville	Canadian Miner	Canadian Voyager
Algolake	Algoway	Canadian Navigator	Gordon C. Leitch
Algomarine	Algowest	Canadian Olympic	James Norris
Algonorth	Algowood	Canadian Progress	Montrealais
Algontario	Agawa Canyon	Canadian Prospector	Quebecois
Algoport	Capt. Henry Jackman	Canadian Provider	Seaway Queen
Algorai	John B. Aird	Canadian Ranger	

SEE RESPECTIVE FLEETS FOR VESSEL DETAILS

Fleet # Fleet Name Vessel Name	Type of Vessel	Year Built	Type of Engine	Cargo Cap. or Gross*	Overal Length	Breadth	Depth or Draft*
S-7	**SELVICK MARINE TOWING CORP., STURGEON BAY, WI**						
Baldy B.	TB	1932	D	36*	62' 00"	16' 01"	7' 00"
Bonnie G. Selvick	TB	1928	D	95*	86' 00"	21' 00"	12' 00"
(E. James Fucik '28 - '77)							

Courtney Burton and Columbia Star in winter lay-up at Toledo, March, 1999. (Roger LeLievre)

Fleet #	Fleet Name Vessel Name	Type of Vessel	Year Built	Type of Engine	Cargo Cap. or Gross*	Overal Length	Breadth	Depth or Draft*
	Carla Anne Selvick	TB	1908	D	191*	96' 00"	23' 00"	11' 02"
	(S.O. Co. No. 19 '08 - '16, S.T. Co. No. 19 '16 - '18, Socony 19 '18 - '47,							
	Esso Tug No. 4 '47 - '53, McAllister 44 '53 - '55, Roderick McAllister '55 - '84)							
	Escort	TB	1955	D	26*	50' 00"	15' 00"	7' 03"
	John M. Selvick	TB	1898	D	256*	118' 00"	24' 00"	12' 07"
	(Illinois {1} 1898 - '41, John Roen III '41 - '74)							
	Mary Page Hannah {1}	TB	1950	D	461*	143' 00"	33' 01"	14' 06"
	(U.S. Army ATA-230 '49 - '72, G. W. Codrington '72 - '73, William P. Feeley {2} '73 - '73,							
	William W. Stender '73 - '78)							
	Moby Dick	DB	1952	B	835	121' 00"	33' 02"	10' 06"
	Sharon M. Selvick	TB	1945	D	28*	45' 06"	13' 00"	7' 01"
	Susan L.	TB	1944	D	163*	86' 00"	23' 00"	10' 04"
	(U.S. Army ST-709 '44 - '47, USCOE Stanley '47 - '99)							
	Timmy L.	TB	1939	D	148*	110' 00"	25' 00"	13' 00"
	(USCG Naugatuck [WYT / WYTM-92] '39 - '80, Timmy B. '80 - '84)							
	William C. Selvick	TB	1944	D	142*	85' 00"	22' 11"	10' 04"
	(U.S. Army ST-500 '44 - '49, Sherman H. Serre '49 - '77)							
S-8	**SHAKER CRUISE LINES, TORONTO, ON**							
	Sunrise V	HY	1990	D		90' 07"	20' 04"	6' 07"*
	Sunrise VI	HY	1990	D		90' 07"	20' 04"	6' 07"*
S-9	**SHAMROCK CHARTERING CO., GROSSE POINT, MI**							
	Helene	ES	1927	D	109*	106' 00"	17' 00"	6' 06"*
S-10	**SHELL CANADIAN TANKERS LTD., MONTREAL, QC**							
	Horizon Montreal	RT	1958	D	32,900	315' 00"	45' 07"	24' 07"
	(Tyee Shell '58 - '69, Arctic Trader '69 - '83, Rivershell {4} '83 - '95)							
S-11	**SHEPHERD BOATS LTD., TORONTO, ON**							
	Glenmont	TB	1943	D	102*	82' 00"	20' 01"	9' 00"
S-12	**SHEPLER'S MACKINAC ISLAND FERRY SERVICE, MACKINAW CITY, MI**							
	Capt. Shepler	PF	1986	D	71*	78' 00"	21' 00"	7' 10"
	Felicity	PF	1972	D	84*	65' 00"	18' 01"	8' 03"
	Sacre Bleu	PK	1959	D	92*	94' 10"	31' 00"	9' 09"
	(Put-In-Bay {2} '59 - '94)							
	The Hope	PF	1975	D	87*	77' 00"	20' 00"	8' 03"
	The Welcome	PF	1969	D	66*	60' 06"	16' 08"	8' 02"
	Wyandot	PF	1979	D	99*	77' 00"	20' 00"	8' 00"
S-13	**SHIPWRECK TOURS, INC., MUNISING, MI**							
	Miss Munising	ES	1967	D	50*	60' 00"	14' 00"	4' 04"
S-14	**SHORELINE MARINE CO., CHICAGO, IL**							
	Marlyn	ES	1961	D	85*	65' 00"	25' 00"	7' 00"*
	Shoreline II	ES	1987	D	89*	75' 00"	26' 00"	7' 01"
S-15	**SIVERTSON'S GRAND PORTAGE - ISLE ROYALE TRANS. LINES, INC., SUPERIOR, WI**							
	A. E. Clifford	TB	1946	D	33*	45' 00"	15' 00"	7' 00"
	Hiawatha {1}	TB	1938	D	63*	58' 00"	15' 00"	8' 00"
	(Apostle Islands '38 - '60)							
	Provider	TB	1959	D		46' 00"	13' 05"	5' 05"
	Sharon Jon	TB	1943	D	17*	32' 04"	11' 06"	5' 00"
	Voyageur II	ES	1970	D		63' 00"	18' 00"	5' 00"
	Wenonah	ES	1960	D	91*	70' 07"	19' 04"	9' 07"
S-16	**SOCIETE DES TRAVERSIERS DU QUEBEC, QUEBEC, QC**							
	Alphonse des Jarnins	CF	1971	D	1,741*	214' 00"	71' 06"	20' 00"
	Armand Imbeau	CF	1980	D	1,285*	203' 07"	72' 00"	18' 04"
	Camille Marcoux	CF	1974	D	6,122*	310' 09"	62' 09"	39' 00"
	Catherine-Legardeur	CF	1985	D	1,348*	205' 09"	71' 10"	18' 10"
	Felix-Antoine-Savard	CF	1997	D	2,489*	272' 00"	70' 00"	
	Grue Des Iles	CF	1981	D	447*	155' 10"	41' 01"	12' 06"
	Jos Deschenes	CF	1980	D	1,287*	203' 07"	72' 00"	18' 04"
	Joseph Savard	CF	1985	D	1,445*	206' 00"	71' 10"	18' 10"
	Lomer Gouin	CF	1971	D	1,741*	214' 00"	71' 06"	20' 00"
	Lucien L.	CF	1967	D	867*	220' 10"	61' 06"	15' 05"
	Radisson {1}	CF	1954	D	1,043*	164' 03"	72' 00"	10' 06"
	Trois Rivieres	CF	1961	D	882*	200' 00"	70' 06"	10' 00"
S-17	**SOCIETE DU PORT DE MONTREAL, MONTREAL, QC**							
	Maisonneuve	TB	1972	D	103*	63' 10"	20' 07"	9' 03"

Fleet #	Fleet Name / Vessel Name	Type of Vessel	Year Built	Type of Engine	Cargo Cap. or Gross*	Overal Length	Breadth	Depth or Draft*
S-18	**SOO LOCKS BOAT TOURS, SAULT STE. MARIE, MI**							
	AMERICAN AND CANADIAN LOCK TOURS, INC. - OWNER							
	Bide-A-Wee {3}	ES	1955	D	99*	64' 07"	23' 00"	7' 11"
	Hiawatha {2}	ES	1959	D	99*	64' 07"	23' 00"	7' 11"
	Holiday	ES	1957	D	99*	64' 07"	23' 00"	7' 11"
	FAMOUS SOO LOCK CRUISES, INC. - OWNER							
	LeVoyageur	ES	1959	D	70*	65' 00"	25' 00"	7' 00"
	Nokomis	ES	1959	D	70*	65' 00"	25' 00"	7' 00"
S-19	**SOUTHDOWN, INC., CLEVELAND, OH**							
	C.T.C. No.1	CC	1943	R	16,300	620' 06"	60' 00"	35' 00"
	(Launched as McIntyre, Frank Purnell {1} '43 - '64, Steelton {3} '64 - '78, Hull No. 3 '78 - '79, Pioneer {3} '79 - '82)							
	(Last operated 12 Novembe, 1981.)							
	(Currently in use as a stationary cement storage/transfer vessel in South Chicago, IL.)							
	Southdown Challenger	CC	1906	S	10,250	552' 01"	56' 00"	31' 00"
	(William P. Snyder '06 - '26, Elton Hoyt II {1} '26 - '52, Alex D. Chisholm '52 - '66, Medusa Challenger '66 - '99)							
	Southdown Conquest	CC	1937	B	8,500	437' 06"	55' 00"	28' 00"
	(Red Crown '37 - '62, Amoco Indiana '62 - '87, Medusa Conquest '87 - '99)							
	HANNAH MARINE CORP. - VESSEL CHARTERED BY SOUTHDOWN, INC.							
	Susan W. Hannah	TBA	1977	D	174*	121' 06"	34' 06"	18' 02"
	(Lady Elda '77 - '78, Kings Challenger '78 - '78, ITM No. 1 '78 - '81, Kings Challenger '81 - '86)							
S-20	**SPECIALTY RESTAURANTS CORP., ANAHEIM, CA**							
	Lansdowne	TF	1884	B	1,571*	319' 00"	41' 03"	13' 00"
	(Last operated in 1974 — Currently laid up in Erie, PA.)							
S-21	**SPIRIT LAKE MARINE, INC., DULUTH, MN**							
	John V. III	TB	1942	D	12*	40' 00"	10' 00"	3' 05"
S-22	**ST. LAWRENCE CRUISE LINES, INC., KINGSTON, ON**							
	Canadian Empress	PA	1981	D	463*	108' 00"	30' 00"	8' 00"
S-23	**ST. LAWRENCE SEAWAY MANAGEMENT CORP., CORNWALL, ON**							
	VM/S Hercules	GL	1962	D	2,107	200' 00"	75' 00"	18' 08"
	VM/S Iroquois	TB	1974	D	20*			
	VM/S Massinouve	SV		D				
	VM/S St. Lambert	TB	1974	D	20*			
S-24	**ST. LAWRENCE SEAWAY DEVELOPMENT CORP., MASSENA, NY**							
	Bge 6704	BT		B				
	Eighth Sea	TB	1958	D	17*	40' 00"	12' 06"	4' 00"
	Performance	TB	1997	D		50' 00"	16' 07"	7' 06"
	Robinson Bay	TB	1958	D	213*	103' 00"	26' 10"	14' 06"
S-25	**STAR LINE MACKINAC ISLAND FERRY, ST. IGNACE, MI**							
	Cadillac {5}	PF	1990	D	73*	64' 07"	20' 00"	7' 07"
	Joliet {3}	PF	1993	D	83*	64' 08"	22' 00"	8' 03"
	La Salle {4}	PF	1983	D	55*	65' 00"	20' 00"	7' 05"
	Marquette {5}	PF	1979	D	55*	62' 03"	22' 00"	7' 01"
	Nicolet {2}	PF	1985	D	51*	65' 00"	20' 00"	7' 05"
	Radisson {2}	PF	1988	D	97*	80' 00"	23' 06"	7' 00"
S-26	**STAR SHIP MANAGEMENT LTD., CORAL GABLES, FL**							
	Feederteam	RR	1973	D	4,658	372' 05"	63' 02"	41' 04"
	Florence Star	GC	1979	D	12,665	492' 02"	69' 01"	37' 01"
	(Pacific Dragon '79 - '84, Huey An '84 - '87, Sea Pearl '87 - '92, Kota Mutiara '92 - '96, Dimko Glory '96 - '96, African Cape '96 - '98)							
	Gulf Star	GC	1979	D	3,458	271' 07"	52' 09"	29' 07"
	(Stentor '79 - '86, Starum '86 - '88, La Paimpolaise '88 - '97, River Ocean I '97 - '98)							
	Kaylin Star	RR	1969	D	2,540	426' 10"	64' 05"	42' 09"
	(Tor Mercia '69 - '75, Jolly Blu '75 - '88, Roro Catania '88 - '94, Christian I '94 - '97)							
	Rodin	TK	1982	D	95,966	444' 07"	65' 07"	32' 10"
	(L' Erable No. 1 '82 - '82, Hubert Gaucher '82 - '96)							
S-27	**STEVEN WALLACE, PENETANGUISHENE, ON**							
	Georgian Storm	TB	1931	D	167*	91' 00"	24' 02"	12' 00"
	(Capitaine Simard '31 - '57, Renee Simard '57 - '86)							
S-28	**STOLT PARCEL TANKERS, INC., GREENWICH, CT**							
	Stolt Alliance	TK	1985	D	88,147	404' 06"	65' 08"	36' 09"
	Stolt Aspiration	TK	1987	D	90,305	422' 11"	66' 04"	36' 01"
	Stolt Egret	TK	1992	D	33,569	327' 09"	56' 00"	28' 03"
	Stolt Kent	TK	1998	D	122,025	487' 00"	75' 06"	42' 06"
	Stolt Taurus	TK	1985	D	89,248	404' 06"	67' 04"	36' 09"

Fleet #	Fleet Name Vessel Name	Type of Vessel	Year Built	Type of Engine	Cargo Cap. or Gross*	Overall Length	Breadth	Depth or Draft*
T-1	**TECHNO-NAVIGATION LTEE., SILLERY, QC**							
	Petrel V	SV	1947	D	955*	195' 00"	30' 01"	16' 00"
	(Currently laid up in Quebec, QC.)							
	Techno St-Laurent	TB	1944	D	261*	111' 00"	27' 00"	13' 00"
	(HMCS Riverton [W-47 / ATA-528] '44 - '79)							
T-2	**TEE DEE ENTERPRISES, INC., CHICAGO, IL**							
	Anita Dee	ES	1972	D	97*	90' 00"	21' 00"	8' 10"
	Anita Dee II	ES	1990	D	81*	140' 00"	33' 00"	8' 06"
T-3	**THE ISLE ROYALE LINE, COPPER HARBOR, MI**							
	Isle Royale Queen III	PK	1959	D	15	85' 00"	18' 04"	9' 05"
T-4	**THOMAS W. MARSHALL, TORONTO, ON**							
	Still Watch	SV	1960	D	390*	134' 02"	28' 00"	13' 09"
	(Currently laid up in Toronto, ON.)							
T-5	**THORNTON CONSTRUCTION CO., INC., HANCOCK, MI**							
	Shannon 66-5							
T-6	**THREE RIVERS BOATMEN LTD., TROIS-RIVIERES, QC**							
	Andre H.	TB	1963	D	317*	126' 00"	28' 06"	15' 06"
	(Foundation Valiant '63 - '73, Point Valiant {1} '73 - '95)							
	Avantage	TB	1969	D	367*	116' 10"	32' 09"	16' 03"
	(Sea Lion '69 - '97)							
	Duga	TB	1977	D	403*	111' 00"	33' 00"	16' 01"
	Escorte	TT	1964	D	120*	85' 00"	23' 08"	11' 00"
	(USS Menasha [YTB/YTM-773, YTM-761] '64 - '92, Menasha {1} '92 - '95)							
	R. F. Grant	TB	1969	D	78*	71' 00"	17' 00"	8' 00"
	Robert H.	TB	1944	D	261*	111' 00"	27' 00"	13' 00"
	(HMCS Heatherton [W-22 / ATA-527] '44 - '77)							
T-7	**THUNDER BAY MARINE SERVICE LTD., THUNDER BAY, ON**							
	Agoming	CS	1926	B	155*	100' 00"	34' 00"	9' 00"
	Coastal Cruiser	TB	1939	D	29*	65' 00"	18' 00"	12' 00"
	Glenada	TB	1944	D	107*	80' 06"	25' 00"	10' 01"
	Robert W.	TB	1949	D	48*	60' 00"	16' 00"	8' 06"
	Rosalee D.	TB	1943	D	22*	55' 00"	16' 00"	10' 00"
T-8	**THUNDER BAY TUG SERVICES LTD., THUNDER BAY, ON**							
	Point Valour	TB	1958	D	246*	97' 08"	28' 02"	13' 10"
	(Foundation Valour '58 - '83)							
T-9	**TORONTO DRYDOCK CORP., TORONTO, ON**							
	Menier Consol	FD	1962	B	2,575*	304' 07"	49' 06"	25' 06"
	(Last operated 13 September 1984 — Currently in use as a floating drydock in Toronto, ON.)							
T-10	**TORONTO FIRE DEPARTMENT, TORONTO, ON**							
	Wm. Lyon Mackenzie	FB	1964	D	102*	81' 01"	20' 00"	10' 00"
T-11	**TORONTO HARBOUR COMMISSIONERS, TORONTO, ON**							
	Fred Scandrett	TB	1963	D	52*	62' 00"	17' 00"	8' 00"
	(C. E. "Ted" Smith '63 - '70)							
	J. G. Langton	TB	1934	D	15*	45' 00"	12' 00"	5' 00"
	Maple City	CF	1951	D	135*	70' 06"	36' 04"	5' 11"
	Ned Hanlan II	TB		D				
	William Rest	TB	1961	D	62*	65' 00"	18' 06"	10' 06"
	Windmill Point	CF	1954	D	118*	65' 00"	36' 00"	10' 00"
T-12	**TORONTO METROPOLITAN PARK DEPARTMENT, TORONTO, ON**							
	Ongiara	PF	1963	D	180*	78' 00"	36' 00"	9' 09"
	Sam McBride	PF	1939	D	412*	129' 00"	34' 11"	6' 00"
	Thomas Rennie	PF	1950	D	419*	129' 00"	32' 11"	6' 00"
	Trillium	PF	1910	R	611*	150' 00"	30' 00"	8' 04"
	William Inglis	PF	1935	D	238*	99' 00"	24' 10"	6' 00"
T-13	**TRANSPORT DESGAGNES, INC., QUEBEC, QC**							
	CROISIERES NORDIK, INC. - A DIVISION OF TRANSPORT DESGAGNES, INC.							
	Nordik Passeur	RR	1962	D	627	285' 04"	62' 00"	20' 01"
	(Confederation {1} '62 - '93, Hull 28 '93 - '94)							
	(5 year survey expired April 1994 — Currently laid up in Quebec, QC.)							
	DESGAGNES SHIPPING INTERNATIONAL, INC. - A DIVISION OF TRANSPORT DESGAGNES, INC.							
	Anna Desgagnes	RR	1986	D	17,850	565' 00"	75' 00"	45' 00"
	(Truskavets '86 - '96, Anna Desgagnes '96 - '98, PCC Panama '98 - '99)							

Fleet #	Fleet Name / Vessel Name	Type of Vessel	Year Built	Type of Engine	Cargo Cap. or Gross*	Overal Length	Breadth	Depth or Draft*
	DESGAGNES TANKER, INC. - A DIVISION OF TRANSPORT DESGAGNES, INC.							
	Maria Desgagnes	TK	1999	D	95,607	393' 08"	68' 11"	40' 04"
	(Kilchem Asia '99 - '99)							
	Petrolia Desgagnes	TK	1975	D	97,725	441' 05"	56' 06"	32' 10"
	(Jorvan '75 - '79, Lido '79 - '84, Ek-Sky '84 - '98)							
	Thalassa Desgagnes	TK	1976	D	104,667	441' 05"	56' 06"	32' 10"
	(Joasla '76 - '79, Orinoco '79 - '82, Rio Orinoco '82 - '93)							
	GROUP DESGAGNES, INC. - A DIVISION OF TRANSPORT DESGAGNES, INC.							
	Alcor	BC	1977	D	27,536	584' 08"	75' 01"	48' 03"
	(Patricia V '77 - '83, Mekhanik Dren '83 - '97)							
	Amelia Desgagnes	GC	1976	D	7,000	355' 00"	49' 00"	30' 06"
	(Soodoc {2} '76 - '90)							
	Catherine Desgagnes	GC	1962	D	8,350	410' 03"	56' 04"	31' 00"
	(Gosforth '62 - '72, Thorold {4} '72 - '85)							
	Cecelia Desgagnes	GC	1971	D	7,875	374' 10"	54' 10"	34' 06"
	(Carl Gorthon '71 - '81, Federal Pioneer '81 - '85)							
	Jacques Desgagnes	GC	1960	D	1,250	208' 10"	36' 00"	14' 00"
	(Loutre Consol '60 - '77)							
	Mathilda Desgagnes	GC	1959	D	6,920	360' 00"	51' 00"	30' 02"
	(Eskimo '59 - '80)							
	Melissa Desgagnes	GC	1975	D	7,000	355' 00"	49' 00"	30' 06"
	(Ontadoc {2} '75 - '90)							
	Nordik Express	CF	1974	D	1,697	219' 11"	44' 00"	16' 01"
	(Theriot Offshore IV '74 - '77, Scotoil 4 '77 - '79, Tartan Sea '79 - '87)							
T-14	**TRANSPORT IGLOOLIK, INC., MONTREAL, QC**							
	Aivik	HL	1980	D	4,860	359' 08"	63' 08"	38' 09"
	(Mont Ventoux '80 - '90, Aivik '90 - '91, Unilifter '91 - '92)							
	LOGISTEC NAVIGATION, INC. - VESSEL MANAGED BY TRANSPORT IGLOOIK, INC.							
	Lucien-Paquin	GC	1969	D	12,802	459' 05"	70' 06"	42' 01"
	(Boreland '69 - '79, Sunemerillon '79 - '82, Mesange '82 - '85)							
T-15	**TRAVERSE TALL SHIP CO., TRAVERSE CITY, MI**							
	Malabar	2S	1975	W	100*	105' 00"	22' 00"	8' 00"
	Manitou {1}	2S	1983	W	78*	114' 00"	21' 00"	9' 00"
T-16	**TRUMP INDIANA, INC., GARY, IN**							
	Trump Casino	GA	1996	D	7,256*	288' 00"	76' 00"	17' 06"
T-17	**30,000 ISLANDS CRUISE LINES, INC., PARRY SOUND, ON**							
	Island Queen V {3}	ES	1990	D	526*	130' 00"	35' 00"	6' 06"
U-1	**UNCLE SAM BOAT TOURS, ALEXANDRIA, NY**							
	Alexandria Belle	ES	1988	D	72*	104' 00"	32' 00"	7' 08"*
	Island Duchess	ES	1988	D	60*	110' 00"	27' 08"	8' 08"*
	Island Wanderer	ES	1971	D	57*	62' 05"	22' 00"	7' 02"
	Riot II	ES	1934	D	15*	27' 10"	7' 05"	2' 04"*
	Uncle Sam Jr.	ES	1958	D	30*	50' 00"	10' 00"	4' 00"*
	Uncle Sam II	ES	1958	D	75*	63' 00"	17' 06"	5' 04"
	Uncle Sam VII	ES	1976	D	55*	60' 04"	22' 00"	7' 01"
U-2	**UNISPEED GROUP, INC., WESTMOUNT, QC**							
	Phoenician Trader	GC	1969	D	12,898	496' 09"	66' 09"	39' 02"
	(Professor Nikolay Baranskiy '69 - '96)							
U-3	**UNITED STATES ARMY CORPS OF ENGINEERS - GREAT LAKES AND OHIO RIVER DIV., CHICAGO, IL**							
	UNITED STATES ARMY CORPS OF ENGINEERS - BUFFALO DISTRICT							
	Buffalo	TB	1953	D	23*	45' 00"	13' 00"	7' 00"*
	Cheraw	TB	1970	D	356*	109' 00"	30' 06"	16' 03"
	(USS Cheraw [YTB-802] '70 - '96)							
	Chetek	TB	1973	D	356*	109' 00"	30' 06"	16' 03"
	(USS Chetek [YTB-827] '73 - '96)							
	McCauley	CS	1948	B		112' 00"	52' 00"	3' 00"*
	Simonsen	CS	1954	B		142' 00"	58' 00"	5' 00"*
	Tonawanda	CS	1935	B		120' 00"	45' 00"	3' 00"*
	Washington	TB	1952	D	390*	107' 00"	26' 06"	14' 10"
	(U.S. Army LT-1944 '52 - '62)							
	Wheeler	DR	1982	B	10,353	384' 00"	78' 00"	39' 00"
	UNITED STATES ARMY CORPS OF ENGINEERS - CHICAGO DISTRICT							
	Kenosha	TB	1954	D	82*	70' 00"	20' 00"	9' 08"
	(U.S. Army ST-2011 '54 - '65)							
	Manitowoc	CS	1976	B		132' 00"	44' 00"	8' 00"*
	Racine	TB	1931	D	61*	66' 03"	18' 05"	7' 08"

1,000-footer Edwin H. Gott, cargo capacity 74,100 tons, docks at Two Harbors, MN, 6 July 1999. (Roger D. White)

Adam E. Cornelius unloads coal at Escanaba in 1999. (Rod Burdick)

ADAM E. CORNELIUS

Vessel Spotlight

ADAM E. CORNELIUS	
Length	680'00"
Beam	78'00"
Depth	42'00"
Built	1973
Tonnage	28,200

The **Adam E. Cornelius** was one of the first American vessels built with all cabins and propulsion aft. She entered service in 1973 after construction at Toledo (the largest vessel ever built there and the first since 1959).

Originally named **Roger M. Kyes**, she was renamed on 15 June 1989 to honor one of the founding partners of the Boland and Cornelius fleet, now American Steamship Co. The Kyes was part of a 10-year building program to modernize the U.S. fleet in general and American Steamship Company (ASC) in particular.

During her 26 years on the lakes, Cornelius has had more than her share of hard luck, with numerous groundings and ice damage, perhaps the worst occurring during spring 1996, when ice conditions were particularly difficult.

During her ASC career, the Cornelius has carried cargoes of ore, coal and aggregates, and visited a variety of Great Lakes ports. From 1994-1998, she was chartered by the Inland Steel Co. (now Central Marine Logistics) sailing under their colors and on their trade routes (but minus the famous "Inland Steel" billboards on her sides).

During fit-out, 1999, the Cornelius' ownership and colors returned to ASC.

— *Rod Burdick*

Fleet #	Fleet Name / Vessel Name	Type of Vessel	Year Built	Type of Engine	Cargo Cap. or Gross*	Overall Length	Breadth	Depth or Draft*
	UNITED STATES ARMY CORPS OF ENGINEERS - DETROIT DISTRICT							
	D. L. Billmaier	TB	1968	D	345*	109' 00"	30' 06"	16' 03"
	(USS Natchitoches [YTB-799] '68 - '95)							
	Duluth	TB	1954	D	82*	70' 00"	20' 00"	9' 08"
	(U.S. Army ST-2015 '54 - '62)							
	Fairchild	TB	1953	D	23*	45' 00"	13' 00"	7' 00"*
	Forney	TB	1944	D	163*	86' 00"	23' 00"	10' 04"
	Hammond Bay	TB	1953	D	23*	45' 00"	13' 00"	7' 00"*
	Harvey	CS	1961	B		122' 00"	40' 00"	4' 10"*
	H. J. Schwartz	CS	1995	B		150' 00"	48' 00"	11' 00"
	Huron	CS	1954	B		100' 00"	34' 00"	4' 06"*
	James M. Bray	SV	1924	D	194*	128' 00"	31' 00"	8' 00"
	Michigan	CS	1971	B		120' 00"	33' 00"	3' 06"*
	Nicolet	CS	1971	B		120' 00"	42' 00"	5' 00"*
	Owen M. Frederick	TB	1942	D	56*	65' 00"	17' 00"	7' 06"
	Paj	SV	1955	D	151*	120' 06"	34' 02"	6' 05"
	Paul Bunyan	GL	1945	B		150' 00"	65' 00"	12' 06"
	Shelter Bay	TB	1953	D	23*	45' 00"	13' 00"	7' 00"*
	Tawas Bay	TB	1953	D	23*	45' 00"	13' 00"	7' 00"*
	Veler	CS	1991	B	613*	150' 00"	46' 00"	10' 06"
	Whitefish Bay	TB	1953	D	23*	45' 00"	13' 00"	7' 00"*
U-4	**UNITED STATES COAST GUARD - 9TH COAST GUARD DISTRICT, CLEVELAND, OH**							
	Acacia [WLB-406]	BT	1944	D	1,025*	180' 00"	37' 00"	17' 04"
	(Launched as USCGC Thistle [WAGL-406])							
	(To be decommissioned in 2004.)							
	Adler [WLB-216]	BT	2004	D	2,000*	225' 09"	46' 00"	19' 08"
	(To be commissioned in January 2004 and stationed at Charlevoix, MI.)							
	Biscayne Bay [WTGB-104]	IB	1979	D	662*	140' 00"	37' 06"	12' 00"*
	Bramble [WLB-392]	BT	1944	D	1,025*	180' 00"	37' 00"	17' 04"
	(To be decommissioned in 2003.)							
	Bristol Bay [WTGB-102]	IB	1979	D	662*	140' 00"	37' 06"	12' 00"*
	Buckthorn [WLI-642]	BT	1963	D	200*	100' 00"	24' 00"	4' 08"*
	CGB-12000 [CGB-12000]	BT	1991	B	700*	120' 00"	50' 00"	6' 00"*
	CGB-12001 [CGB-12001]	BT	1991	B	700*	120' 00"	50' 00"	6' 00"*
	Hollyhock [WLB-215]	BT	2003	D	2,000*	225' 09"	46' 00"	19' 08"
	(To be commissioned in September 2003 and stationed at Port Huron, MI.)							
	Katmai Bay [WTGB-101]	IB	1978	D	662*	140' 00"	37' 06"	12' 00"*
	Mackinaw [WAGB-83]	IB	1944	D	5,252*	290' 00"	74' 00"	29' 00"
	(Launched as USCGC Manitowoc [WAG-83])							
	Mobile Bay [WTGB-103]	IB	1979	D	662*	140' 00"	37' 06"	12' 00"*
	Neah Bay [WTGB-105]	IB	1980	D	662*	140' 00"	37' 06"	12' 00"*
	Sundew [WLB-404]	BT	1944	D	1,025*	180' 00"	37' 00"	17' 04"
	NEW BUILDING, UNITED STATES COAST GUARD - "JUNIPER" CLASS - MARINETTE, WI.							
	Spar [WLB-206]	BT	2001	D	2,000*	225' 09"	46' 00"	19' 08"
	(To be commissioned in January 2001 and stationed at Kodiak, AK in the 17th CG District.)							
	Maple [WLB-207]	BT	2001	D	2,000*	225' 09"	46' 00"	19' 08"
	(To be commissioned in April 2001 and stationed at Sitka, AK in the 17th CG District.)							
	Aspen [WLB-208]	BT	2001	D	2,000*	225' 09"	46' 00"	19' 08"
	(To be commissioned in June 2001 and stationed at San Francisco, CA in the 11th CG District.)							
	Sycamore [WLB-209]	BT	2001	D	2,000*	225' 09"	46' 00"	19' 08"
	(To be commissioned in September 2001 and stationed at Cordova, AK in the 17th CG District.)							
	Cypress [WLB-210]	BT	2002	D	2,000*	225' 09"	46' 00"	19' 08"
	(To be commissioned in January 2002 and stationed at Mobile, AL in the 8th CG District.)							
	Oak [WLB-211]	BT	2002	D	2,000*	225' 09"	46' 00"	19' 08"
	(To be commissioned in June 2002 and stationed at Miami, FL in the 7th CG District.)							
	Hickory [WLB-212]	BT	2002	D	2,000*	225' 09"	46' 00"	19' 08"
	(To be commissioned in September 2002 and stationed at Homer, AK in the 17th CG District.)							
	Fir [WLB-213]	BT	2003	D	2,000*	225' 09"	46' 00"	19' 08"
	(To be commissioned in January 2003 and stationed at Astoria, OR in the 13th CG District.)							
	Sequoia [WLB-214]	BT	2003	D	2,000*	225' 09"	46' 00"	19' 08"
	(To be commissioned in June 2003 and stationed at Apra Harbor, Guam in the 14th CG District.)							
	NEW BUILDING, UNITED STATES COAST GUARD - "IDA LEWIS" CLASS, MARINETTE, WI.							
	Maria Bray [WLM-562]	BT	2000	D	840*	175' 00"	36' 00"	14' 03"
	(To be commissioned in February 2000 and stationed at Charleston, SC in the 7th CG District.)							
	Henry Blake [WLM-563]	BT	2000	D	840*	175' 00"	36' 00"	14' 03"
	(To be commissioned in June 2000 and stationed at Seattle, WA in the 13th CG District.)							
	George Cobb [WLM-564]	BT	2000	D	840*	175' 00"	36' 00"	14' 03"
	(To be commissioned in August 2000 and stationed at San Pedro, CA in the 11th CG District.)							

Fleet #	Fleet Name / Vessel Name	Type of Vessel	Year Built	Type of Engine	Cargo Cap. or Gross*	Overall Length	Breadth	Depth or Draft*
U-5	**UNITED STATES DEPT. OF THE INTERIOR - FISH & WILDLIFE SERVICE, ANN ARBOR, MI**							
	Cisco	RV	1951	D		60' 06"	16' 08"	7' 08"
	Grayling	RV	1977	D		75' 00"	22' 00"	9' 10"
	Kaho	RV	1961	D		64' 10"	17' 10"	9' 00"
	Musky II	RV	1960	D	25*	45' 00"	14' 04"	5' 00"
	Siscowet	RV	1946	D	54*	57' 00"	14' 06"	7' 00"
U-6	**UNITED STATES ENVIRONMENTAL PROTECTION AGENCY - REGION 5, CHICAGO, IL**							
	Lake Explorer	RV	1962	D	69*	82' 10"	17' 07"	5' 11"*
	Lake Guardian	RV	1989	D	282*	180' 00"	40' 00"	11' 00"
U-7	**UNITED STATES NATIONAL PARK SERV. - ISLE ROYALE NATL. PARK, HOUGHTON, MI**							
	Beaver	GC	1952	B	550	110' 00"	32' 00"	6' 05"
	Charlie Mott	PF	1953	D	28*	56' 00"	14' 00"	4' 07"
	Greenstone	TK	1977	B	30	81' 00"	24' 00"	6' 01"
	J. E. Colombe	TB	1953	D	25*	45' 00"	12' 05"	5' 03"
	Ranger III	PK	1958	D	140	165' 00"	34' 00"	15' 03"
U-8	**UNITED STATES NAVAL SEA CADET CORPS - FC SHERMAN DIVISION, PORT HURON, MI**							
	Grey Fox [TWR-825]	TV	1985	D	213*	120' 00"	25' 00"	12' 00"*
	Pride of Michigan [YP-673]	TV	1977	D	70*	80' 06"	17' 08"	5' 03"*
U-9	**UNIVERSITE DU QUEBEC, RIMOUSKI, QC**							
	Alcide C. Horth	RV	1965	D	135*	89' 02"	22' 09"	11' 00"
U-10	**UNIVERSITY OF MICHIGAN, ANN ARBOR, MI**							
	CENTER FOR GREAT LAKES AND AQUATIC SCIENCES							
	Laurentian	RV	1977	D	129*	80' 00"	21' 06"	11' 00"
U-11	**UNIVERSITY OF MINNESOTA - DULUTH, DULUTH, MN**							
	Blue Heron	RV	1985	D	175*	119' 06"	28' 00"	15' 06"
U-12	**UNIVERSITY OF WISCONSIN - SUPERIOR, SUPERIOR, WI**							
	L. L. Smith Jr.	RV	1950	D	38*	57' 06"	16' 06"	6' 06"
U-13	**UPPER CANADA STEAMBOATS, INC., BROCKVILLE, ON**							
	Miss Brockville	ES		D		48' 00"	10' 00"	4' 00"
	Miss Brockville IV	ES		D		45' 00"	10' 00"	5' 00"
	Miss Brockville V	ES		D		62' 00"	13' 00"	5' 00"
	Miss Brockville VI	ES		D		38' 00"	8' 00"	3' 00"
	Miss Brockville VII	ES		D		66' 00"	15' 00"	5' 00"
	Miss Brockville VIII	ES		D		48' 00"	12' 00"	5' 00"
U-14	**UPPER LAKES BARGE LINE, INC., BARK RIVER, MI**							
	McKee Sons	SU	1945	B	19,900	579' 02"	71' 06"	38' 06"
	(USNS Marine Angel '45 - '52)							
	Olive M. Moore	TB	1928	D	301*	125' 00"	27' 01"	13' 09"
	(John F. Cushing '28 - '66, James E. Skelly '66 - '66)							
U-15	**UPPER LAKES GROUP, INC., TORONTO, ON**							
	HAMILTON MARINE & ENGINEERING LTD. - A DIVISION OF UPPER LAKES GROUP, INC.							
	James E. McGrath	TB	1963	D	90*	77' 00"	20' 00"	10' 09"
	JACKES SHIPPING, INC. - A DIVISION OF UPPER LAKES GROUP, INC.							
	Canadian Trader	BC	1969	D	28,300	730' 00"	75' 00"	39' 08"
	(Ottercliffe Hall '69 - '83, Royalton {2} '83 - '85, Ottercliffe Hall '85 - '88, Peter Misener '88 - '94)							
	Canadian Venture	BC	1965	D	28,050	730' 03"	75' 00"	39' 02"
	(Lawrencecliffe Hall {2} '65 - '88, David K. Gardiner '88 - '94)							
	Gordon C. Leitch {2}	BC	1968	D	29,700	730' 00"	75' 00"	42' 00"
	(Ralph Misener '68 - '94)							
	MARBULK SHIPPING, INC. - A DIVISION OF UPPER LAKES GROUP, INC.							
	Ambassador	SU	1983	D	37,800	730' 00"	75' 10"	50' 00"
	(Canadian Ambassador '83 - '85)							
	Nelvana	SU	1983	D	74,973	797' 05"	105' 11"	66' 04"
	Pioneer	SU	1981	D	37,900	730' 00"	75' 10"	50' 00"
	(Canadian Pioneer '81 - '86)							
	PROVMAR FUELS, INC. - A DIVISION OF UPPER LAKES GROUP, INC.							
	Hamilton Energy	TK	1965	D	8,622	201' 05"	34' 01"	14' 09"
	(Partington '65 - '79, Shell Scientist '79 - '81, Metro Sun '81 - '85)							
	Provmar Terminal	TK	1959	B	60,000	403' 05"	55' 06"	28' 05"
	(Varangnes '59 - '70, Tommy Wiborg '70 - '74, Ungava Transport '74 - '85)							
	(Last operated in 1984 — Currently in use as a stationary fuel storage barge in Hamilton, ON.)							
	Provmar Terminal II	TK	1948	B	73,740	408' 08"	53' 00"	26' 00"
	(Imperial Sarnia {2} '48 - '89)							
	(Last operated 13 December 1986.)							
	(Currently in use as a stationary fuel storage barge in Hamilton, ON.)							

Fleet #	Fleet Name / Vessel Name	Type of Vessel	Year Built	Type of Engine	Cargo Cap. or Gross*	Overall Length	Breadth	Depth or Draft*
	ULS CORPORATION - A DIVISION OF UPPER LAKES GROUP, INC.							
	Canadian Century	SU	1967	D	31,600	730' 00"	75' 00"	45' 00"
	Canadian Enterprise	SU	1979	D	35,100	730' 00"	75' 08"	46' 06"
	Canadian Leader	BC	1967	T	28,300	730' 00"	75' 00"	39' 08"
	(Feux - Follets '67 - '72)							
	Canadian Mariner	BC	1963	T	27,700	730' 00"	75' 00"	39' 03"
	(Newbrunswicker '63 - '68, Grande Hermine '68 - '72)							
	Canadian Miner	BC	1966	D	28,050	730' 00"	75' 00"	39' 01"
	(Maplecliffe Hall '66 - '88, Lemoyne {2} '88 - '94)							
	Canadian Navigator	SU	1967	D	30,925	728' 11"	75' 10"	40' 06"
	(Demeterton '67 - '75, St. Lawrence Navigator '75 - '80)							
	Canadian Olympic	SU	1976	D	35,100	730' 00"	75' 00"	46' 06"
	Canadian Progress	SU	1968	D	32,700	730' 00"	75' 00"	46' 06"
	Canadian Prospector	BC	1964	D	30,500	730' 00"	75' 10"	40' 06"
	(Carlton '64 - '75, Federal Wear '75 - '75, St. Lawrence Prospector '75 - '79)							
	Canadian Provider	BC	1963	T	27,450	730' 00"	75' 00"	39' 02"
	(Murray Bay {3} '63 - '94)							
	Canadian Ranger	GU	1943	D	25,900	729' 10"	75' 00"	39' 03"
	([Fore Section] Grande Ronde '43 - '48, Kate N. L. '48 - '61, Hilda Marjanne '61 - '84)							
	([Stern Section] Chimo '67 - '83)							
	Canadian Transfer	SU	1943	D	16,235	650' 06"	60' 00"	35' 00"
	([Fore Section] J. H. Hillman Jr. '43 - '74, Crispin Oglebay {2} '74 - '95, Hamilton '95 - '96, Hamilton Transfer '96 - '98)							
	([Stern Section] Cabot '65 - '83, Canadian Explorer '83 - '98)							
	Canadian Transport {2}	SU	1979	D	35,100	730' 00"	75' 08"	46' 06"
	Canadian Voyager	BC	1963	T	27,050	730' 00"	75' 00"	39' 02"
	(Black Bay '63 - '94)							
	James Norris	SU	1952	U	18,600	663' 06"	67' 00"	35' 00"
	Montrealais	BC	1962	T	27,800	730' 00"	75' 00"	39' 00"
	(Launched as Montrealer)							
	Quebecois	BC	1963	T	27,800	730' 00"	75' 00"	39' 00"
	Seaway Queen	BC	1959	T	24,300	713' 03"	72' 00"	37' 00"
	BARBER SHIP MANAGEMENT LTD. - MANAGED BY UPPER LAKES GROUP, INC.							
	Thornhill	SU	1981	D	37,939	635' 11"	90' 08"	48' 07"
	(Frotabrasil '81 - '87, Athos '87 - '89, Chennai Perumai '89 - '93)							
	ESSROC CANADA, INC. - VESSELS MANAGED BY UPPER LAKES GROUP, INC.							
	Metis	CC	1956	B	5,800	331' 00"	43' 09"	26' 00"
	(Last operated 19 August 1993.)							
	(Currently in use as a stationary cement storage barge in Windsor, ON.)							
	Stephen B. Roman	CC	1965	D	7,600	488' 09"	56' 00"	35' 06"
	(Fort William '65 - '83)							
U-16	**UPPER LAKES TOWING, INC., ESCANABA, MI**							
	Joseph H. Thompson	SU	1944	B	21,200	706' 06"	71' 06"	38' 06"
	(USNS Marine Robin '44 - '52)							
	Joseph H. Thompson Jr.	TBA	1990	D	841*	146' 06"	38' 00"	35' 00"
U-17	**USS GREAT LAKES FLEET, INC., DULUTH, MN**							
	Arthur M. Anderson	SU	1952	T	25,300	767' 00"	70' 00"	36' 00"
	Calcite II	SU	1929	D	12,650	604' 09"	60' 00"	32' 00"
	(William G. Clyde '29 - '61)							
	Cason J. Callaway	SU	1952	T	25,300	767' 00"	70' 00"	36' 00"
	Edgar B. Speer	SU	1980	D	73,700	1,004' 00"	105' 00"	56' 00"
	Edwin H. Gott	SU	1979	D	74,100	1,004' 00"	105' 00"	56' 00"
	George A. Sloan	SU	1943	D	15,800	620' 06"	60' 00"	35' 00"
	(Hill Annex '43 - '43)							
	John G. Munson {2}	SU	1952	T	25,550	768' 03"	72' 00"	36' 00"
	Myron C. Taylor	SU	1929	D	12,450	603' 09"	60' 00"	32' 00"
	Ojibway {1}	SB	1945	D	65*	53' 00"	28' 00"	7' 00"
	Philip R. Clarke	SU	1952	T	25,300	767' 00"	70' 00"	36' 00"
	Presque Isle {2}	TBA	1973	D	1,578*	153' 03"	54' 00"	31' 03"
	Presque Isle {2}	SU	1973	B	57,500	974' 06"	104' 07"	46' 06"
	[Presque Isle {2} overall dimensions together]					1,000' 00"	104' 07"	46' 06"
	Roger Blough	SU	1972	D	43,900	858' 00"	105' 00"	41' 06"
V-1	**VERREAULT NAVIGATION, INC., LES MACHINS, QC**							
	I.V. No. 9	GC	1936	D	320	110' 00"	23' 10"	8' 05"
	(A.C.D. '36 - '69)							
	I.V. No. 10	GC	1936	D	320	110' 00"	23' 10"	8' 05"
	(G.T.D. ' 36 - '69)							
	I.V. No. 14	GC	1937	D	229	113' 00"	22' 05"	8' 06"
	(Kermic '37 - '74)							

Fleet #	Fleet Name / Vessel Name	Type of Vessel	Year Built	Type of Engine	Cargo Cap. or Gross*	Overal Length	Breadth	Depth or Draft*
	Keta V	TB	1961	D	236*	98' 00"	26' 00"	12' 06"
	(Kelligrews '61 - '89, Verreault '89 - '89, Verreault No. 25 '89 - '89)							
	Port Mechins	DR	1949	R	1,321	200' 00"	40' 02"	18' 00"
	(Haffar '49 - '61, Lockeport '61 - '92)							
V-2	**VINCENT KLAMERUS EXCAVATING, DRUMMOND ISLAND, MI**							
	Lime Island	TB	1957	D	21*	42' 10"	12' 00"	12' 00"
V-3	**VISTA FLEET, DULUTH, MN**							
	Vista King	ES	1978	D	60*	78' 00"	28' 00"	5' 02"
	Vista Star	ES	1987	D	95*	91' 00"	24' 09"	7' 08"
V-4	**V. M. SHIPPING L.L.C., BARK RIVER, MI**							
	Great Lakes Trader	SU	2000	B	38,200	740' 00"	78' 00"	45' 00"
	Joyce L. Van Enkevort	TBA	1998	D	1,179*	135' 04"	50' 00"	26' 00"
	[Great Lakes Trader/Joyce L. Van Enkevort overall dimensions together]					844' 10"	78' 00"	45' 00"
V-5	**VOIGHT'S MARINE SERVICES, ELLISON BAY, WI**							
	Bounty	ES	1968	D		40' 00"	14' 00"	3' 03"
	Island Clipper {2}	ES	1987	D	149*	65' 00"	20' 00"	5' 00"
	Yankee Clipper	ES	1971	D		54' 00"	17' 00"	5' 00"
V-6	**VOYAGEUR CRUISES, INC., CHARLEVOIX, MI**							
	Voyageur	ES	1981	D	72*	105' 00"	21' 06"	6' 00"*
V-7	**VOYAGEURS MARINE CONSTRUCTION LTEE., VAUDREUIL-DORION, QC**							
	Glenlivet II	TB	1944	D	111*	76' 08"	20' 09"	10' 02"
	Soulanges	TB	1905	D	72*	77' 00"	17' 00"	8' 00"
W-1	**WAGNER CHARTER CO., INC., CAROL STREAM, IL**							
	Buccaneer	ES	1925	D	98*	100' 00"	23' 00"	14' 06"
	Jamica	ES	1967	D	88*	105' 00"	25' 00"	10' 06"
	Trinidad {2}	ES	1926	D	98*	100' 00"	23' 00"	14' 06"
W-2	**WASHINGTON ISLAND FERRY LINE, INC., WASHINGTON ISLAND, WI**							
	C. G. Richter	CF	1950	D	82*	70' 06"	25' 00"	9' 05"
	Eyrarbakki	CF	1970	D	95*	87' 00"	36' 00"	7' 06"
	Robert Noble	CF	1979	D	97*	90' 04"	36' 00"	8' 03"
	Voyager	CF	1960	D	98*	65' 00"	35' 00"	8' 00"
	Washington {2}	CF	1989	D	93*	100' 00"	37' 00"	9' 00"
W-3	**WATERWAYS TRANSPORTATION SERVICES CORP., TORONTO, ON**							
	Waterways 1	PC	1988	D	387*	119' 02"	30' 11"	11' 04"
W-4	**WELLINGTON MARITIME, SAULT STE. MARIE, MI**							
	Linda Jean	PB	1950	D	17*	38'00"	10'00"	5'00"
	Soo River Belle	PB	1961	D	25*	40'00"	14'00"	6'00"
W-5	**WENDELLA SIGHTSEEING CO., CHICAGO, IL**							
	Queen of Andersonville	ES	1962	D	23*	40' 00"	15' 00"	3' 05"
	Wendella Clipper	ES	1958	D	41*	67' 00"	20' 00"	4' 00"
	Wendella Limited	ES	1992	D	66*	68' 00"	20' 00"	4' 09"
	Wendella Sunliner	ES	1961	D	35*	68' 00"	17' 00"	6' 05"
W-6	**WINDSOR DETROIT BARGE, DETROIT, MI**							
	Manco	TB	1951	D	263*	100' 00"	28' 00"	10' 00"
Y-1	**YANKEE LADY YACHT CHARTERS, TORONTO, ON**							
	Yankee Lady	ES	1965	D	56*	42' 10"	16' 06"	9' 02"
	Yankee Lady II	ES	1980	D	68*	75' 00"	16' 00"	9' 08"

FOOTER FACTS

A Great Lakes 1,000 footer carries, in one trip, enough ore to make the steel used in 6,000 cars — or enough coal to power a midsized city for one month.

In one trip, a 1,000-footer carries the equivalent of six 100-car trains.

A 1,000-footer that makes 45 trips a season will carry approximately 31 million tons between fit-out and lay-up.

The Cliffs Victory was scrapped overseas in 1986. (Roger LeLievre)

CLIFFS VICTORY

Classic Spotlight

The **Cliffs Victory**, a familiar sight on the Great Lakes 1951-1985, was also one of the most distinctive vessels to ever serve in the iron ore trade.

Built in 1945 as the fast, Victory-class cargo ship **Notre Dame Victory** for the U.S. Maritime Commission, she sailed on the high seas until 1948. As hostilities in Korea increased, Great Lakes fleets, in need of more tonnage, turned to surplus World War II hulls. Notre Dame Victory was bought by the Cleveland Cliffs Iron Co., converted to a rather non-traditional Great Lakes bulk carrier at Baltimore, MD, and renamed Cliffs Victory. The end product was unusual since it boasted a cargo hold, five hatches and a second hatch crane astern of the aft cabin, as well as a propeller shaft running through the after hold. After her arrival in the lakes, she quickly became known for speed ... as high as 23 mph on the open lake. Unofficial races among her and other World War II converts, such as the **Charles M. White**, were the talk of the lakes at the time.

After the Korean War ended, Cliffs Victory was lengthened 96 feet and returned to service, quite often on the Marquette to Cleveland ore run. Her rudder was torn off in a late 1979 grounding in the St. Mary's River, but the Cliffs Victory's fate was really sealed a few years later when her high cost of operation coupled with a downturn in the steel industry led to her sale for scrap to foreign interests. The vessel, renamed **Savic** (a combination of letters from her old name), sailed under her own power out of the Great Lakes during the final days of 1985. In September 1986, after hull reinforcements were installed at Quebec, Savic sailed, with a cargo for South Korea, via the Panama Canal. Scrapping was completed at Masan, South Korea, shortly thereafter.

— Roger LeLievre

International Fleets

Millenium Falcon, upbound for Lake Superior. (Roger LeLievre)

Space does not permit listing every potential saltwater visitor to the Great Lakes and Seaway. At the end of 1997, the world fleet totaled 85,494 vessels over 100 gross tons, according to Lloyd's Register of Shipping. Therefore we have included only those fleets and vessels that make regular transits of the St. Lawrence Seaway and Great Lakes system, according to reports compiled by the St. Lawrence Seaway Authority. We have also included some vessels that are too large to transit the Seaway but are frequent visitors to St. Lawrence River ports.

Fleet #	Fleet Name Vessel Name	Type of Vessel	Year Built	Type of Engine	Cargo Cap. or Gross*	Overal Length	Breadth	Depth or Draft*
IA-1	**ACOMARIT (U.K.) LTD., GLASGOW, SCOTLAND**							
	Echo Pioneer	GC	1981	D	11,464	479' 09"	70' 08"	37' 01"
IA-2	**AEGEUS SHIPPING S.A., PIREAUS, GREECE**							
	George	GC	1977	D	16,875	530' 00"	70' 03"	43' 00"
	Nini	GC	1976	D	16,291	529' 10"	70' 03"	43' 00"
IA-3	**AKMAR SHIPPING & TRADING CO., INC., ISTANBUL, TURKEY**							
	Ayse Ana	BC	1979	D	25,452	607' 08"	75' 05"	46' 05"
IA-4	**ALBA SHIPPING LTD. A/S, AALBORG, DENMARK**							
	Kasla	TK	1974	D	8,639	427' 07"	57' 10"	26' 03"
IA-5	**ALL TRUST SHIPPING CO. S.A., PIRAEUS, GREECE**							
	Aghia Marina	BC	1978	D	16,868	481' 03"	75' 02"	40' 01"
	Akrathos	BC	1981	D	25,817	605' 08"	75' 05"	46' 05"
	Calliope	BC	1978	D	30,353	622' 07"	76' 05"	47' 05"
	Dora	BC	1978	D	30,350	622' 07"	76' 05"	47' 05"
IA-6	**ALVARGONZALEZ S.A., GIJON, SPAIN**							
	Flag Adrienne	BC	1968	D	18,289	518' 11"	71' 05"	42' 08"
IA-7	**AMASUS SHIPPING B.V., FARMSUM, NETHERLANDS**							
	Aldebaran	GC	1997	D	2,270	270' 06"	37' 05"	13' 02"
	Antares	GC	1984	D	1,576	258' 08"	33' 02"	13' 10"
	Aquatique	GC	1962	D	580	180' 05"	23' 08"	10' 02"
	Auriga	GC	1978	D	1,670	276' 04"	35' 03"	17' 03"
	Bolder	GC	1986	D	1,500	266' 06"	34' 03"	15' 02"
	Christiaan	GC	1984	D	2,280	261' 09"	36' 05"	17' 01"
	Compaen	GC	1975	D	1,458	262' 09"	29' 07"	14' 05"
	Daan	GC	1979	D	1,163	204' 11"	30' 11"	13' 01"
	Diamant	GC	1985	D	1,497	255' 09"	32' 08"	13' 10"
	Eemshorn	GC	1995	D	4,250	293' 10"	43' 03"	23' 04"
	Elisabeth G	GC	1978	D	1,163	204' 11"	32' 06"	13' 01"
	Gitana	GC	1970	D	830	219' 10"	26' 08"	12' 03"
	Laurina Neeltje	GC	1995	D	2,310	279' 04"	35' 05"	17' 07"
	Miska	GC	1963	D	507	182' 03"	23' 11"	8' 10"
	Morgenstond	GC	1967	D	530	203' 10"	23' 06"	10' 00"
	Njord	GC	1985	D	1,490	258' 06"	34' 09"	13' 10"
	Quo-Vadis	GC	1983	D	1,564	259' 03"	32' 08"	14' 10"
	Ulmo	GC	1961	D	700	188' 00"	23' 06"	10' 02"
	Vega	GC	1992	D	2,880	371' 09"	50' 04"	11' 06"
	Vesting	GC	1992	D	2,166	288' 07"	39' 02"	15' 09"
	Vikingbank	GC	1978	D	3,040	268' 01"	46' 10"	21' 02"
	Vios	GC	1984	D	1,485	255' 09"	33' 00"	13' 10"
IA-8	**ANANGEL SHIPPING ENTERPRISES S.A., PIRAEUS, GREECE**							
	Amilla	BC	1972	D	22,589	539' 02"	75' 02"	44' 06"
	Anangel Ares	GC	1980	D	17,154	477' 04"	68' 11"	43' 00"
	Anangel Endeavor	GC	1978	D	23,130	539' 02"	75' 00"	44' 06"
	Anangel Fidelity	BC	1979	D	22,000	539' 02"	75' 00"	44' 06"
	Anangel Honesty	BC	1983	D	31,774	598' 07"	77' 05"	50' 06"
	Anangel Honour	BC	1976	D	22,600	539' 02"	75' 00"	44' 06"
	Anangel Hope	BC	1974	D	22,670	539' 02"	75' 00"	44' 06"
	Anangel Horizon	BC	1977	D	27,090	580' 10"	75' 02"	46' 03"
	Anangel Liberty	BC	1976	D	22,668	539' 02"	75' 00"	44' 06"
	Anangel Might	BC	1978	D	23,130	539' 02"	75' 00"	46' 06"
	Anangel Prosperity	BC	1976	D	22,314	539' 02"	75' 00"	44' 06"
	Anangel Sky	GC	1979	D	17,199	477' 04"	68' 11"	43' 00"
	Anangel Spirit	GC	1978	D	22,109	539' 02"	75' 00"	44' 06"
	Anangel Triumph	BC	1976	D	22,311	539' 02"	75' 00"	44' 06"
	Anangel Victory	GC	1979	D	17,188	477' 04"	68' 11"	44' 06"
	Anangel Wisdom	BC	1974	D	22,353	539' 02"	75' 02"	44' 05"
	Evimeria	BC	1973	D	22,630	539' 02"	75' 02"	44' 06"
	Maria Angelicoussi	GC	1978	D	16,934	477' 05"	69' 00"	43' 00"

Fleet #	Fleet Name Vessel Name	Type of Vessel	Year Built	Type of Engine	Cargo Cap. or Gross*	Overal Length	Breadth	Depth or Draft*
IA-9	ARMADA (GREECE) CO. LTD., PIRAEUS, GREECE							
	Adamas	GC	1978	D	22,823	539' 02"	75' 00"	46' 04"
	Anthos	GC	1979	D	16,897	477' 05"	69' 00"	43' 00"
	Atlas	GC	1984	D	17,249	477' 05"	69' 00"	43' 00"
	Magic	GC	1983	D	3,960	309' 09"	50' 07"	27' 03"
	Prudence	GC	1984	D	17,297	477' 04"	69' 01"	43' 00"
IA-10	ARGOSY SHIPMANAGEMENT, INC. LIBERIA, PIRAEUS, GREECE							
	Alba Sierra	GC	1979	D	14,900	472' 05"	73' 07"	38' 07"
IA-11	ASLAN DENIZCILIK A.S., ISTANBUL, TURKEY							
	Aslan-1	GC	1990	D	8,284	395' 10"	55' 09"	30' 06"
IA-12	ASTRON MARITIME CO. S.A., PIRAEUS, GREECE							
	Agamemnon	GC	1983	D	23,443	539' 02"	75' 02"	46' 06"
	Akragas	GC	1978	D	23,168	539' 02"	75' 00"	46' 06"
	Amfitriti	GC	1978	D	17,224	477' 05"	69' 00"	43' 00"
	Arabella	GC	1983	D	23,440	539' 00"	75' 01"	46' 05"
	Aristotelis	GC	1985	D	23,286	539' 02"	75' 00"	46' 05"
IA-13	ATLANTIS MANAGEMENT, INC., PIRAEUS, GREECE							
	Atlantis Charm	BC	1982	D	22,558	539' 02"	75' 02"	44' 06"
	Atlantis Joy	BC	1977	D	18,216	511' 11"	73' 10"	39' 05"
	Atlantis Spirit	BC	1977	D	19,019	497' 10"	75' 00"	42' 00"
IA-14	ATLANTSKA PLOVIDBA D.D., DUBROVNIK, CROATIA							
	Kupari	HL	1979	D	2,720	266' 05"	48' 09"	21' 08"
	Lapad	HL	1978	D	1,970	307' 11"	52' 07"	24' 00"
	Mljet	BC	1982	D	29,643	622' 01"	74' 11"	49' 10"
	Orsula	BC	1996	D	34,198	656' 02"	77' 01"	48' 11"
	Petka	BC	1986	D	34,685	728' 09"	75' 11"	48' 05"
	Plitvice	HL	1979	D	2,720	266' 05"	48' 09"	21' 08"
	Ruder Boskovic	BC	1974	D	27,020	599' 05"	73' 09"	46' 07"
	Slano	HL	1978	D	2,811	289' 04"	51' 02"	24' 10"
IA-15	AURORA SHIPPING, INC., MANILA, PHILIPPINES							
	Aurora Gold	GC	1976	D	10,027	419' 10"	60' 02"	32' 06"
	Aurora Jade	BC	1979	D	13,206	436' 04"	67' 08"	37' 09"
	Aurora Topaz	BC	1982	D	28,268	639' 09"	75' 10"	46' 11"
IA-16	AZOV SHIPPING CO., MARIUPOL, UKRAINE							
	Avdeevka	BC	1977	D	26,398	570' 11"	75' 03"	47' 07"
	Dobrush	BC	1982	D	28,160	644' 06"	75' 10"	46' 11"
	Fatezh	GC	1981	D	7,805	399' 08"	57' 09"	32' 06"
	General Blazhevich	GC	1981	D	7,805	399' 09"	67' 00"	27' 03"
	Kramatorsk	GC	1980	D	7,805	399' 09"	57' 09"	32' 06"
	Makeevka	BC	1982	D	28,136	644' 06"	75' 07"	46' 11"
	Mekhanik Aniskin	GC	1973	D	8,264	426' 04"	58' 06"	32' 02"
	Sumy	BC	1978	D	22,904	540' 00"	75' 00"	45' 00"
IB-1	B & N B. V. KUSTVAARTBEDRIJF MOERMAN, RIDDERKERK, NETHERLANDS							
	Forte	RR	1989	D	4,001	298' 00"	53' 01"	32' 10"
	Swallow	GC	1996	D	4,250	296' 09"	43' 04"	23' 11"
IB-2	B & N, BYLOCK & NORDSJOFRAKT AS, OSLO, NORWAY							
	Bergon	GC	1978	D	5,449	330' 10"	54' 02"	26' 03"
	Bremon	GC	1976	D	8,650	393' 10"	54' 06"	33' 04"
	Concord	GC	1985	D	9,260	404' 11"	65' 08"	34' 05"
	Corner Brook	GC	1976	D	7,173	445' 06"	61' 00"	40' 01"
	Holmon	GC	1978	D	10,900	442' 11"	59' 06"	32' 10"
	Humber Arm	GC	1976	D	7,173	426' 07"	61' 00"	40' 01"
	Neva Trader	GC	1977	D	7,884	370' 09"	63' 00"	28' 07"
	Norcove	RR	1977	D	6,671	466' 07"	63' 02"	47' 08"
	Storon	BC	1975	D	10,880	470' 02"	61' 00"	33' 04"
	Tofton	GC	1980	D	14,883	522' 02"	70' 03"	41' 04"
	Tor Belgia	RR	1979	D	8,400	558' 07"	69' 00"	42' 00"
	Weston	GC	1979	D	14,938	522' 02"	70' 03"	41' 04"
IB-3	B+H EQUIMAR SINGAPORE PTE. LTD., SINGAPORE, MALAYSIA							
	Narragansett	BC	1977	D	35,910	729' 11"	76' 00"	47' 00"
IB-4	BALTIMAR APS LTD., HUMLEBAEK, DENMARK							
	Baltimar Boreas	GC	1989	D	2,742	299' 07"	49' 03"	25' 00"
	Baltimar Euros	GC	1991	D	3,181	299' 04"	49' 04"	24' 11"
	Baltimar Notos	GC	1988	D	3,168	299' 05"	50' 10"	24' 11"

Fleet #	Fleet Name / Vessel Name	Type of Vessel	Year Built	Type of Engine	Cargo Cap. or Gross*	Overall Length	Breadth	Depth or Draft*
	Baltimar Orion	GC	1990	D	3,168	299' 04"	49' 05"	24' 11"
	Baltimar Saturn	GC	1991	D	2,700	299' 03"	49' 05"	24' 11"
	Baltimar Sirius	GC	1991	D	3,181	299' 04"	49' 07"	24' 11"
	Baltimar Venus	GC	1990	D	2,700	299' 04"	49' 03"	25' 00"
IB-5	**BARU KAHA, INC., PIRAEUS, GREECE**							
	Elite B	BC	1979	D	19,009	509' 07"	74' 10"	41' 01"
	Iron B	GC	1981	D	21,889	584' 08"	75' 03"	46' 00"
	Runner B	GC	1983	D	14,930	532' 06"	72' 10"	44' 00"
IB-6	**BELUGA SHIPPING GMBH, BREMEN, GERMANY**							
	Beluga Obsession	GC	1982	D	5,327	270' 03"	51' 11"	29' 06"
	Beluga Performer	GC	1982	D	6,081	303' 04"	52' 00"	33' 06"
IB-7	**BERGEN BULK CARRIERS A/S, BERGEN, NORWAY**							
	Bergen Bay	BC	1977	D	27,765	579' 11"	75' 02"	48' 03"
	Bergen Sea	BC	1977	D	28,218	579' 11"	75' 02"	48' 03"
IB-8	**BIRLIK DENIZCILIK ISLETMECILIGI SANAYI VE TICARET A.S., ISTANBUL, TURKEY**							
	Haci Hilmi Bey	BC	1977	D	24,354	607' 07"	75' 00"	46' 05"
	Riza Sonay	GC	1989	D	8,219	380' 07"	56' 06"	32' 02"
IB-9	**BISON SHIPMANAGEMENT & CHARTERING CO. PTE. LTD., SINGAPORE, MALAYASIA**							
	Olga	BC	1996	D	18,319	486' 01"	74' 10"	40' 00"
IB-10	**BLUE MARINE S.A. LIBERIA, PIRAEUS, GREECE**							
	Anthony	GC	1981	D	15,883	532' 09"	73' 00"	44' 02"
IB-11	**BLUE PLANET SHIPPING LTD., PIRAEUS, GREECE**							
	Akmi	BC	1977	D	26,874	580' 09"	75' 04"	47' 07"
	Evmar	BC	1976	D	29,212	593' 02"	76' 00"	47' 07"
IB-12	**BOTANY BAY MANAGEMENT SERVICES PTY. LTD., SYDNEY, AUSTRALIA**							
	Marinor	TK	1992	D	53,464	368' 01"	59' 02"	31' 02"
	Tradewind Express	TK	1986	D	87,719	404' 06"	65' 09"	36' 09"
IB-13	**BURMA NAVIGATION CORP., YANGON, UNION OF MYANMAR**							
	Great Laker	BC	1987	D	28,358	590' 07"	75' 10"	48' 07"
	Sea Eagle	GC	1984	D	17,330	519' 03"	75' 09"	44' 00"
IC-1	**CANADA MARITIME LTD., HAMILTON, BERMUDA**							
	Canmar Bravery	CO	1978	D	33,869	717' 02"	101' 11"	54' 03"
	Canmar Conquest	CO	1979	D	18,643	580' 09"	88' 10"	44' 03"
	Canmar Courage	CO	1996	D	34,330	709' 01"	105' 10"	62' 04"
	Canmar Fortune	CO	1995	D	34,330	709' 01"	105' 10"	62' 04"
	Canmar Glory	CO	1979	D	18,964	580' 10"	88' 09"	44' 04"
	Canmar Honour	CO	1998	D	40,879	803' 10"	105' 08"	62' 04"
	Canmar Pride	CO	1998	D	40,879	803' 10"	105' 08"	62' 04"
	Canmar Spirit	CO	1971	D	16,963	548' 02"	84' 02"	50' 01"
	Canmar Triumph	CO	1978	D	18,606	580' 10"	88' 10"	44' 04"
	Canmar Valour	CO	1979	D	18,643	580' 09"	88' 10"	44' 03"
	Canmar Venture	CO	1971	D	16,963	548' 02"	84' 02"	50' 00"
	Canmar Victory	CO	1979	D	18,381	580' 09"	88' 10"	44' 04"
	Contship Endeavour	CO	1983	D	32,424	727' 02"	105' 08"	49' 03"
	Contship Success	CO	1982	D	32,207	730' 00"	105' 10"	61' 08"
IC-2	**CAPE SHIPPING S.A., PIRAEUS, GREECE**							
	Cape Kennedy	GC	1971	D	14,934	466' 09"	65' 01"	40' 06"
	Cape Syros	GC	1978	D	14,948	470' 06"	65' 01"	40' 06"
	Radnor	GC	1975	D	14,970	470' 06"	65' 01"	40' 06"
	Shannon	GC	1976	D	14,829	470' 06"	65' 01"	40' 06"
IC-3	**CAPELLE CHARTERING EN TRADING B.V., CAPELLE A/D IJSSEL, NETHERLANDS**							
	Blue Moon	GC	1975	D	1,559	216' 00"	35' 06"	16' 09"
	Irene	GC	1978	D	1,548	216' 00"	36' 05"	16' 09"
	Wijmers	GC	1984	D	5,050	301' 05"	49' 08"	26' 07"
IC-4	**CARISBROOKE SHIPPING PLC, COWES, ISLE OF WIGHT**							
	Anja C	GC	1991	D	3,222	327' 03"	41' 00"	20' 10"
	Cheryl C	GC	1983	D	2,367	230' 01"	42' 11"	19' 09"
	Elizabeth C	GC	1971	D	2,823	278' 11"	41' 10"	20' 04"
	Emily C	GC	1996	D	4,650	294' 07"	43' 02"	23' 05"
	Klazina C	GC	1983	D	2,554	266' 09"	39' 04"	17' 09"
	Mark C	GC	1996	D	4,620	294' 11"	43' 04"	23' 05"
	Mary C	GC	1977	D	2,440	216' 10"	42' 11"	20' 05"
	Minka C	GC	1975	D	2,657	258' 00"	40' 10"	20' 00"

Antalina unloads steel at Detroit. *(Gene W. Peterson)*

Turkish saltie Mina Cebi heads out of the MacArthur Lock at Sault Ste. Marie and onto Lake Superior.

(Roger LeLievre)

Nordstrand	GC	1991	D	2,800	289' 08"	41' 00"	21' 04"
Tina C	GC	1974	D	2,591	258' 02"	40' 10"	20' 00"
Vanessa C	GC	1974	D	3,165	262' 11"	44' 08"	22' 01"
Vectis Falcon	GC	1978	D	3,564	285' 06"	45' 01"	22' 04"
Vectis Isle	GC	1990	D	3,222	327' 02"	41' 00"	20' 10"

IC-5 CARSTEN REHDER SCHIFFSMAKLER UND REEDEREI GMBH & CO., HAMBURG, GERMANY

Arosette	GC	1971	D	1,968	244' 06"	35' 06"	19' 09"
Industrial Advantage	GC	1984	D	17,330	519' 03"	75' 08"	44' 00"
Vento Del Golfo	GC	1983	D	9,300	416' 11"	65' 03"	35' 02"

IC-6 CATSAMBIS SHIPPING LTD., PIRAEUS, GREECE

Adimon	BC	1977	D	30,880	644' 11"	75' 04"	47' 06"

IC-7 CERES HELLENIC SHIPPING ENTERPRISES LTD., PIRAEUS, GREECE

George L.	BC	1975	D	27,419	597' 01"	75' 02"	48' 03"
Kalliopi L.	BC	1974	D	26,998	585' 08"	75' 01"	47' 06"
Marka L.	BC	1975	D	27,418	597' 01"	75' 02"	48' 03"
Mini Lace	GC	1969	D/W	3,217	214' 11"	50' 03"	21' 08"
Pantazis L.	BC	1974	D	27,434	597' 02"	75' 02"	48' 03"
Tatiana L.	GC	1978	D	16,251	482' 00"	72' 04"	39' 05"

IC-8 CHARTWORLD SHIPPING CORP., PIRAEUS, GREECE

Golden Sky	BC	1975	D	30,449	625' 06"	75' 00"	47' 11"
Golden Sun	BC	1977	D	22,647	539' 03"	75' 01"	44' 06"

IC-9 CHELLARAM SHIPPING LTD., HONG KONG, PEOPLE'S REPUBLIC OF CHINA

Darya Devi	BC	1985	D	28,019	584' 08"	75' 11"	48' 05"
Darya Kamal	BC	1981	D	30,900	617' 04"	76' 00"	47' 07"
Darya Ma	BC	1983	D	30,750	617' 04"	76' 00"	47' 07"

IC-10 CHEMICO NAVIGATION LTD., ATHENS, GREECE

Gulfbreeze	TK	1982	D	85,191	416' 08"	65' 09"	36' 09"

IC-11 CHEMOIL INTERNATIONAL LTD., ATHENS, GREECE

Martinique	TK	1974	D	46,470	360' 11"	54' 07"	28' 01"

IC-12 CHINA OCEAN SHIPPING (GROUP) CO., BEIJING, PEOPLE'S REPUBLIC OF CHINA

An Guang Jiang	GC	1987	D	14,913	491' 02"	71' 06"	41' 00"
An Kang Jiang	GC	1985	D	15,852	487' 02"	74' 07"	43' 04"
An Qing Jiang	GC	1985	D	14,913	491' 02"	71' 06"	41' 00"
An Ze Jiang	GC	1987	D	14,913	491' 02"	71' 06"	41' 00"
Aptmariner	BC	1979	D	31,000	619' 03"	75' 11"	47' 07"
Da Hua	GC	1998	D	16,957	502' 00"	75' 08"	46' 03"
Handymariner	BC	1978	D	31,200	619' 03"	75' 11"	47' 07"
Hui Fu	BC	1978	D	35,887	734' 02"	76' 08"	47' 05"
Hun Jiang	GC	1981	D	15,265	474' 11"	67' 01"	38' 07"
Jing Hong Hai	BC	1976	D	28,863	594' 01"	76' 01"	47' 07"
Ocean Priti	BC	1982	D	27,019	599' 05"	75' 04"	46' 08"
Rong Cheng	GC	1977	D	18,687	484' 07"	75' 00"	42' 08"
Rong Jiang	GC	1978	D	15,189	462' 07"	67' 05"	38' 06"
Yick Hua	BC	1984	D	28,086	584' 08"	75' 11"	48' 05"

IC-13 CLIPPER GREECE LTD., ATHENS, GREECE

Clipper Spirit	BC	1985	D	17,825	481' 08"	74' 10"	40' 01"

IC-14 COLONIAL MARINE INDUSTRIES, INC., SAVANNAH, GA

Eagle	BC	1972	D	10,079	464' 07"	70' 01"	40' 04"

IC-15 COMMERCIAL TRADING & DISCOUNT CO. LTD., ATHENS, GREECE

Ira	BC	1979	D	26,697	591' 02"	75' 10"	45' 08"
Ivi	BC	1979	D	26,697	591' 04"	75' 10"	45' 08"

IC-16 COMMON PROGRESS COMPANIA NAVIERA S.A., PIRAEUS, GREECE

Angelia P	BC	1979	D	22,549	539' 02"	75' 02"	44' 06"
Athinais P	BC	1973	D	22,631	539' 02"	75' 02"	44' 06"
Ellinis P.	BC	1974	D	22,669	539' 02"	75' 01"	44' 06"
Kastor P	BC	1983	D	22,713	528' 03"	75' 07"	45' 07"
Nereis P.	BC	1974	D	22,631	539' 02"	74' 11"	44' 05"
Polydefkis P.	BC	1982	D	22,713	528' 03"	75' 07"	45' 07"
Treasure Island	BC	1974	D	22,647	539' 02"	75' 02"	44' 06"

IC-17 COMPAGNIE DES ILES DU PONANT, NANTES, FRANCE

Le Levant	PA	1998	D	3,500*	326' 09"	45' 07"	11' 00"*
Le Ponant	PA	1991	W	1,189*	290' 06"	39' 01"	17' 00"

IC-18 COMPAGNIE TUNISIENNE DE NAVIGATION S.A., TUNIS, TUNISIA

Bizerte	GC	1979	D	8,312	450' 06"	64' 01"	34' 05"
El Kef	BC	1982	D	26,355	599' 10"	75' 08"	46' 00"

	Habib	RR	1978	D	3,372	478' 01"	77' 02"	27' 05"
	Kairouan	GC	1979	D	8,345	450' 06"	64' 01"	34' 05"
	Tabarka	GC	1952	D	1,651	272' 04"	39' 02"	15' 04"

IC-19 COMPANIA DE NAVIGATIE MARITIMA PETROMIN S.A., CONSTANTZA, ROMANIA

	Costesti	TK	1994	D		337' 05"	53' 10"	26' 11"
	Lotru	BC	1976	D	24,854	607' 07"	75' 00"	46' 05"
	Pionierul	BC	1976	D	18,295	477' 06"	68' 11"	43' 04"
	Tirgu Bujor	BC	1977	D	18,295	476' 01"	68' 10"	43' 04"
	Tirgu Frumos	BC	1977	D	18,295	476' 01"	68' 10"	43' 04"
	Vidraru	BC	1976	D	24,850	607' 07"	75' 00"	46' 05"
	Vulcan	BC	1971	D	12,548	487' 11"	66' 10"	35' 01"

IC-20 COMPAGNIE DE MANAGEMENT D' ORBIGNY (C.M.O.), PARIS, FRANCE

	Clipper Cheyenne	HL	1986	D	4,244	341' 03"	67' 05"	29' 03"
	Petra	RR	1983	D	3,550	303' 01"	59' 06"	28' 03"

IC-21 CORAL CONTAINER LINES S.A., HAVANA, CUBA

	Giorita	GC	1988	D	13,226	482' 04"	73' 10"	35' 10"

IC-22 CROATIA LINE, RIJEKA, CROATIA

	Bribir	RR	1979	D	7,478	482' 03"	71' 04"	43' 11"
	Buzet	GC	1979	D	12,430	474' 10"	75' 07"	35' 02"
	Grobnik	GC	1981	D	14,425	514' 07"	71' 08"	39' 01"
	Hreljin	CO	1977	D	11,031	504' 10"	70' 09"	36' 09"
	Karlobag	GC	1980	D	24,432	634' 04"	75' 04"	46' 05"
	Krk	GC	1977	D	13,694	514' 07"	71' 08"	39' 01"
	Ledenice	RR	1979	D	7,478	473' 09"	71' 04"	43' 11"
	Moscenice	GC	1976	D	13,914	514' 07"	71' 08"	39' 01"
	Motovun	GC	1977	D	13,914	514' 07"	71' 08"	39' 01"
	Opatija	GC	1973	D	15,142	485' 07"	67' 09"	41' 01"
	Pionir	CO	1973	D	5,580	390' 00"	53' 03"	27' 03"
	Rab	GC	1972	D	14,956	482' 10"	67' 09"	41' 00"
	Rijeka	GC	1981	D	16,728	525' 00"	77' 02"	46' 00"
	Slavonija	GC	1980	D	24,432	634' 04"	75' 04"	46' 05"
	Slovenija	GC	1980	D	14,425	514' 07"	71' 08"	39' 01"
	Susak	CO	1977	D	11,031	504' 09"	70' 09"	36' 09"
	Triglav	GC	1981	D	15,642	500' 04"	74' 04"	41' 11"
	Tuhobic	GC	1983	D	16,648	524' 11"	77' 02"	46' 00"
	Velebit	GC	1981	D	15,709	500' 04"	74' 04"	41' 11"

ID-1 DALEX SHIPPING CO. S.A., PIRAEUS, GREECE

	Arabian Express	GC	1977	D	17,089	483' 05"	72' 04"	39' 01"
	Caribbean Express I	GC	1977	D	17,057	483' 05"	72' 04"	39' 01"
	Pol Daisy	GC	1982	D	17,279	509' 03"	74' 10"	43' 04"
	Pol Iris	GC	1982	D	16,467	509' 03"	74' 10"	43' 04"
	Pol Pansy	GC	1982	D	17,279	509' 03"	74' 10"	43' 04"
	Pol Primrose	GC	1984	D	17,279	509' 03"	74' 10"	43' 04"

ID-2 DALNAVE NAVIGATION, INC., ATHENS, GREECE

	DS Pioneer	BC	1978	D	29,696	584' 00"	75' 04"	48' 03"

ID-3 DENSAN SHIPPING CO. LTD., ISTANBUL, TURKEY

	Gunay A	BC	1981	D	30,900	617' 04"	76' 00"	47' 07"
	Necat A	BC	1981	D	28,645	655' 06"	75' 00"	45' 11"

ID-4 DET NORDENFJELDSKE D/S AS, TRONDHEIM, NORWAY

	Consensus Manitou	BC	1983	D	28,192	584' 08"	75' 11"	48' 05"

ID-5 DIANA SHIPPING AGENCIES S.A., PIRAEUS, GREECE

	Elm	BC	1984	D	21,978	509' 02"	75' 01"	44' 07"
	Maple	BC	1977	D	19,020	497' 10"	75' 00"	42' 00"
	Oak	BC	1981	D	21,951	509' 02"	75' 02"	44' 07"

ID-6 DILMUN SHIPPING CO. LTD., MANAMA, BAHRAIN

	Dilmun Fulmar	TK	1980	D	10,150	361' 04"	60' 02"	32' 10"
	Dilmuan Shearwater	TK	1983	D	19,217	486' 06"	69' 00"	38' 03"
	Dilmun Tern	TK	1980	D	21,770	496' 05"	74' 10"	39' 05"

ID-7 DOBSON FLEET MANAGEMENT LTD., LIMASSOL, CYPRUS

	Evangeline	GC	1975	D	4,250	316' 07"	52' 07"	28' 11"
	Fetish	GC	1977	D	4,240	309' 09"	50' 08"	27' 03"
	Jenny D	BC	1972	D	19,306	508' 11"	74' 11"	41' 06"
	Nicola D	BC	1977	D	9,267	439' 01"	59' 03"	29' 06"
	Scarab	GC	1983	D	4,240	309' 01"	50' 07"	27' 03"

ID-8 DOCKENDALE SHIPPING CO. LTD., NASSAU, BAHAMAS

	Attica	GC	1984	D	20,412	503' 07"	74' 08"	45' 04"
	Clipper Arita	GC	1984	D	17,247	477' 05"	69' 00"	43' 01"

Fleet #	Fleet Name / Vessel Name	Type of Vessel	Year Built	Type of Engine	Cargo Cap. or Gross*	Overal Length	Breadth	Depth or Draft*
	Clipper Mandarin	GC	1985	D	17,247	477' 05"	69' 01"	43' 00"
	Okim	GC	1989	D	23,270	539' 02"	75' 01"	46' 05"
	Sakura	GC	1987	D	23,209	539' 02"	75' 00"	46' 05"
ID-9	**DONNELLY SHIPMANAGEMENT LTD., LIMASSOL, CYPRUS**							
	Finnsnes	BC	1978	D	12,394	441' 04"	67' 11"	37' 09"
	Fonnes	BC	1978	D	5,753	346' 09"	50' 07"	26' 03"
	Frines	BC	1978	D	12,358	441' 04"	67' 11"	37' 09"
	Fullnes	BC	1979	D	12,274	441' 04"	67' 11"	37' 09"
	Garnes	GC	1980	D	5,995	351' 01"	49' 04"	28' 09"
	Rafnes	BC	1976	D	6,351	339' 09"	52' 06"	28' 11"
	Risnes	BC	1976	D	5,699	339' 09"	52' 10"	28' 11"
	Rollnes	BC	1976	D	5,789	334' 09"	52' 00"	28' 09"
	Vigsnes	BC	1979	D	6,105	352' 04"	49' 03"	28' 09"
ID-10	**DORVAL KAIUN K.K., TOKYO, JAPAN**							
	Golden Fumi	TK	1996	D	78,895	383' 10"	65' 07"	36' 09"
	Golden Georgia	TK	1996	D		452' 09"	72' 02"	38' 03"
	Tenyu	GC	1985	D	4,240	277' 09"	47' 07"	28' 07"
ID-11	**DYNASTY SHIPPING CO. LTD., ATHENS, GREECE**							
	Seaglory	BC	1978	D	29,212	593' 03"	75' 11"	47' 07"
IE-1	**EGON OLDENDORFF LTD., LUEBECK, GERMANY**							
	Anna Oldendorff	BC	1994	D	18,355	486' 05"	74' 10"	40' 00"
	Elise Oldendorff	BC	1998	D	20,100	488' 10"	75' 11"	44' 03"
	Erna Oldendorff	BC	1994	D	18,355	486' 05"	74' 10"	40' 00"
	Helena Oldendorff	BC	1984	D	28,354	644' 06"	75' 10"	46' 11"
	Jobst Oldendorff	GC	1983	D	14,279	462' 06"	67' 01"	38' 06"
	Mathilde Oldendorff	BC	1999	D	20,427	488' 10"	75' 11"	44' 04"
	Regina Oldendorff	BC	1986	D	28,031	639' 09"	75' 10"	46' 11"
	Rixta Oldendorff	BC	1986	D	28,031	639' 09"	75' 10"	46' 11"
	T. A. Adventurer	GC	1988	D	20,586	595' 06"	77' 01"	44' 00"
	T. A. Discoverer	GC	1989	D	28,386	595' 06"	75' 08"	44' 00"
	T. A. Explorer	GC	1987	D	22,500	614' 10"	75' 11"	42' 08"
	T. A. Voyager	GC	1987	D	22,800	614' 10"	75' 11"	44' 04"
IE-2	**ELITE-SHIPPING A/S, COPENHAGEN, DENMARK**							
	Arktis Atlantic	GC	1992	D	4,110	290' 01"	49' 08"	24' 07"
	Arktis Blue	GC	1992	D	4,110	290' 01"	49' 08"	24' 07"
	Arktis Breeze	GC	1987	D	2,671	261' 01"	44' 02"	21' 00"
	Arktis Carrier	GC	1988	D	2,671	261' 01"	44' 02"	21' 00"
	Arktis Crystal	GC	1994	D	5,401	319' 07"	53' 08"	27' 11"
	Arktis Dream	GC	1993	D	4,110	290' 01"	49' 08"	24' 07"
	Arktis Fantasy	GC	1994	D	7,120	331' 08"	63' 00"	30' 06"
	Arktis Fighter	GC	1994	D	7,120	331' 08"	63' 00"	30' 06"
	Arktis Future	GC	1994	D	7,120	331' 08"	63' 00"	30' 06"
	Arktis Grace	GC	1988	D	2,671	261' 01"	44' 02"	21' 00"
	Arktis Hope	GC	1994	D	5,401	319' 07"	53' 08"	27' 11"
	Arktis Hunter	GC	1995	D	5,401	319' 07"	53' 08"	27' 11"
	Arktis Light	GC	1993	D	5,401	319' 07"	53' 08"	27' 11"
	Arktis Mariner	GC	1996	D	8,972	330' 09"	67' 01"	36' 01"
	Arktis Mayflower	GC	1996	D	8,973	330' 09"	67' 01"	36' 01"
	Arktis Meadow	GC	1995	D	8,970	330' 09"	66' 03"	36' 01"
	Arktis Meridian	GC	1996	D	8,900	330' 08"	67' 01"	36' 01"
	Arktis Mirage	GC	1999	D	8,943	330' 09"	67' 01"	36' 01"
	Arktis Mistral	GC	1998	D	8,950	330' 09"	66' 03"	36' 01"
	Arktis Ocean	GC	1987	D	2,433	249' 07"	38' 03"	21' 00"
	Arktis Pearl	GC	1984	D	2,298	243' 10"	37' 03"	22' 01"
	Arktis Pride	GC	1991	D	4,110	290' 01"	49' 08"	24' 07"
	Arktis Princess	GC	1989	D	2,671	261' 01"	44' 02"	21' 00"
	Arktis Queen	GC	1989	D	2,676	261' 01"	44' 02"	21' 00"
	Arktis River	GC	1986	D	2,433	249' 07"	38' 03"	21' 00"
	Arktis Sea	GC	1984	D	2,298	243' 10"	37' 03"	22' 01"
	Arktis Sirius	GC	1989	D	2,671	261' 01"	44' 02"	21' 00"
	Arktis Sky	GC	1987	D	2,671	261' 01"	44' 02"	21' 00"
	Arktis Spring	GC	1993	D	4,110	290' 01"	49' 08"	24' 07"
	Arktis Star	CO	1993	D	12,200	488' 10"	75' 11"	37' 01"
	Arktis Sun	CO	1993	D	12,216	488' 10"	75' 11"	37' 01"
	Arktis Trader	GC	1987	D	2,433	249' 07"	38' 03"	21' 00"
	Arktis Venture	GC	1992	D	4,110	290' 01"	49' 08"	24' 07"
	Arktis Vision	GC	1994	D	5,401	319' 07"	53' 08"	27' 11"
	Industrial Ace	GC	1993	D	4,111	290' 01"	49' 08"	24' 07"

Fleet #	Fleet Name Vessel Name	Type of Vessel	Year Built	Type of Engine	Cargo Cap. or Gross*	Overal Length	Breadth	Depth or Draft*
IE-3	**ELMIRA SHIPPING & TRADING S.A., ATHENS, GREECE**							
	Aegean Sea	BC	1983	D	31,431	598' 09"	77' 06"	50' 06"
	Mecta Sea	BC	1984	D	28,166	584' 08"	75' 11"	48' 05"
	Tecam Sea	BC	1984	D	28,166	584' 08"	75' 11"	48' 05"
IE-4	**EPIDAURUS S.A., PIRAEUS, GREECE**							
	Phoenix M	BC	1976	D	26,874	580' 08"	75' 04"	47' 07"
IE-5	**ER DENIZCILIK SANAYI NAKLIYAT VE TICARET A.S., ISTANBUL, TURKEY**							
	Balaban I	BC	1979	D	24,747	562' 06"	75' 00"	46' 00"
IE-6	**ERSHIP INTERNACIONAL S.A., MADRID, SPAIN**							
	La Rabida	BC	1988	D	11,901	468' 10"	65' 10"	33' 04"
	Manjoya	BC	1974	D	11,848	445' 02"	63' 05"	35' 09"
	Milanos	BC	1975	D	11,849	445' 02"	63' 05"	35' 09"
	Sac Flix	BC	1982	D	15,855	479' 09"	70' 03"	40' 00"
	Sac Huelva	BC	1972	D	5,645	379' 02"	50' 07"	28' 08"
	Sac Malaga	BC	1976	D	30,499	625' 06"	75' 00"	47' 10"
IE-7	**ESTONIAN SHIPPING CO., TALLINN, ESTONIA**							
	Aleksander Kolmpere	BC	1987	D	24,105	605' 09"	74' 10"	46' 06"
	Gustav Sule	BC	1986	D	24,150	605' 00"	75' 00"	46' 06"
	Valga	RR	1979	D	4,600	458' 01"	63' 01"	43' 00"
	Viljandi	RR	1978	D	4,600	458' 01"	63' 01"	43' 00"
IE-8	**EUROCARRIERS S.A., ATHENS, GREECE**							
	Anastasia	BC	1974	D	17,567	502' 04"	73' 00"	39' 04"
	Golden Venture	BC	1971	D	16,887	486' 11"	74' 00"	35' 00"
	Mitsa	BC	1973	D	20,815	514' 08"	74' 11"	44' 03"
	Queen	BC	1968	D	19,297	512' 04"	74' 04"	42' 04"
IF-1	**FABRICIUS & CO. A/S, MARSTAL, DENMARK**							
	Emilie K	GC	1982	D	2,150	237' 08"	37' 04"	22' 00"
	Gimo One	GC	1986	D	7,310	350' 06"	54' 07"	31' 03"
	Greenland Saga	GC	1989	D	3,200	285' 07"	47' 10"	25' 03"
	Industrial Faith	GC	1993	D	4,000	290' 00"	49' 03"	24' 07"
	Laola	GC	1980	D	2,920	327' 06"	37' 05"	14' 02"
	Malene	GC	1984	D	922	176' 08"	31' 06"	18' 05"
	Sea Flower	GC	1982	D	1,630	237' 09"	36' 11"	22' 06"
	Sea Maid	GC	1984	D/W	1,632	237' 08"	36' 09"	22' 00"
	Sea Rose	GC	1980	D	1,304	229' 00"	34' 03"	19' 09"
	Susan K	GC	1982	D	2,158	237' 08"	37' 03"	22' 00"
	Vinland Saga	GC	1982	D	932	207' 04"	31' 06"	18' 05"
IF-2	**FAFALIOS SHIPPING S.A., PIRAEUS, GREECE**							
	Irene	BC	1993	D	65,671	738' 02"	72' 02"	59' 01"
	Nea Doxa	BC	1984	D	30,900	617' 03"	76' 00"	47' 07"
	Nea Elpis	BC	1978	D	29,300	593' 03"	76' 00"	47' 07"
	Nea Tyhi	BC	1978	D	29,300	593' 03"	76' 00"	47' 07"
IF-3	**FAIRMONT SHIPPING (H.K.) LTD., HONG KONG, PEOPLE'S REPUBLIC OF CHINA**							
	Gefion	GC	1985	D	12,363	399' 07"	65' 08"	36' 02"
IF-4	**FAR-EASTERN SHIPPING CO., VLADIVOSTOK, RUSSIA**							
	Argut	BC	1990	D	3,600	311' 08"	51' 10"	25' 07"
	Cheremkhovo	GC	1984	D	24,200	579' 05"	75' 00"	45' 11"
	Kapitan Milovzorov	BC	1975	D	14,204	497' 10"	69' 01"	38' 00"
IF-5	**FEEDERLINES B.V., GRONINGEN, NETHERLANDS**							
	Johannes Boele	GC	1997	D	7,761	415' 00"	65' 00"	27' 07"
IF-6	**FG-SHIPPING OY AB, HELSINKI, FINLAND**							
	Astrea	RR	1990	D	6,672	423' 07"	70' 01"	43' 06"
	Finnfighter	GC	1978	D	14,931	522' 02"	70' 03"	41' 05"
	Finnmaster	RR	1973	D	5,710	451' 02"	73' 04"	52' 10"
	Finnpine	RR	1984	D	7,669	394' 05"	69' 00"	47' 07"
	Kemira	BK	1981	D	19,323/8,250	369' 09"	57' 05"	34' 06"
	Railship I	RR	1975	D	8,970	581' 04"	71' 00"	43' 00"
IF-7	**FRANCO COMPANIA NAVIERA S.A., ATHENS, GREECE**							
	Rhea	BC	1978	D	29,300	593' 10"	76' 00"	47' 07"
	Stefania I	BC	1985	D	28,269	584' 08"	75' 11"	48' 05"
IF-8	**FREJA TANKERS A/S, COPENHAGEN, DENMARK**							
	Freja Scandic	TK	1981	D	77,442	405' 07"	59' 09"	32' 02"

Fleet #	Fleet Name / Vessel Name	Type of Vessel	Year Built	Type of Engine	Cargo Cap. or Gross*	Overal Length	Breadth	Depth or Draft*
IG-1	**GALATIA SHIPPING CO. S.A., PIRAEUS, GREECE**							
	Agios Georgios	GC	1970	D	3,062	214' 10"	50' 03"	21' 08"
	Captain Christos	GC	1976	D	11,775	419' 03"	67' 04"	33' 09"
	Dimitra	GC	1973	D	5,792	309' 00"	49' 06"	29' 07"
IG-2	**GANYMED (MALTA) LTD., BIRZEBBUGA, MALTA**							
	MSC Boston	CO	1993	D	41,750	794' 00"	105' 09"	75' 06"
	MSC Houston	CO	1994	D	41,570	794' 00"	105' 09"	75' 06"
	Norasia Chicago	CO	1977	D	14,520	556' 06"	83' 04"	57' 03"
	Norasia Montreal	CO	1996	D	18,355	522' 05"	78' 09"	45' 07"
	Norasia Samantha	CO	1998	D	14,310	708' 08"	87' 06"	62' 02"
	Norasia Savannah	CO	1998	D	14,310	708' 08"	87' 06"	62' 02"
IG-3	**GANYMED SHIPPING GMBH, HAMBURG, GERMANY**							
	Morillo	GC	1971	D	10,800	511' 02"	70' 01"	41' 08"
	MSC New York	CO	1994	D	41,570	794' 00"	106' 00"	75' 06"
	Norasia Malta	CO	1994	D	41,722	773' 04"	106' 00"	63' 04"
	Norasia Salome	CO	1998	D	14,310	708' 08"	87' 06"	71' 06"
	Norasia Scarlet	CO	1999	D	14,310	708' 08"	87' 06"	62' 02"
	Norasia Sharjah	CO	1994	D	41,570	794' 00"	105' 09"	75' 06"
	Norasia Shanghai	CO	1996	D	41,460	794' 02"	106' 00"	75' 06"
	Norasia Sheba	CO	1998	D	14,310	708' 08"	87' 06"	62' 02"
	Norasia Singa	CO	1996	D	41,460	794' 02"	106' 00"	75' 06"
	Norasia Sultana	CO	1999	D	11,000	711' 07"	87' 06"	62' 04"
IG-4	**GEORGIAN SHIPPING CO. LTD., BATUMI, GEORGIA**							
	Bakradze	TK	1985	D	126,377	496' 05"	73' 07"	40' 00"
	Chavchavadze	TK	1988	D	126,377	496' 05"	73' 07"	40' 00"
	Davitaja	BC	1983	D	24,150	605' 00"	75' 05"	46' 06"
	G. Ordzhonikidze	TK	1988	D	126,377	496' 05"	73' 07"	40' 00"
	Gonio	TK	1984	D	126,377	496' 05"	73' 07"	39' 10"
	Kacharava	TK	1984	D	126,377	496' 05"	73' 07"	40' 00"
	Kobuleti	TK	1985	D	126,377	496' 05"	73' 07"	39' 11"
	Makatsarija	TK	1984	D	126,377	496' 05"	73' 07"	40' 00"
	Poti	TK	1981	D	167,174	505' 03"	74' 07"	45' 04"
	Sedoy	BC	1984	D	24,105	605' 08"	75' 00"	46' 05"
	Uznadze	TK	1988	D	128,956	496' 05"	73' 07"	39' 10"
	Vachnadze	TK	1985	D	126,377	496' 05"	73' 07"	39' 10"
	Vakhtangov	BC	1984	D	24,105	605' 00"	75' 00"	46' 05"
	Vekua	TK	1987	D	126,377	496' 05"	73' 07"	39' 10"
IG-5	**GODBY SHIPPING A/B, GODBY, FINLAND**							
	Jenolin	GC	1992	D	5,314	345' 04"	55' 11"	27' 01"
	Julia	GC	1993	D	5,314	345' 04"	55' 11"	27' 01"
	Link Star	RR	1989	D	4,453	349' 05"	56' 05"	32' 06"
	Mimer	RR	1990	D	4,232	355' 06"	57' 04"	42' 00"
	Mini Star	RR	1988	D	4,452	352' 06"	56' 05"	32' 06"
	Miniforest	GC	1972	D	2,545	290' 04"	42' 01"	26' 02"
IG-6	**GOLDENPORT SHIPSMANAGEMENT LTD., ATHENS, GREECE**							
	Golden D	BC	1977	D	24,738	565' 02"	75' 02"	44' 08"
IG-7	**GOOD FAITH SHIPPING CO. S.A., PIRAEUS, GREECE**							
	Amitie	AC	1970	D	20,139	485' 07"	74' 10"	44' 03"
	Encouragement	GC	1974	D	19,920	537' 01"	75' 02"	47' 03"
	Enterprise I	GC	1974	D	19,920	537' 01"	75' 02"	47' 03"
	Epos	BC	1975	D	24,482	608' 04"	74' 10"	46' 04"
	Krissa	BC	1979	D	20,698	521' 00"	74' 03"	43' 08"
	Mana	GC	1978	D	17,089	505' 03"	72' 11"	41' 03"
	Ocean Grace	GC	1976	D	1,381	212' 01"	31' 06"	16' 01"
	Ocean Lake	GC	1976	D	20,950	521' 08"	75' 06"	44' 03"
IG-8	**GORTHON LINES, HELSINGBORG, SWEDEN**							
	Ada Gorthon	RR	1984	D	9,981	512' 07"	73' 00"	46' 09"
	Alida Gorthon	GC	1977	D	14,299	463' 09"	71' 04"	38' 08"
	Ingrid Gorthon	GC	1977	D	14,298	463' 10"	73' 00"	38' 09"
	Ivan Gorthon	RR	1974	D	3,500	387' 08"	51' 02"	37' 03"
	Joh. Gorthon	RR	1977	D	7,182	512' 07"	69' 07"	47' 01"
	Lovisa Gorthon	RR	1979	D	6,420	440' 07"	69' 01"	37' 09"
	Margit Gorthon	GC	1977	D	14,298	463' 10"	73' 00"	38' 09"
	Maria Gorthon	RR	1984	D	9,995	512' 07"	73' 00"	48' 09"
	Ragna Gorthon	RR	1979	D	7,583	442' 07"	69' 01"	37' 09"
	Stig Gorthon	RR	1979	D	6,382	440' 08"	69' 01"	37' 09"
	Viola Gorthon	RR	1987	D	10,917	544' 08"	75' 08"	43' 02"

Fleet #	Fleet Name / Vessel Name	Type of Vessel	Year Built	Type of Engine	Cargo Cap. or Gross*	Overal Length	Breadth	Depth or Draft*
IG-9	**GOURDOMICHALIS MARITIME S.A., PIRAEUS, GREECE**							
	Kavo Alexandros	BC	1977	D	26,414	567' 09"	74' 10"	48' 05"
	Kavo Sidero	BC	1976	D	26,671	592' 11"	75' 04"	47' 07"
	Kavo Yerakas	BC	1981	D	25,854	585' 00"	75' 08"	45' 11"
IG-10	**GRAIG SHIP MANAGEMENT, CARDIFF, ENGLAND**							
	Clipper Cowbridge	GC	1998	D	8,874	329' 08"	66' 11"	36' 05"
	Clipper Westoe	GC	1998	D	8,874	329' 08"	66' 11"	36' 05"
IG-11	**GREAT CIRCLE SHIPPING AGENCY LTD., BANGKOK, THAILAND**							
	Chada Naree	BC	1981	D	18,668	479' 03"	75' 01"	41' 04"
	Chalothorn Naree	GC	1977	D	16,953	505' 07"	73' 00"	39' 08"
	Fujisan Maru	BC	1976	D	16,883	481' 03"	75' 02"	40' 00"
	Wana Naree	BC	1980	D	26,977	566' 00"	75' 11"	48' 05"
IG-12	**GREAT LAKES EUROPEAN SHIPPING AS, ORNSKOLDSVIK, SWEDEN**							
	Marinette	GC	1967	D	12,497	503' 03"	66' 07"	36' 09"
	Menominee	GC	1967	D	12,497	503' 03"	66' 07"	36' 09"
	Munksund	GC	1968	D	12,497	503' 03"	66' 07"	36' 09"
IG-13	**GRECOMAR SHIPPING AGENCY LTD., PIRAEUS, GREECE**							
	Lamda	BC	1978	D	16,644	465' 08"	71' 07"	40' 00"
IG-14	**GREEN MANAGEMENT AS, MINDE, NORWAY**							
	Nomadic Patria	GC	1978	D	17,160	511' 09"	73' 11"	45' 10"
	Nomadic Pollux	GC	1977	D	17,161	511' 10"	73' 11"	46' 00"
	Nomadic Princess	BC	1978	D	26,991	564' 04"	75' 02"	47' 03"
IH-1	**H.C. GRUBE, MARSTAL, DENMARK**							
	Jenclipper	GC	1976	D	710	163' 00"	27' 02"	18' 01"
IH-2	**H.S.S. HOLLAND SHIP SERVICE B.V., ROTTERDAM, NETHERLANDS**							
	Carola I	GC	1983	D	9,620	372' 04"	56' 02"	37' 01"
	Margaretha Green	GC	1999	D	15,970	468' 07"	70' 07"	43' 08"
	Maria Green	GC	1998	D	17,539	468' 07"	70' 07"	43' 08"
	Marion Green	GC	1999	D	17,538	468' 07"	70' 07"	43' 08"
IH-3	**HANS PETER WEGENER KG, JORK, GERMANY**							
	Atria	GC	1986	D	2,973	288' 08"	42' 09"	24' 05"
	Containerships III	CO	1990	D	6,350	400' 03"	62' 02"	29' 02"
	Containerships IV	CO	1994	D	8,932	495' 10"	64' 06"	30' 06"
	Containerships V	CO	1996	D	8,912	495' 10"	64' 06"	30' 06"
IH-4	**HANSEATIC SHIPPING CO. LTD., LIMASSOL, CYPRUS**							
	Cape Confidence	BC	1982	D	18,649	506' 11"	75' 01"	41' 00"
	Jo Hassel	TK	1986	D	8,139	356' 00"	58' 05"	32' 02"
IH-5	**HAPAG-LLOYD CRUISES GMBH, HAMBURG, GERMANY**							
	c. Columbus	PA	1997	D	14,000*	472' 06"	70' 06"	18' 06"*
	Europa	PA	1999	D	28,437*	651' 07"	78' 09"	59' 01"
IH-6	**HARBOR SHIPPING & TRADING CO. S.A., CHIOS, GREECE**							
	Chios Charity	BC	1981	D	29,002	589' 11"	76' 01"	47' 07"
	Chios Charm	BC	1976	D	26,541	600' 06"	74' 11"	47' 01"
	Chios Glory	BC	1972	D	29,197	593' 02"	76' 00"	47' 07"
	Chios Harmony	BC	1977	D	29,337	594' 01"	75' 11"	47' 07"
	Chios Pride	BC	1981	D	28,500	627' 07"	75' 03"	44' 04"
	Chios Spirit	BC	1977	D	17,769	479' 00"	73' 03"	40' 10"
	Elpida	BC	1971	D	25,635	591' 06"	75' 02"	45' 00"
	Galini	BC	1971	D	25,651	591' 06"	75' 02"	45' 00"
IH-7	**HARREN & PARTNER SCHIFFAHRTS GMBH, EMS, GERMANY**							
	Nenufar Atlantico	CO	1996	D	7,200	387' 02"	64' 08"	31' 00"
	Opdr Douro	GC	1994	D	4,766	330' 00"	54' 02"	24' 07"
	Padua	GC	1992	D	3,735	288' 05"	42' 00"	23' 04"
	Pampero	GC	1995	D	5,660	371' 11"	53' 10"	25' 09"
	Pandora	GC	1992	D	3,735	288' 05"	42' 00"	23' 04"
	Rhein Master	GC	1994	D	4,766	330' 00"	54' 02"	24' 07"
	Rheintal	GC	1996	D	4,750	305' 01"	54' 02"	24' 07"
	Scan Pacific	RR	1996	D	5,100	329' 01"	61' 00"	31' 10"
	Scan Partner	RR	1997	D	5,147	331' 00"	62' 04"	23' 02"
IH-8	**HELIKON SHIPPING ENTERPRISES LTD., LONDON, ENGLAND**							
	Arcadia	BC	1973	D	22,587	539' 02"	75' 02"	44' 06"
	Elikon	BC	1980	D	16,106	582' 00"	75' 02"	44' 04"

Fleet #	Fleet Name / Vessel Name	Type of Vessel	Year Built	Type of Engine	Cargo Cap. or Gross*	Overal Length	Breadth	Depth or Draft*
IH-9	**HELLENIC STAR SHIPPING CO. S.A., ATHENS, GREECE**							
	Faith Star	BC	1972	D	16,914	486' 11"	74' 00"	39' 00"
	Glory Star	GC	1977	D	16,543	483' 05"	72' 07"	39' 01"
	Winter Star	BC	1978	D	28,660	655' 06"	75' 09"	45' 11"
	World Star	GC	1980	D	16,640	548' 11"	75' 02"	42' 08"
IH-10	**HERMAN BUSS GMBH & CIE., LEER, GERMANY**							
	Baltic Trader	CO	1995	D	6,928	381' 11"	64' 00"	30' 02"
	Edda	GC	1985	D	2,812	322' 07"	44' 04"	23' 00"
IH-11	**HERMANN C. BOYE & CO., MARSTAL, DENMARK**							
	Andreas Boye	GC	1979	D	1,304	229' 00"	34' 03"	19' 09"
	Anne Boye	GC	1985	D	1,680	251' 02"	36' 09"	22' 00"
	Birthe Boye	GC	1983	D/W	1,630	237' 08"	36' 11"	22' 00"
	Elisabeth Boye	GC	1990	D	2,650	251' 06"	36' 09"	17' 03"
	Hermann C. Boye	GC	1980	D	1,525	229' 00"	34' 03"	19' 09"
IH-12	**HILAL SHIPPING TRADING & INDUSTRY CO., ISTANBUL, TURKEY**							
	Hilal II	BC	1981	D	25,845	585' 00"	75' 09"	45' 11"
II-1	**INTERSCAN SCHIFFAHRTSGESELLSCHAFT MBH, HAMBURG, GERMANY**							
	Pamela	GC	1985	D	1,738	273' 07"	37' 01"	17' 09"
	Patria	GC	1995	D	3,519	270' 03"	41' 02"	23' 07"
	Pinta	GC	1993	D	2,795	270' 00"	41' 02"	21' 08"
	Pionier	GC	1989	D	2,801	270' 00"	41' 00"	23' 07"
	Premiere	GC	1985	D	1,631	270' 06"	37' 02"	17' 09"
	Sooneck	GC	1986	D	2,019	270' 07"	37' 01"	17' 09"
IJ-1	**J. BEKKERS CO. B.V., ROTTERDAM, NETHERLANDS**							
	Falcon Carrier	GC	1975	D	21,367	531' 08"	75' 02"	45' 11"
IJ-2	**J. G. GOUMAS (SHIPPING) CO. S.A., PIRAEUS, GREECE**							
	Washington Rainbow II	BC	1984	D	22,828	515' 11"	75' 07"	44' 08"
IJ-3	**J. G. ROUSSOS SHIPPING S.A., ATHENS, GREECE**							
	Pany R	BC	1978	D	22,174	528' 00"	75' 02"	44' 04"
	Smaragda	BC	1985	D	17,825	481' 08"	74' 10"	40' 01"
IJ-4	**J. POULSEN SHIPPING A/S, KORSOR, DENMARK**							
	Ocean Bird	GC	1991	D	4,222	309' 09"	50' 10"	25' 11"
	Sky Bird	GC	1977	D	4,305	298' 11"	47' 08"	27' 11"
IJ-5	**JAISING MARITIME LTD., MUMBAI, INDIA**							
	Jaising Energy	GC	1995	D	2,873	269' 00"	46' 07"	16' 05"
	Jaising Frontier	GC	1995	D	2,873	269' 00"	46' 07"	16' 05"
	Jaising Trinity	BC	1982	D	28,076	646' 10"	75' 10"	46' 11"
IJ-6	**JAN WIND SHIPPING, NANSUM, NETHERLANDS**							
	Lida	GC	1974	D	1,448	214' 03"	35' 05"	16' 01"
IJ-7	**JARDINE SHIP MANAGEMENT LTD. ,HONG KONG, PEOPLE'S REPUBLIC OF CHINA**							
	Golden Laker	BC	1996	D	30,838	607' 01"	77' 05"	48' 11"
IJ-8	**JAYSHIP LTD., LONDON, ENGLAND**							
	Gur Maiden	GC	1976	D	16,251	491' 06"	69' 01"	40' 03"
	Gur Master	GC	1978	D	15,767	492' 00"	69' 00"	40' 03"
	M. Melody	GC	1978	D	15,765	491' 06"	69' 00"	40' 03"
IJ-9	**JO TANKERS B.V., SPIJKENISSE, NETHERLANDS**							
	Jo Adler	TK	1992	D	89,632	456' 00"	69' 09"	34' 03"
	Jo Aspen	TK	1991	D	87,839	456' 00"	69' 09"	34' 03"
	Jo Calluna	TK	1986	D	93,865	448' 02"	68' 00"	35' 02"
	Jo Ebony	TK	1986	D	88,443	422' 11"	66' 04"	36' 01"
	Jo Hegg	TK	1985	D	51,200	356' 00"	58' 07"	32' 02"
	Jo Maple	TK	1991	D	60,968	377' 11"	59' 05"	31' 02"
	Jo Palm	TK	1991	D	60,968	377' 11"	59' 05"	31' 02"
	Jo Spirit	TK	1998	D	33,205	352' 02"	52' 02"	30' 02"
IJ-10	**JUGOSLAVENSKA OCEANSKA PLOVIDBA, KOTOR, YUGOSLAVIA**							
	Durmitor	GC	1982	D	17,400	519' 03"	75' 09"	39' 01"
	Grant Carrier	BC	1984	D	30,850	617' 04"	75' 11"	47' 07"
IJ-11	**JUHL & EHRHORN, ESBJERG, DENMARK**							
	Elisabeth Clipper	GC	1983	D	1,490	222' 00"	40' 00"	21' 04"
	Karen Clipper	GC	1978	D	1,285	206' 04"	36' 09"	20' 04"
	Mette Clipper	GC	1977	D	1,281	206' 05"	36' 09"	12' 00"

Kroonborg, owned by Wagenborg Shipping B.V., The Netherlands. (Roger LeLievre)

Fleet #	Fleet Name Vessel Name	Type of Vessel	Year Built	Type of Engine	Cargo Cap. or Gross*	Overal Length	Breadth	Depth or Draft*
IJ-12	**JUMBO SHIPPING CO. S.A., GENEVA, SWITZERLAND**							
	Daniella	HL	1989	D	7,600	322' 09"	68' 06"	37' 02"
	Fairlift	HL	1990	D	7,780	329' 02"	68' 10"	43' 08"
	Fairload	HL	1995	D	7,500	313' 11"	60' 03"	37' 02"
	Fairmast	HL	1983	D	6,833	360' 07"	63' 07"	34' 05"
	Gajah Borneo	HL	1978	D	5,076	327' 05"	59' 02"	32' 00"
	Jumbo Challenger	HL	1983	D	6,375	360' 11"	63' 00"	34' 05"
	Jumbo Spirit	HL	1995	D	5,200	313' 11"	60' 03"	37' 02"
	Stellamare	HL	1982	D	2,850	289' 04"	51' 02"	24' 00"
	Stellanova	HL	1996	D	5,198	313' 08"	60' 03"	37' 02"
	Stellaprima	GC	1991	D	7,600	329' 02"	68' 10"	43' 08"
IK-1	**KG PAUL HEINRICH GMBH & CO., STEINKIRCHEN, GERMANY**							
	Frauke	GC	1994	D	7,713	352' 06"	64' 06"	34' 09"
IK-2	**KIL SHIPPING A/S, GENTOFTE, DENMARK**							
	Baltic Sif	TK	1984	D	47,124	371' 10"	59' 02"	26' 03"
	Celtic Sif	TK	1985	D	48,124	371' 10"	59' 02"	26' 03"
	Kilchem America	TK	1999	D	95,607	393' 08"	68' 11"	40' 04"
	Malene Sif	TK	1994	D	68,811	382' 06"	62' 04"	33' 02"
IK-3	**KIRAN GROUP OF SHIPPING COMPANIES, ISTANBUL, TURKEY**							
	TK Barcelona	GC	1985	D	6,596	345' 01"	54' 02"	27' 07"
	TK Bremen	GC	1982	D	6,605	357' 09"	53' 10"	27' 01"
	TK Captain Kadir	GC	1982	D	6,251	353' 05"	54' 01"	26' 09"
	TK London	GC	1982	D	8,535	390' 11"	59' 02"	29' 06"
	TK Odessa	GC	1982	D	6,524	357' 09"	53' 11"	27' 01"
	TK Valletta	GC	1985	D	6,607	345' 01"	54' 02"	27' 07"
	TK Venice	GC	1985	D	6,596	345' 01"	54' 02"	27' 07"
IK-4	**KNUTSEN O.A.S. SHIPPING A/S, HAUGESUND, NORWAY**							
	Ellen Knutsen	TK	1992	D	105,193	464' 03"	75' 07"	38' 09"
	Helene Knutsen	TK	1992	D	114,577	464' 08"	75' 07"	39' 10"
	Hilda Knutsen	TK	1989	D	112,275	464' 08"	75' 07"	39' 10"
	Pascale Knutsen	TK	1993	D	112,275	464' 08"	75' 07"	38' 09"
	Sidsel Knutsen	TK	1993	D	163,463	533' 02"	75' 05"	48' 07"
	Synnove Knutsen	TK	1992	D	105,193	464' 03"	75' 07"	38' 09"
	Torill Knutsen	TK	1990	D	112,275	464' 08"	75' 07"	38' 09"
	Turid Knutsen	TK	1993	D	163,463	533' 03"	75' 07"	48' 07"
IL-1	**LATMAR COLUMBIA LTD., LIMASSOL, CYPRUS**							
	Dzintari	TK	1985	D	128,818	497' 01"	73' 07"	39' 11"
IL-2	**LATVIAN SHIPPING CO., RIGA, LATVIA**							
	Juris Avots	RR	1983	D	5,500	501' 00"	63' 01"	43' 00"
IL-3	**LIBANFRACHT SARL., BEIRUT, LEBANON**							
	Baalbeck	CO	1979	D	7,285	414' 03"	59' 03"	24' 06"
	Carl Metz	GC	1980	D	7,796	417' 05"	58' 11"	32' 00"
	Metz Beirut	GC	1967	D	10,150	492' 07"	66' 05"	38' 05"
	Metz Italia	GC	1967	D	10,080	493' 01"	66' 05"	38' 06"
	Pablo Metz	CO	1970	D	4,250	375' 08"	68' 03"	26' 11"
	Pauline Metz	GC	1970	D	3,030	313' 08"	52' 10"	25' 07"
IL-4	**LINK LINE LTD., PIREAUS, GREECE**							
	Aktis	GC	1976	D	18,627	532' 02"	75' 02"	44' 00"
	Beluga	BC	1977	D	23,725	585' 02"	74' 04"	44' 02"
	Ochimos	GC	1976	D	17,000	521' 11"	75' 00"	43' 04"
	Phaethon	GC	1977	D	24,300	567' 07"	75' 00"	47' 11"
IL-5	**LITHUANIAN SHIPPING CO., KLAIPEDA, LITHUANIA**							
	Asta	GC	1996	D	5,805	337' 04"	52' 00"	26' 07"
	Kapitonas A. Lucka	BC	1980	D	14,550	479' 08"	67' 09"	42' 04"
	Kapitonas Andzejauskas	BC	1978	D	14,550	479' 08"	67' 09"	42' 04"
	Kapitonas Daugela	BC	1975	D	14,631	479' 08"	67' 09"	42' 04"
	Kapitonas Daugirdas	BC	1976	D	14,631	479' 08"	67' 09"	42' 04"
	Kapitonas Domeika	BC	1979	D	14,550	479' 08"	67' 09"	42' 04"
	Kapitonas Kaminskas	BC	1978	D	14,550	479' 08"	67' 09"	42' 04"
	Kapitonas Marcinkus	BC	1977	D	14,550	479' 08"	67' 09"	42' 04"
	Kapitonas Serafinas	BC	1980	D	14,550	479' 08"	67' 09"	42' 04"
	Kapitonas Sevcenko	BC	1977	D	14,550	479' 08"	67' 09"	42' 04"
	Kapitonas Simkus	BC	1976	D	14,550	479' 08"	67' 09"	42' 04"
	Kapitonas Stulpinas	BC	1981	D	14,550	479' 08"	67' 09"	42' 04"
	Rasa	GC	1998	D	5,836	337' 04"	52' 04"	26' 07"

Fleet #	Fleet Name / Vessel Name	Type of Vessel	Year Built	Type of Engine	Cargo Cap. or Gross*	Overal Length	Breadth	Depth or Draft*
IM-1	**M. ODYSSEOS SHIPMANAGEMENT LTD., NICOSIA, CYPRUS**							
	Bluebill	BC	1977	D	30,242	621' 06"	75' 00"	47' 11"
	Hellenic Confidence	BC	1977	D	17,616	479' 00"	73' 04"	40' 10"
	Tropic Confidence	BC	1986	D	17,832	473' 03"	75' 06"	40' 00"
IM-2	**M. T. M. SHIP MANAGEMENT PTE. LTD., SINGAPORE, SINGAPORE**							
	Chembulk Fortitude	TK	1989	D	104,036	432' 01"	66' 11"	36' 09"
	Chembulk Singapore	TK	1989	D	104,036	433' 01"	66' 11"	36' 09"
	Encounter	TK	1983	D	89,386	413' 05"	65' 09"	36' 09"
	Entity	TK	1985	D	89,474	404' 06"	65' 09"	36' 09"
	Equity	TK	1985	D	89,386	404' 06"	65' 08"	36' 09"
	Espoir	TK	1979	D	105,193	438' 00"	72' 03"	39' 01"
	Kwan Siu	TK	1976	D	16,203	264' 10"	40' 01"	21' 02"
	Pacific Star	TK	1984	D	38,922	351' 01"	52' 07"	26' 11"
IM-3	**MAMMOET SHIPPING (NETHERLAND ANTILLES) B.V., ROOSENDAAL, NETHERLANDS**							
	Enchanter	HL	1998	D	16,069	452' 09"	74' 10"	31' 03"
	Happy Ranger	HL	1998	D	15,065	452' 09"	74' 10"	31' 03"
	Happy River	HL	1998	D	15,700	452' 09"	74' 10"	31' 03"
	Happy Rover	HL	1997	D	15,700	452' 09"	74' 10"	31' 03"
	Project Americas	HL	1979	D	12,811	455' 10"	70' 08"	42' 08"
	Project Arabia	HL	1982	D	12,800	455' 11"	70' 08"	42' 08"
	Project Europa	HL	1983	D	13,493	456' 02"	75' 02"	42' 08"
	Project Orient	HL	1981	D	10,434	454' 07"	70' 08"	42' 08"
	Thor Scan	HL	1982	D	9,800	404' 08"	67' 09"	33' 10"
	Titan Scan	HL	1982	D	9,864	404' 08"	67' 11"	33' 10"
	Tracer	HL	2000	D	8,874	329' 09"	73' 06"	26' 11"
	Tramper	HL	2000	D	8,874	329' 09"	73' 06"	26' 11"
	Transporter	HL	2000	D	8,874	329' 09"	73' 06"	26' 11"
	Traveller	HL	2000	D	8,874	329' 09"	73' 06"	26' 11"
IM-4	**MARINE MANAGERS LTD., PIRAEUS, GREECE**							
	Trident Mariner	BC	1984	D	28,503	590' 03"	75' 04"	47' 07"
IM-5	**MARINE TRUST LTD., ATHENS, GREECE**							
	Tribels	GC	1974	D	18,029	484' 07"	75' 03"	42' 08"
	Vulcan	BC	1975	D	30,499	625' 06"	75' 00"	47' 10"
IM-6	**MARMARAS NAVIGATION LTD., PIRAEUS, GREECE**							
	Artaki	BC	1977	D	19,077	508' 10"	74' 11"	41' 06"
	Kydonia	BC	1977	D	18,737	479' 03"	75' 00"	41' 04"
	Kyzikos	BC	1978	D	19,374	496' 01"	75' 01"	42' 08"
	Proussa	BC	1979	D	18,750	504' 07"	75' 00"	41' 01"
	Redestos	GC	1977	D	15,180	462' 07"	67' 01"	38' 06"
IM-7	**MARTI SHIPPING & TRADING CO., INC., ISTANBUL, TURKEY**							
	Tevfik Kaptan I	GC	1977	D	1,036	212' 05"	28' 03"	13' 02"
	Zafer Tomba	GC	1970	D	979	189' 01"	31' 00"	13' 05"
IM-8	**MEDITERRANEA DI NAVIGAZIONE S.R.L., RAVENNA, ITALY**							
	Barbarossa	TK	1982	D	163,538	517' 01"	75' 04"	43' 00"
	Fradiavolo	TK	1973	D	31,324	333' 10"	41' 11"	21' 04"
	Longobarda	TK	1992	D		411' 01"	62' 04"	30' 00"
	Metauro	TK	1991	D	29,972	323' 06"	49' 03"	23' 00"
IM-9	**METRON SHIPPING & AGENCIES S.A., PIRAEUS, GREECE**							
	Pontokratis	BC	1981	D	28,738	590' 02"	75' 11"	47' 07"
	Pontoporos	BC	1984	D	29,155	590' 02"	75' 11"	47' 07"
IM-10	**MILLENIUM MARITIME SERVICES LTD., PIRAEUS, GREECE**							
	Clipper Atlantic	GC	1975	D	7,923	399' 05"	57' 09"	32' 06"
	Clipper Pacific	GC	1976	D	7,923	399' 08"	57' 11"	32' 06"
	Millenium Amethyst	GC	1978	D	23,536	539' 02"	75' 00"	46' 05"
	Millenium Condor	BC	1981	D	27,036	627' 07"	75' 03"	44' 03"
	Millenium Eagle	BC	1983	D	28,788	606' 11"	75' 11"	48' 01"
	Millenium Falcon	BC	1981	D	27,048	627' 07"	75' 00"	44' 03"
	Millenium Golden Hind	BC	1978	D	16,560	537' 11"	75' 03"	38' 09"
	Millenium Harmony	GC	1978	D	16,711	537' 11"	75' 03"	38' 09"
	Millenium Hawk	BC	1984	D	28,791	606' 11"	75' 11"	48' 01"
	Millenium Leader	BC	1984	D	37,489	599' 09"	93' 03"	49' 11"
	Millenium Majestic	GC	1979	D	17,154	477' 05"	69' 00"	43' 00"
	Millenium Osprey	BC	1984	D	28,786	606' 11"	75' 11"	48' 01"
	Millenium Raptor	BC	1982	D	30,670	617' 04"	76' 00"	47' 07"
	Millenium Yama	GC	1979	D	23,169	539' 02"	75' 00"	46' 04"

Fleet #	Fleet Name / Vessel Name	Type of Vessel	Year Built	Type of Engine	Cargo Cap. or Gross*	Overal Length	Breadth	Depth or Draft*
IM-11	**MONTEVERDE DI NAVIGAZIONE S.R.L., NAPLES, ITALY**							
	Serenade	BC	1972	D	6,341	332' 07"	52' 07"	30' 03"
IM-12	**MURMANSK SHIPPING CO., MURMANSK, RUSSIA**							
	Admiral Ushakov	BC	1979	D	19,885	531' 07"	75' 01"	44' 05"
	Aleksandr Nevskiy	BC	1978	D	19,590	532' 02"	75' 02"	44' 05"
	Aleksandr Suvorov	BC	1979	D	19,590	532' 02"	75' 02"	44' 05"
	Dmitriy Donskoi	BC	1977	D	19,885	531' 10"	75' 02"	44' 05"
	Dmitriy Pozharskiy	BC	1977	D	19,885	531' 10"	75' 02"	44' 05"
	Ivan Bogun	BC	1981	D	19,885	531' 10"	75' 02"	44' 05"
	Ivan Susanin	BC	1981	D	19,885	531' 10"	75' 02"	44' 05"
	Kapitan Bochek	BC	1982	D	19,253	531' 10"	75' 02"	44' 05"
	Kapitan Chukhchin	BC	1981	D	19,240	531' 10"	75' 02"	44' 05"
	Kapitan Kudley	BC	1983	D	19,252	531' 10"	75' 02"	44' 05"
	Kuzma Minin	BC	1980	D	19,885	531' 10"	75' 02"	44' 05"
	Mikhail Kutuzov	BC	1979	D	19,590	531' 10"	75' 01"	44' 05"
	Mikhail Strekalovskiy	BC	1981	D	19,252	531' 10"	75' 02"	44' 05"
	Pyotr Velikiy	BC	1978	D	19,885	531' 10"	75' 02"	44' 05"
	Stepan Razin	BC	1980	D	19,590	531' 09"	75' 01"	44' 05"
	Tonya Bondarchuk	GC	1972	D	4,687	346' 07"	51' 04"	26' 03"
	Yuriy Dolgorukiy	BC	1980	D	19,885	532' 02"	75' 02"	44' 05"
IN-1	**NARVAL SHIPPING CORP., PIRAEUS, GREECE**							
	Cay	BC	1976	D	18,726	507' 09"	73' 11"	41' 01"
	Lyra	BC	1976	D	27,140	579' 10"	75' 00"	46' 04"
	Paragon	BC	1977	D	29,039	593' 02"	75' 11"	47' 07"
IN-2	**NAUTILUS CHARTERING N.V., KALMTHOUT, BELGIUM**							
	Dennis Danielsen	GC	1978	D	2,537	261' 10"	43' 00"	24' 08"
IN-3	**NAVARONE S.A., PIRAEUS, GREECE**							
	Mallard	GC	1977	D	18,791	479' 03"	75' 01"	41' 05"
IN-4	**NAVIERA PENINSULAR S.A., BILBAO, SPAIN**							
	Misty	GC	1983	D	8,150	392' 01"	60' 10"	31' 03"
IN-5	**NAVIERA POSEIDON, HAVANA, CUBA**							
	Lilac Islands	GC	1983	D	15,175	472' 05"	67' 02"	38' 07"
	South Islands	GC	1986	D	15,147	472' 05"	67' 02"	38' 07"
IN-6	**NAVIGATION MARITIME BULGARE LTD., VARNA, BULGARIA**							
	Balkan	BC	1975	D	25,714	607' 08"	74' 10"	46' 05"
	Kamenitza	BC	1980	D	24,150	605' 08"	75' 00"	46' 05"
	Kapitan Georgi Georgiev	BC	1980	D	24,150	605' 08"	75' 00"	46' 05"
	Kom	BC	1997	D	13,971	437' 10"	73' 00"	36' 06"
	Malyovitza	BC	1983	D	24,456	605' 00"	75' 05"	46' 06"
	Milin Kamak	BC	1979	D	24,285	607' 07"	75' 00"	46' 05"
	Okoltchitza	BC	1982	D	24,148	605' 08"	75' 05"	46' 06"
	Perelik	BC	1998	D	13,971	437' 10"	73' 00"	36' 06"
	Persensk	BC	1998	D	13,971	437' 10"	73' 00"	36' 06"
	Shipka	BC	1979	D	24,285	607' 07"	75' 00"	46' 05"
IN-7	**NEPTUNE TRADING, INC., BASSETERRE, ST. KITTS-NEVIS**							
	Altair	GC	1979	D	2,534	261' 10"	42' 10"	24' 08"
IN-8	**NESTE OYJ, ESPOO, FINLAND**							
	Kihu	TK	1984	D	160,507	527' 11"	76' 00"	46' 08"
	Lunni	TK	1976	D	108,231	539' 06"	72' 09"	39' 04"
	Melkki	TK	1982	D	82,417	461' 11"	69' 08"	32' 04"
	Rankki	TK	1982	D	82,417	461' 11"	69' 08"	32' 04"
	Sirri	TK	1981	D	47,502	351' 01"	59' 00"	30' 01"
	Sotka	TK	1976	D	101,991	539' 07"	73' 00"	39' 05"
	Tavi	TK	1985	D	160,507	527' 11"	76' 00"	58' 05"
	Tiira	TK	1977	D	108,231	539' 07"	72' 10"	39' 05"
	Uikku	TK	1977	D	108,231	539' 07"	73' 00"	39' 05"
	Vikla	TK	1982	D	53,490	437' 04"	63' 02"	31' 03"
IN-9	**NISSEN KAIUN K.K., HAKATA, JAPAN**							
	Rubin Eagle	BC	1995	D	18,315	447' 10"	74' 10"	40' 00"
	Rubin Falcon	BC	1996	D	18,000	486' 01"	74' 10"	40' 00"
	Rubin Halcyon	BC	1997	D	18,315	486' 01"	74' 10"	40' 00"
	Rubin Hawk	BC	1995	D	18,233	486' 01"	74' 10"	40' 00"
	Rubin Lark	BC	1997	D	18,315	486' 01"	74' 10"	40' 00"
	Rubin Stork	BC	1996	D	18,315	446' 00"	74' 10"	40' 00"

Fleet # Fleet Name Vessel Name	Type of Vessel	Year Built	Type of Engine	Cargo Cap. or Gross*	Overal Length	Breadth	Depth or Draft*
IN-10	**NORDANE SHIPPING A/S, SVENDBORG, DENMARK**						
Gerda Vesta	GC	1983	D	2,610	243' 03"	36' 10"	22' 00"
Helle Stevns	GC	1980	D	7,909	349' 08"	54' 03"	29' 06"
Stevnsland	GC	1972	D	2,510	290' 04"	45' 05"	26' 03"
Stevns Bulk	GC	1975	D	3,320	246' 01"	43' 08"	25' 04"
Stevns Pearl	GC	1984	D	5,900	327' 09"	58' 06"	29' 07"
Stevns Sea	GC	1972	D	3,610	290' 04"	45' 04"	26' 03"
Stevns Trader	GC	1970	D	2,245	290' 04"	45' 05"	26' 03"
IN-11	**NORTHERN SHIPPING CO., ARKHANGELSK, RUSSIA**						
Fyodor Varaksin	BC	1977	D	14,220	497' 10"	69' 01"	38' 00"
Kapitan Alekseyev	GC	1971	D	16,618	556' 05"	71' 07"	43' 05"
Kapitan Glazachev	BC	1976	D	14,200	497' 10"	69' 01"	38' 00"
Kapitan Zamyatin	BC	1976	D	14,200	497' 10"	69' 01"	38' 00"
Nikolay Novikov	BC	1973	D	13,955	492' 11"	69' 01"	38' 00"
Petr Strelkov	BC	1977	D	14,200	497' 10"	69' 01"	38' 00"
Vasiliy Musinskiy	BC	1974	D	14,200	497' 10"	69' 01"	38' 00"
Vladimir Timofeyev	BC	1973	D	14,204	493' 00"	69' 01"	38' 00"
IO-1	**O. T. TONNEVOLD AS, GRIMSTAD, NORWAY**						
Thornburg	GC	1981	D	4,447	332' 04"	56' 02"	29' 07"
Thorndale	GC	1981	D	4,380	332' 04"	55' 11"	29' 06"
IO-2	**OCEANBULK MARITIME S.A., ATHENS, GREECE**						
Aurora	GC	1976	D	15,513	491' 05"	69' 00"	40' 03"
Etoile	GC	1990	D	17,430	520' 10"	75' 00"	44' 00"
Strange Attractor	BC	1978	D	28,873	593' 02"	76' 00"	47' 07"
Thorsriver	GC	1992	D	17,510	569' 03"	75' 07"	45' 01"
IO-3	**ODYSSEY INVESTMENTS CO. LTD.**						
Ziria	GC	1983	D	16,208	532' 06"	73' 00"	44' 00"
IO-4	**OLYMPIC SHIPPING AND MANAGEMENT S.A., ATHENS, GREECE**						
Calliroe Patronicola	BC	1985	D	29,608	599' 09"	75' 11"	48' 07"
Olympic Melody	BC	1984	D	29,640	599' 09"	75' 11"	48' 07"
Olympic Mentor	BC	1984	D	29,693	599' 09"	75' 11"	48' 07"
Olympic Merit	BC	1985	D	29,611	599' 09"	75' 11"	48' 07"
Olympic Miracle	BC	1984	D	29,670	599' 09"	75' 11"	48' 07"
IO-5	**"ORION" SCHIFFAHRTS-GESELLSCHAFT REITH & CO., HAMBURG, GERMANY**						
Baltia	BC	1986	D	12,337	399' 07"	65' 07"	36' 01"
Caro	BC	1984	D	19,429	485' 07"	75' 09"	41' 08"
Concordia	GC	1985	D	8,881	378' 00"	61' 01"	32' 02"
Crio	BC	1984	D	19,483	485' 07"	75' 09"	41' 08"
Fortuna	GC	1984	D	8,875	378' 00"	61' 01"	32' 02"
Gotia	GC	1985	D	12,349	399' 07"	65' 07"	36' 01"
Hero	BC	1984	D	19,505	485' 11"	75' 10"	41' 08"
Ida	BC	1995	D	18,172	486' 01"	74' 10"	40' 00"
Lita	BC	1995	D	18,173	486' 01"	74' 10"	40' 00"
Meta	BC	1987	D	18,612	477' 04"	75' 11"	40' 08"
Patria	GC	1985	D	8,880	377' 11"	61' 01"	32' 02"
Rugia	BC	1986	D	12,342	399' 07"	65' 08"	36' 02"
IP-1	**P&O NEDLLOYD B.V., ROTTERDAM, NETHERLANDS**						
APL France	CO	1996	D	60,200	962' 11"	105' 11"	70' 02"
APL Germany	CO	1996	D	60,200	962' 11"	105' 11"	70' 02"
APL Indonesia	CO	1996	D	60,219	964' 03"	105' 11"	70' 03"
Aramae	CO	1977	D	49,262	848' 01"	106' 00"	79' 03"
Armada Trader	CO	1990	D	10,345	459' 08"	70' 08"	35' 09"
Heemskerck	CO	1978	D	49,730	848' 02"	106' 00"	68' 03"
Nedlloyd Africa	CO	1992	D	47,157	873' 08"	106' 00"	76' 03"
Nedlloyd America	CO	1992	D	47,042	872' 08"	105' 10"	76' 03"
Nedlloyd Asia	CO	1991	D	46,985	872' 08"	105' 10"	76' 03"
Nedlloyd Clarence	CO	1983	D	35,890	689' 00"	106' 00"	61' 08"
Nedlloyd Clement	CO	1983	D	35,890	689' 00"	106' 00"	61' 08"
Nedlloyd Colombo	CO	1982	D	32,841	692' 10"	105' 10"	62' 05"
Nedlloyd Dejima	CO	1973	D	46,984	941' 08"	106' 00"	67' 01"
Nedlloyd Delft	CO	1973	D	46,984	941' 08"	106' 00"	67' 01"
Nedlloyd Europa	CO	1991	D	47,157	872' 08"	106' 00"	76' 03"
Nedlloyd Hongkong	CO	1994	D	51,151	915' 09"	124' 02"	76' 03"
Nedlloyd Honshu	CO	1995	D	55,242	915' 09"	124' 02"	76' 03"
Nedlloyd Hoorn	CO	1979	D	48,439	848' 01"	106' 00"	79' 03"
Nedlloyd Marne	CO	1989	D	14,101	514' 08"	75' 00"	36' 09"
Nedlloyd Musi	CO	1989	D	14,170	514' 07"	75' 00"	36' 09"

Fleet #	Fleet Name / Vessel Name	Type of Vessel	Year Built	Type of Engine	Cargo Cap. or Gross*	Overal Length	Breadth	Depth or Draft*
	Nedlloyd Oceania	CO	1992	D	46,985	872' 08"	105' 10"	76' 03"
	P&O Nedlloyd Brisbane	CO	1985	D	53,726	798' 09"	105' 10"	61' 09"
	P&O Nedlloyd Buenos Aires	CO	1984	D	29,930	598' 09"	100' 03"	53' 02"
	P&O Nedlloyd Houston	CO	1983	D	29,730	599' 07"	100' 03"	53' 02"
	P&O Nedlloyd Los Angeles	CO	1980	D	23,678	675' 09"	101' 08"	61' 07"
	P&O Vera Cruz	CO	1984	D	29,730	599' 07"	100' 01"	53' 02"
IP-2	**PACC SHIP MANAGERS PTE. LTD., SINGAPORE, MALAYSIA**							
	Alam Jaya	GC	1996	D	2,500	226' 04"	59' 00"	15' 08"
	Alam Karang	TK	1985	D	51,621	377' 04"	58' 05"	28' 11"
	Alam Kembong	TK	1985	D	63,736	383' 06"	59' 09"	32' 02"
	Alam Kerisi	TK	1982	D	57,867	372' 08"	57' 05"	31' 06"
	Alam Pari	TK	1981	D	27,191	308' 06"	47' 04"	24' 08"
	Alam Sejahtera	BC	1985	D	29,692	599' 09"	75' 10"	48' 07"
	Alam Sempurna	BC	1984	D	28,094	584' 08"	75' 11"	48' 05"
	Alam Senang	BC	1984	D	28,098	584' 08"	75' 11"	48' 05"
	Alam Tabah	GC	1977	D	15,098	470' 06"	65' 02"	40' 06"
	Alam Talang	GC	1985	D	17,322	477' 05"	69' 00"	43' 01"
	Alam Tangkas	GC	1979	D	15,097	470' 06"	65' 01"	40' 06"
	Alam Tegas	GC	1979	D	17,187	477' 05"	69' 00"	43' 00"
	Alam Teguh	GC	1980	D	17,169	477' 06"	69' 00"	43' 00"
	Alam Teladan	GC	1979	D	17,168	477' 04"	69' 01"	43' 00"
	Alam Tenega	GC	1977	D	15,097	470' 06"	65' 01"	40' 06"
	Alam Tenggiri	GC	1985	D	17,322	477' 05"	69' 00"	43' 01"
	Alam Tenteram	BC	1979	D	16,902	477' 04"	69' 00"	43' 00"
	Ikan Selar	BC	1978	D	21,652	539' 02"	75' 02"	44' 06"
	Ikan Sepat	BC	1984	D	28,503	590' 03"	75' 04"	47' 07"
	Ikan Tamban	GC	1980	D	17,159	477' 05"	69' 00"	43' 00"
	Ikan Tanda	GC	1979	D	16,916	477' 05"	69' 00"	43' 00"
	Ulloa	BC	1983	D	28,126	584' 08"	75' 11"	48' 05"
	Union	BC	1984	D	28,166	584' 08"	75' 11"	48' 05"
	United	BC	1984	D	27,223	584' 08"	75' 11"	48' 05"
IP-3	**PAN NAUTIC S.A., LUGANO, SWITZERLAND**							
	Anita G.	GC	1979	D	7,800	321' 10"	56' 01"	33' 03"
IP-4	**PAN OCEAN SHIPPING CO. LTD., SEOUL, SOUTH KOREA**							
	Pan Hope	BC	1977	D	22,289	539' 02"	75' 03"	44' 06"
	Pan Noble	BC	1977	D	27,307	580' 10"	75' 02"	46' 03"
	Pan Voyager	BC	1985	D	29,432	589' 11"	75' 09"	47' 07"
	Sammi Aurora	BC	1978	D	23,101	559' 08"	75' 00"	45' 00"
	Sammi Herald	BC	1978	D	24,231	559' 05"	75' 00"	45' 11"
IP-5	**PEGASUS DENIZEILIK, ISTANBUL, TURKEY**							
	Mina Cebi	BC	1980	D	27,311	627' 07"	75' 03"	44' 03"
IP-6	**PERGAMOS SHIPPING CO. S.A., PIRAEUS, GREECE**							
	Adventure	GC	1971	D	15,178	466' 09"	65' 00"	40' 06"
	Astron	GC	1976	D	14,800	462' 06"	67' 04"	38' 06"
IP-7	**PETER DOHLE SCHIFFAHRTS-KG (GMBH & CO.), HAMBURG, GERMANY**							
	Alexandria	GC	1994	D	6,918	351' 04"	59' 11"	26' 03"
	Skagen	GC	1999	D	3,440	283' 06"		
IP-8	**PHOENOCEAN LTD., SURREY, ENGLAND**							
	Falknes	BC	1983	D	12,296	423' 04"	65' 08"	36' 09"
	Nornes	BC	1976	D	6,258	339' 09"	52' 06"	28' 11"
IP-9	**PINAT GIDA SANAYI VE TICARET A.S., ISTANBUL, TURKEY**							
	Ihsan	GC	1993	D	10,560	420' 05"	59' 01"	34' 05"
	Kevser Gunes	GC	1994	D	11,307	441' 01"	59' 01"	34' 09"
	Maersk Manila	CO	1996	D	12,630	460' 11"	68' 03"	38' 05"
	Nimet	GC	1991	D	7,416	376' 04"	54' 02"	30' 06"
	Suat Ulusoy	GC	1995	D	11,366	441' 01"	59' 01"	34' 09"
IP-10	**POLCLIP (LUXEMBOURG) S.A., LUXEMBOURG, LUXEMBOURG**							
	Clipper Eagle	BC	1994	D	16,900	490' 04"	76' 00"	39' 08"
	Clipper Falcon	BC	1994	D	16,900	490' 04"	76' 00"	39' 08"
IP-11	**POLISH STEAMSHIP CO., SZCZECIN, POLAND**							
	Irma	BC	2000	D	34,939	655' 10"	77' 05"	50' 02"
	Iryda	BC	2000	D	34,939	655' 10"	77' 05"	50' 02"
	Isa	BC	1999	D	34,939	655' 10"	77' 05"	50' 02"
	Isadora	BC	1999	D	34,939	655' 10"	77' 05"	50' 02"
	Isolda	BC	1999	D	34,939	655' 10"	77' 05"	50' 02"

Federal Rhine at dusk, 21 September 1999. (Roger LeLievre)

Fleet #	Fleet Name / Vessel Name	Type of Vessel	Year Built	Type of Engine	Cargo Cap. or Gross*	Overal Length	Breadth	Depth or Draft*
	Kopalnia Borynia	BC	1989	D	11,898	471' 08"	63' 08"	36' 05"
	Kopalnia Halemba	BC	1990	D	11,715	471' 01"	63' 08"	36' 05"
	Kopalnia Jeziorko	BC	1971	D	13,665	481' 06"	65' 09"	37' 01"
	Kopalnia Machow	BC	1972	D	14,036	475' 05"	67' 11"	37' 05"
	Kopalnia Piaseczno	BC	1971	D	13,665	481' 04"	65' 09"	37' 01"
	Kopalnia Rydultowy	BC	1990	D	11,702	471' 01"	63' 08"	36' 05"
	Kopalnia Sosnowiec	BC	1974	D	14,179	477' 09"	67' 09"	37' 03"
	Kopalnia Szczyglowice	BC	1969	D	12,480	465' 04"	63' 01"	37' 05"
	Kopalnia Walbrzych	BC	1975	D	14,176	477' 05"	67' 09"	37' 03"
	Kopalnia Ziemowit	BC	1991	D	11,722	471' 05"	63' 08"	36' 05"
	Kopalnia Zofiowka	BC	1975	D	14,176	477' 09"	67' 09"	37' 03"
	Nogat	BC	1999	D	17,064	490' 02"	76' 00"	39' 08"
	Odranes	BC	1992	D	13,790	471' 05"	68' 08"	37' 02"
	Pomorze Zachodnie	BC	1985	D	26,696	591' 04"	75' 11"	45' 08"
	Warta	BC	1992	D	13,790	471' 05"	68' 08"	37' 02"
	Wislanes	BC	1992	D	13,770	471' 05"	68' 08"	37' 02"
	Ziemia Chelminska	BC	1984	D	26,700	591' 04"	75' 11"	45' 08"
	Ziemia Gnieznienska	BC	1985	D	26,696	591' 04"	75' 11"	45' 08"
	Ziemia Suwalska	BC	1984	D	26,706	591' 04"	75' 11"	45' 08"
	Ziemia Tarnowska	BC	1985	D	26,700	591' 04"	75' 11"	45' 08"
	Ziemia Zamojska	BC	1984	D	26,600	591' 04"	75' 11"	45' 08"
IP-12	**PREKOOKEANSKA PLOVIDBA, BAR, YUGOSLAVIA**							
	Obod	GC	1988	D	18,235	543' 00"	75' 07"	44' 00"
IP-13	**PRIME ORIENT SHIPPING S.A., PANAMA CITY, PANAMA**							
	Luna Verde	BC	1986	D	26,706	591' 06"	75' 10"	48' 07"
IP-14	**PRISCO (UK) LTD., LONDON, ENGLAND**							
	Jakov Sverdlov	TK	1989	D	20,502	496' 01"	73' 05"	39' 10"
	Kapitan Rudnev	TK	1988	D	20,502	496' 01"	73' 05"	41' 01"
IP-15	**PROJECT SHIPPING, INC., PIRAEUS, GREECE**							
	Elena G	GC	1978	D	16,436	475' 10"	71' 03"	29' 06"
	Kathrin	GC	1981	D	11,301	392' 01"	65' 09"	34' 09"
	Marinik G	BC	1972	D	25,635	591' 06"	75' 02"	45' 01"
	Silvia	GC	1981	D	11,274	392' 01"	65' 09"	33' 00"
IP-16	**PROSPERITY BAY SHIPPING CO. LTD., PIRAEUS, GREECE**							
	Anna	BC	1976	D	26,702	600' 06"	74' 08"	47' 01"
IP-17	**PYRSOS MANAGING CO., PIRAEUS, GREECE**							
	Anax	BC	1979	D	30,084	622' 00"	74' 10"	49' 10"
	Anemi	BC	1978	D	14,840	469' 02"	65' 00"	40' 06"
	Anemone	GC	1979	D	17,179	477' 04"	68' 11"	43' 00"
	Audacious	BC	1977	D	27,560	600' 06"	74' 08"	43' 09"
	Clipper Amaryllis	GC	1983	D	23,000	539' 02"	75' 02"	46' 05"
	Clipper Antares	BC	1986	D	17,777	481' 05"	74' 10"	40' 01"
	Eagle Quick	GC	1990	D	3,168	299' 03"	49' 05'	24' 11"
	Industrial Hope	GC	1990	D	3,194	299' 04"	49' 03"	25' 00"
IR-1	**RASSEM SHIPPING AGENCY, BEIRUT, LEBANON**							
	Seba M.	GC	1976	D	11,680	424' 01"	64' 05"	34' 06"
IR-2	**REDERI DONSOTANK A/B, DONSO, SWEDEN**							
	Credo	GC	1978	D	10,620	449' 02"	56' 00"	36' 01"
	Madzy	BC	1976	D	11,065	470' 02"	61' 00"	33' 04"
	Navigo	TK	1992	D	123,471	466' 10"	72' 06"	42' 00"
IR-3	**REEDEREI "NORD" KLAUS E. OLDENDORFF LTD., LIMASSOL, CYPRUS**							
	San Marino	TK	1988	D	71,189	414' 10"	68' 07"	32' 04"
IR-4	**REEDEREI HANS-PETER ECKHOFF GMBH CO. HG, HOLLENSTEDT, GERMANY**							
	Kamilla	GC	1985	D	2,785	322' 06"	44' 07"	23' 00"
IR-5	**REEDEREI WESER-SCHIFFAHRTS-AGENTUR GMBH & CO. KG, BRAKE, GERMANY**							
	Abitibi Claiborne	GC	1986	D	7,879	403' 07"	65' 08"	34' 06"
	Abitibi Orinoco	GC	1986	D	7,875	404' 11"	65' 09"	34' 06"
IR-6	**REGAL AGENCIES CORP., PIRAEUS, GREECE**							
	Dali	GC	1977	D	18,784	479' 03"	75' 00"	41' 04"
	Kent Forest	BC	1978	D	14,931	522' 02"	69' 02"	41' 04"
IR-7	**REX SHIPPING CORP., ATHENS, GREECE**							
	Atticos	BC	1976	D	29,165	593' 03"	75' 11"	47' 07"

Fleet #	Fleet Name Vessel Name	Type of Vessel	Year Built	Type of Engine	Cargo Cap. or Gross*	Overal Length	Breadth	Depth or Draft*
IR-8	**RIGEL SCHIFFAHRTS GMBH, BREMEN, GERMANY**							
	Alsterstern	TK	1994	D	125,327	529' 05"	75' 05"	38' 05"
	Donaustern	TK	1995	D	123,371	529' 05"	75' 05"	38' 05"
	Havelstern	TK	1994	D	126,264	529' 05"	75' 05"	38' 05"
	Isarstern	TK	1995	D	123,830	529' 05"	75' 05"	38' 05"
	Ledastern	TK	1993	D	76,737	405' 11"	58' 01"	34' 09"
	Oderstern	TK	1992	D	65,415	360' 00"	58' 02"	34' 09"
	Rheinstern	TK	1993	D	127,937	529' 05"	75' 05"	38' 05"
	Travestern	TK	1993	D	123,346	529' 05"	75' 05"	38' 05"
	Weserstern	TK	1992	D	65,415	360' 00"	58' 02"	34' 09"
IS-1	**S. FRANGOULIS (SHIP MANAGEMENT) LTD., PIRAEUS, GREECE**							
	Stamon	BC	1977	D	17,509	485' 11"	71' 04"	40' 00"
	Vini	BC	1977	D	15,202	472' 05"	69' 08"	40' 07"
IS-2	**SAMALI SHIPPING CO. S.A., PANAMA CITY, PANAMA**							
	Raby S.	BC	1976	D	8,186	385' 10"	59' 02"	29' 07"
IS-3	**SAMIN SHIPPING CO. LTD., CONSTANTZA, ROMANIA**							
	Abdul S	GC	1971	D	16,829	508' 01"	75' 03"	42' 08"
	Abeer S	GC	1974	D	8,001	399' 08"	57' 09"	32' 06"
	Ahmad S	GC	1966	D	2,780	281' 06"	41' 05"	18' 04"
	Ali S	GC	1969	D	15,251	458' 05"	69' 01"	40' 04"
	Amna S	GC	1969	D	15,210	458' 05"	69' 01"	40' 04"
	Hasan S	BC	1976	D	8,159	385' 10"	59' 03"	29' 07"
	Mohamed S	BC	1975	D	8,163	385' 09"	59' 03"	29' 06"
	Mona S	GC	1968	D	2,560	307' 09"	47' 09"	25' 11"
	Raby S	BC	1976	D	8,186	385' 10"	59' 02"	29' 07"
	Sea Lily	GC	1963	D	4,064	300' 03"	48' 01"	23' 00"
	Tartousi	GC	1965	D	1,265	236' 05"	37' 03"	21' 04"
	Zenobia S	BC	1976	D	8,197	385' 10"	59' 02"	29' 07"
IS-4	**SANDFORD SHIP MANAGEMENT LTD., VENTNOR, ISLE OF WIGHT**							
	Clipper Fidelity	GC	1978	D	15,078	470' 06"	65' 02"	40' 06"
	Genie	GC	1979	D	17,179	477' 04"	69' 00"	43' 00"
	Prestigious	BC	1978	D	23,573	539' 02"	75' 00"	46' 06"
	Rothnie	GC	1978	D	17,199	477' 05"	69' 00"	43' 00"
IS-5	**SARK VENUS DENIZCILIK A/S, ISTANBUL, TURKEY**							
	Snowrose	BC	1979	D	24,326	565' 03"	75' 03"	44' 08"
IS-6	**SCANDIA SHIPPING HELLAS, INC., PIRAEUS, GREECE**							
	Armonikos	BC	1979	D	30,689	674' 03"	75' 08"	47' 07"
IS-7	**SCANSCOT SHIPPING SERVICES (DEUTSCHLAND) GMBH, HAMBURG, GERMANY**							
	Scan Atlantic	RR	1999	D	7,100	405' 08"	64' 08"	33' 02"
	Scan Arctic	HL	1998	D	7,270	415' 01"	66' 07"	33' 02"
	Scan Bothnia	HL	1998	D	7,270	415' 01"	66' 07"	33' 02"
	Scan Polaris	HL	1996	D	4,800	331' 00"	61' 00"	31' 10"
IS-8	**SEAARLAND SHIPPING MANAGEMENT GMBH, VILLACH, AUSTRIA**							
	Allegra	TK	1986	D	179,112	536' 07"	75' 06"	37' 09"
	Conny	TK	1984	D	176,879	536' 07"	75' 06"	37' 09"
	Giacinta	TK	1984	D	176,879	536' 07"	75' 06"	37' 09"
	Grazia	TK	1987	D	176,879	536' 07"	75' 06"	37' 09"
	Peonia	BC	1983	D	27,995	647' 08"	75' 10"	46' 11"
IS-9	**SEAGER CORP., ATHENS, GREECE**							
	Ithaki	BC	1977	D	27,540	600' 06"	74' 08"	47' 01"
IS-10	**SEA-PRAXIS MARITIME CO. LTD., NICOSIA, CYPRUS**							
	Apollo C	GC	1983	D	12,665	492' 08"	69' 01"	33' 00"
IS-11	**SEALINK MARINE, INC., PIRAEUS, GREECE**							
	Finikas	BC	1979	D	26,796	599' 05"	73' 09"	46' 08"
IS-12	**SEASCOT SHIPTRADING LTD., GLASGOW, SCOTLAND**							
	Nyanza	GC	1978	D	16,923	497' 10"	71' 08"	40' 09"
IS-13	**SEASTAR NAVIGATION CO. LTD., ATHENS, GREECE**							
	Periandros	BC	1974	D	26,784	579' 10"	75' 01"	46' 03"
	Polydefkis	BC	1976	D	30,244	621' 06"	75' 00"	47' 11"
	Praxitelis	BC	1976	D	30,242	621' 06"	75' 00"	47' 11"
IS-14	**SEA SUPERIORITY SA, ATHENS, GREECE**							
	Gulfbreeze	TK	1982	D	85,191	416' 08"	65' 09"	36' 09"

Fleet #	Fleet Name / Vessel Name	Type of Vessel	Year Built	Type of Engine	Cargo Cap. or Gross*	Overal Length	Breadth	Depth or Draft*
IS-15	**SEAWAYS SHIPPING ENTERPRISES LTD., PIRAEUS, GREECE**							
	Triena	GC	1991	D	16,979	520' 10"	75' 00"	44' 00"
IS-16	**SEVEN SEAS MARITIME LTD., LONDON, ENGLAND**							
	Alma	GC	1980	D	17,520	502' 10"	70' 07"	42' 04"
	Alycia	GC	1975	D	20,950	521' 08"	75' 06"	44' 03"
	Amazonia	BC	1977	D	15,661	479' 00"	69' 08"	38' 09"
	Arethusa	BC	1973	D	22,593	539' 02"	75' 02"	44' 06"
	Arosa	BC	1975	D	30,499	625' 06"	75' 00"	47' 10"
IS-17	**SHERIMAR MANAGEMENT CO. LTD., ATHENS, GREECE**							
	A. M. Spiridon	GC	1968	D	3,780	309' 02"	47' 11"	26' 00"
	Blue Bay	BC	1972	D	22,302	522' 04"	75' 02"	42' 11"
	Blue Lagoon	GC	1979	D	5,500	417' 11"	59' 00"	33' 09"
	Blue Marine	GC	1974	D	15,107	454' 02"	70' 04"	39' 05"
	Blue Moon	GC	1975	D	11,612	404' 06"	67' 05"	34' 09"
	Noor	GC	1967	D	5,912	353' 05"	50' 09"	27' 07"
	S. M. Spiridon	GC	1967	D	2,730	287' 05"	42' 10"	23' 00"
IS-18	**SHUNZAN KAIUN CO. LTD., EHIME, JAPAN**							
	Spring Laker	BC	1996	D	30,855	577' 05"	77' 05"	48' 11"
	Spring Ocean	BC	1986	D	11,769	382' 00"	75' 05"	44' 00"
	Spring Trader	RR	1989	D	8,242	377' 04"	63' 00"	26' 03"
IS-19	**SIDEMAR SERVIZI ACCESSORI S.P.A., GENOA, ITALY**							
	Cygnus	BC	1987	D	28,500	610' 03"	75' 11"	46' 11"
	Galassia	BC	1987	D	29,369	610' 03"	75' 11"	46' 11"
	Gemini	BC	1986	D	28,500	610' 03"	75' 11"	46' 11"
	Sagittarius	BC	1987	D	29,365	610' 03"	75' 10"	46' 11"
	Sideracrux	GC	1983	D	7,988	328' 09"	57' 10"	29' 07"
	Sidercastor	GC	1982	D	7,988	328' 09"	57' 10"	29' 07"
	Siderpollux	GC	1982	D	8,010	328' 09"	57' 10"	29' 07"
IS-20	**SILVER SHIPPING LTD., KINGSTON, ST. VINCENT & THE GRENADINES**							
	Concorde	TK	1975	D	24,518	319' 11"	52' 06"	24' 11"
IS-21	**SLOBODNA PLOVIDBA, SIBENIK, CROATIA**							
	Bilice	BC	1976	D	19,056	319' 11"	74' 11"	41' 01"
	Biograd	GC	1988	D	8,490	392' 01"	60' 10"	31' 03"
	Dinara	BC	1974	D	26,962	599' 04"	73' 09"	46' 07"
	Drnis	GC	1972	D	7,702	404' 08"	55' 10"	29' 06"
	Humbolt Current	GC	1981	D	24,432	634' 04"	75' 04"	46' 05"
	Primosten	BC	1972	D	7,580	404' 05"	56' 00"	29' 07"
	Prvic	GC	1973	D	6,450	370' 02"	54' 00"	27' 07"
	Rossel Current	GC	1981	D	24,432	634' 04"	75' 04"	46' 05"
	Skradin	BC	1976	D	19,055	506' 03"	74' 10"	41' 01"
	Zlarin	GC	1985	D	9,246	392' 01"	60' 10"	31' 03"
IS-22	**SOCIETE ANONYME MONEGASQUE D' ADMINISTRATION MARITIME ET AERIENNE MONTE CARLO, MONACO**							
	Emerald Wave	TK	1992	D	61,560	341' 02"	61' 08"	31' 04"
	Gemini	BC	1977	D	27,106	585' 11"	75' 00"	47' 04"
	Haight	BC	1977	D	26,779	580' 10"	75' 04"	47' 07"
	Holland Park	TK	1983	D	59,440	387' 00"	57' 06"	32' 08"
	Hydra	BC	1977	D	26,715	567' 08"	74' 10"	48' 05"
IS-23	**SOCIETE NATIONALE DE TRANSPORT MARITIME & COMPAGNIE NATIONALE ALGERIENNE DE NAVIGATION MARITIME ALGIERS, ALGERIA**							
	Batna	BC	1978	D	20,586	512' 04"	74' 10"	44' 04"
	Nememcha	BC	1978	D	26,145	565' 02"	75' 11"	47' 01"
IS-24	**SOENDERBORG REDERIAKTIESELSKAB, EGERNSUND, DENMARK**							
	Bison	GC	1977	D	1,370	238' 02"	43' 00"	22' 02"
IS-25	**SOHTORIK DENIZCILIK SANAYI VE TICARET A.S., ISTANBUL, TURKEY**							
	Duden	BC	1981	D	26,975	567' 07"	74' 11"	48' 05"
	Eber	BC	1978	D	18,739	504' 07"	75' 01"	41' 00"
	Med Transporter	BC	1973	D	21,570	510' 03"	75' 02"	44' 00"
	Sapanca	BC	1975	D	19,030	506' 04"	75' 00"	41' 00"
IS-26	**SOLAR SCHIFFAHRTSGES MBH & CO. KG, BREMEN, GERMANY**							
	Argonaut	GC	1978	D	2,384	283' 10"	42' 09"	24' 11"

Fleet # Fleet Name Vessel Name	Type of Vessel	Year Built	Type of Engine	Cargo Cap. or Gross*	Overal Length	Breadth	Depth or Draft*
IS-27 SPAR SHIPPING A.S., BERGEN, NORWAY							
Spar Garnet	BC	1984	D	30,686	589' 11"	75' 10"	50' 11"
Spar Jade	BC	1984	D	30,674	589' 11"	75' 10"	50' 11"
Spar Opal	BC	1984	D	28,214	585' 00"	75' 10"	48' 05"
IS-28 SPLIETHOFF'S BEVRACHTINGSKANTOOR LTD., AMSTERDAM, NETHERLANDS							
Aalsmeergracht	GC	1992	D	12,150	425' 10"	62' 05"	38' 03"
Achtergracht	GC	1990	D	12,150	425' 10"	62' 05"	38' 03"
Admiralengracht	GC	1990	D	12,150	425' 10"	62' 05"	38' 03"
Alblasgracht	GC	1991	D	12,150	425' 10"	62' 05"	38' 03"
Alexandergracht	GC	1991	D	12,150	425' 10"	62' 05"	38' 03"
Amstelgracht	GC	1990	D	12,150	425' 10"	62' 05"	38' 03"
Anjeliersgracht	GC	1990	D	12,150	425' 10"	62' 05"	38' 03"
Ankergracht	GC	1991	D	12,150	425' 10"	62' 05"	38' 03"
Apollogracht	GC	1991	D	12,150	425' 10"	62' 05"	38' 03"
Archangelgracht	GC	1990	D	12,150	425' 10"	62' 05"	38' 03"
Artisgracht	GC	1990	D	12,150	425' 10"	62' 05"	38' 03"
Atlasgracht	GC	1991	D	12,150	425' 10"	62' 05"	38' 03"
Barentzgracht	GC	1981	D	3,444	263' 02"	52' 10"	34' 06"
Bataafgracht	GC	1981	D	3,444	263' 02"	52' 10"	34' 06"
Beursgracht	GC	1981	D	3,448	263' 02"	52' 10"	34' 06"
Bickersgracht	GC	1981	D	3,488	263' 02"	52' 10"	34' 06"
Bloemgracht	GC	1980	D	3,444	263' 02"	52' 10"	34' 06"
Bontegracht	GC	1981	D	3,437	263' 02"	52' 10"	34' 06"
Edamgracht	GC	1995	D	12,754	447' 04"	62' 05"	38' 03"
Edisongracht	GC	1994	D	12,760	447' 04"	62' 05"	38' 03"
Eemsgracht	GC	1995	D	12,754	447' 04"	62' 05"	38' 03"
Egelantiersgracht	GC	1994	D	12,760	447' 10"	62' 05"	38' 03"
Egmondgracht	GC	1994	D	12,760	447' 04"	62' 05"	38' 03"
Elandsgracht	GC	1995	D	12,754	447' 04"	62' 05"	38' 03"
Emmagracht	GC	1995	D	12,760	447' 04"	62' 05"	38' 03"
Erasmusgracht	GC	1994	D	13,000	447' 04"	62' 05"	38' 03"
Eurogracht	GC	1995	D	12,754	447' 04"	62' 05"	38' 03"
Heemskerkgracht	GC	1982	D	4,553	318' 10"	52' 10"	34' 06"
Houtmangracht	GC	1982	D	4,553	319' 00"	52' 10"	34' 06"
Hudsongracht	GC	1982	D	4,510	312' 11"	52' 10"	34' 06"
Humbergracht	GC	1982	D	4,517	312' 11"	52' 10"	34' 06"
Kaapgracht	GC	1984	D	8,038	348' 09"	52' 11"	34' 05"
Keizersgracht	GC	1983	D	4,990	348' 07"	52' 11"	34' 06"
Kielgracht	GC	1984	D	5,022	348' 09"	52' 11"	34' 05"
Klippergracht	GC	1984	D	5,022	348' 09"	52' 11"	34' 05"
Koggegracht	GC	1983	D	5,022	348' 09"	54' 06"	34' 05"
Koningsgracht	GC	1983	D	5,022	348' 09"	54' 06"	34' 05"
Lauriergracht	GC	1988	D	9,656	371' 02"	63' 07"	37' 01"
Leliegracht	GC	1987	D	9,601	371' 02"	63' 01"	37' 01"
Lemmergracht	GC	1988	D	9,682	371' 02"	63' 01"	37' 00"
Levantgracht	GC	1988	D	9,595	371' 03"	63' 01"	37' 00"
Lijnbaansgracht	GC	1988	D	9,606	371' 02"	63' 07"	37' 01"
Lindengracht	GC	1988	D	9,682	371' 02"	63' 01"	37' 00"
Looiersgracht	GC	1987	D	9,606	371' 02"	63' 07"	37' 01"
Lootsgracht	GC	1989	D	9,682	371' 03"	63' 01"	37' 00"
Paleisgracht	GC	1985	D	9,498	370' 09"	62' 05"	36' 05"
Palmgracht	GC	1985	D	9,536	370' 09"	62' 05"	36' 05"
Parkgracht	GC	1986	D	9,656	371' 02"	62' 03"	37' 01"
Pauwgracht	GC	1986	D	9,340	370' 09"	62' 05"	36' 05"
Pietersgracht	GC	1986	D	9,340	370' 09"	62' 05"	37' 01"
Pijlgracht	GC	1985	D	9,650	370' 09"	62' 05"	36' 05"
Poolgracht	GC	1986	D	9,672	371' 02"	62' 03"	37' 01"
IS-29 SPLIT SHIP MANAGEMENT LTD., SPLIT, CROATIA							
Alka	GC	1979	D	14,930	532' 07"	73' 00"	43' 11"
Bol	GC	1980	D	14,930	532' 07"	73' 00"	43' 11"
Hope I	BC	1982	D	30,900	617' 03"	76' 00"	47' 07"
Jelsa	GC	1977	D	13,450	532' 07"	73' 00"	43' 11"
Kairos	GC	1977	D	8,538	424' 03"	63' 02"	33' 08"
Kraljica Mira	RR	1965	D	752	283' 04"	53' 10"	17' 05"
Marjan I	GC	1978	D	13,450	532' 07"	73' 00"	43' 11"
Omis	GC	1977	D	13,450	532' 07"	73' 00"	43' 11"
Pharos	GC	1977	D	8,512	424' 03"	63' 02"	33' 08"
Solin	GC	1985	D	23,240	579' 05"	75' 00"	45' 11"
Solta	BC	1984	D	29,785	622' 00"	74' 11"	49' 10"
Split	GC	1981	D	22,042	585' 08"	75' 02"	46' 00"

Fleet #	Fleet Name / Vessel Name	Type of Vessel	Year Built	Type of Engine	Cargo Cap. or Gross*	Overal Length	Breadth	Depth or Draft*
IS-30	**SPRANTE SCHIFFAHRTS-VERWALTUNGS GMBH, BRUNSBUTTEL, GERMANY**							
	St. George	GC	1979	D	7,309	395' 03"	57' 10"	32' 06"
	St. Martin	GC	1980	D	7,250	395' 04"	57' 10"	32' 06"
	St. Thomas	GC	1976	D	7,496	395' 07"	57' 10"	32' 06"
	Topaz	GC	1975	D	4,798	288' 09"	42' 08"	25' 07"
IS-31	**STEVNS LINE APS, SVENDBORG, DENMARK**							
	Stevnsland	GC	1972	D	2,510	290' 04"	45' 05"	26' 03"
IS-32	**STFA MARITIME INDUSTRY & TRADING CO., ISTANBUL, TURKEY**							
	Danis Koper	BC	1978	D	22,174	528' 00"	75' 02"	44' 04"
	Inanc	BC	1986	D	23,929	579' 03"	75' 00"	45' 11"
	R. Dedeoglu	BC	1986	D	23,930	579' 05"	75' 00"	45' 11"
IS-33	**SURRENDRA OVERSEAS LTD., CALCUTTA, INDIA**							
	APJ Anand	BC	1977	D	16,882	459' 04"	73' 04"	41' 00"
	APJ Angad	BC	1977	D	27,305	581' 08"	75' 02"	47' 11"
	APJ Anjli	BC	1982	D	27,192	577' 05"	75' 11"	47' 11"
	APJ Karan	BC	1977	D	27,305	581' 08"	75' 02"	47' 11"
	APJ Sushma	BC	1983	D	27,213	577' 05"	75' 11"	47' 11"
IT-1	**T. S. SHIPPING, INC., PANAMA CITY, PANAMA**							
	Med Glory	BC	1975	D	16,549	465' 09"	71' 07"	40' 00"
	Sun Glory	GC	1989	D	6,836	318' 08"	59' 01"	42' 08"
IT-2	**TARGET MARINE S.A., PIRAEUS, GREECE**							
	Corithian Trader	BC	1973	D	27,398	599' 10"	73' 06"	46' 07"
IT-3	**TEAM SHIP MANAGEMENT AS, BERGEN, NORWAY**							
	Daviken	BC	1987	D	34,752	729' 00"	75' 11"	48' 05"
	Goviken	BC	1987	D	34,752	729' 00"	75' 11"	48' 05"
	Inviken	BC	1984	D	30,052	621' 05"	75' 01"	47' 11"
	Utviken	BC	1985	D	30,052	621' 05"	75' 01"	47' 11"
IT-4	**TECHNOMAR SHIPPING, INC., ATHENS, GREECE**							
	CMBT Esprit	GC	1982	D	21,894	549' 03"	75' 02"	46' 00"
IT-5	**TEO SHIPPING CORP., PIRAEUS, GREECE**							
	Antalina	BC	1984	D	28,082	584' 08"	75' 11"	48' 05"
	Erikousa Wave	BC	1986	D	26,858	600' 08"	73' 08"	46' 08"
	Marilis T.	BC	1984	D	28,097	584' 08"	75' 11"	47' 10"
	Sevilla Wave	BC	1986	D	26,858	600' 08"	73' 08"	46' 08"
	Vamand Wave	BC	1985	D	28,303	580' 08"	75' 11"	47' 07"
IT-6	**THE EGYPTIAN NAVIGATION CO., ALEXANDRIA, EGYPT**							
	Abu Egila	GC	1984	D	12,600	436' 00"	67' 05"	40' 00"
	Alexandria	GC	1991	D	12,802	436' 00"	67' 04"	40' 00"
IT-7	**THE SHIPPING CORP. OF INDIA LTD., BOMBAY, INDIA**							
	Lok Maheshwari	BC	1986	D	26,728	605' 03"	75' 03"	47' 03"
	Lok Pragati	BC	1984	D	26,928	564' 11"	75' 00"	48' 03"
	Lok Prakash	BC	1989	D	26,790	606' 11"	75' 04"	47' 03"
	Lok Pratap	BC	1993	D	26,718	605' 09"	75' 04"	47' 04"
	Lok Pratima	BC	1989	D	26,925	565' 00"	74' 11"	48' 03"
	Lok Prem	BC	1990	D	26,714	605' 08"	75' 04"	47' 03"
	Lok Rajeshwari	BC	1988	D	26,639	605' 08"	75' 04"	47' 03"
	State of Haryana	GC	1983	D	16,799	465' 07"	75' 02"	47' 04"
IT-8	**THENAMARIS (SHIPS MANAGEMENT), INC., ATHENS, GREECE**							
	Sealink	BC	1983	D	28,234	639' 09"	75' 10"	46' 11"
	Sealuck V	BC	1984	D	28,251	639' 09"	75' 10"	46' 11"
	Searanger II	BC	1976	D	29,300	594' 01"	76' 00"	47' 07"
IT-9	**THORESEN & CO. (BANGKOK) LTD., BANGKOK, THAILAND**							
	Stefania I	BC	1985	D	28,269	584' 08"	75' 11"	48' 05"
IT-10	**TRANSMAN SHIPPING ENTERPRISES S.A., ATHENS, GREECE**							
	Luckyman	BC	1980	D	27,000	584' 08"	75' 10"	48' 05"
IU-1	**UNICOM MANAGEMENT SERVICES (CYPRUS) LTD., LIMASSOL, CYPRUS**							
	Kapitan Vaga	GC	1988	D	9,576	371' 02"	63' 01"	37' 01"
	Lesozavodsk	GC	1992	D	6,100	366' 02"	59' 03"	24' 11"
IU-2	**UNION MARINE ENTERPRISES S.A. OF PANAMA, PIRAEUS, GREECE**							
	Capetan Michalis	BC	1981	D	28,600	593' 03"	75' 11"	47' 07"

Fleet #	Fleet Name / Vessel Name	Type of Vessel	Year Built	Type of Engine	Cargo Cap. or Gross*	Overal Length	Breadth	Depth or Draft*
IU-3	**UNIVAN SHIP MANAGEMENT LTD., HONG KONG, PEOPLE'S REPUBLIC OF CHINA**							
	Pathum Navee	GC	1972	D	20,814	515' 00"	75' 00"	44' 03"
IV-1	**V. SHIPS (CYPRUS) LTD., LIMASSOL, CYPRUS**							
	Cheetah	BC	1977	D	27,535	584' 08"	75' 02"	48' 03"
	Chelsea Bridge	GC	1978	D	22,356	549' 07"	75' 03"	45' 11"
	Lynx	BC	1978	D	29,536	584' 07"	75' 00"	48' 03"
IV-2	**V. SHIPS MARINE LTD., MINEOLA, NY**							
	Spear	GC	1983	D	5,233	379' 00"	57' 07"	29' 07"
IV-3	**VANG SHIPMANAGEMENT A/S, GREAKER, NORWAY**							
	Allvag	GC	1983	D	950	251' 01"	40' 07"	13' 07"
	Allvang	GC	1984	D	1,150	251' 01"	40' 07"	22' 04"
	Stalvang	GC	1983	D	950	251' 01"	40' 07"	13' 07"
	Steinvang	GC	1982	D	950	251' 01"	40' 07"	13' 07"
IV-4	**VANGUARD ENTERPRISE CO. LTD., HIROSHIMA, JAPAN**							
	Moor Laker	BC	1984	D	27,915	584' 08"	69' 03"	48' 05"
IV-5	**VENTURE SHIPPING (MANAGERS) LTD., HONG KONG, PEOPLE'S REPUBLIC OF CHINA**							
	Rose Islands	BC	1984	D	15,175	472' 05"	67' 01"	38' 07"
IV-6	**VENUS SHIPPING CORP., MANILA, PHILIPPINES**							
	Baltic Confidence	BC	1979	D	17,686	481' 03"	75' 01"	40' 01"
	Euorpean Confidence	BC	1980	D	16,533	465' 11"	71' 07"	40' 01"
IV-7	**VERGOS MARINE MANAGEMENT, PIRAEUS, GREECE**							
	Verdon	BC	1981	D	26,350	594' 09"	75' 00"	47' 01"
	Verily	BC	1982	D	26,450	594' 09"	75' 00"	47' 01"
IW-1	**WAGENBORG SHIPPING B.V., DELFZIJL, NETHERLANDS**							
	Arion	GC	1997	D	9,100	441' 04"	54' 02"	32' 02"
	Dintelborg	GC	1999	D	8,865	437' 08"	52' 02"	32' 02"
	Dongeborg	GC	1999	D	9,000	437' 08"	52' 02"	32' 02"
	Egbert Wagenborg	GC	1998	D	9,100	441' 04"	54' 02"	32' 02"
	Flinterborg	GC	1990	D	3,015	269' 02"	41' 04"	21' 08"
	Flinterdam	GC	1995	D	4,506	327' 07"	44' 09"	23' 07"
	Flinterdijk	GC	1978	D	2,955	263' 02"	41' 00"	21' 08"
	Flinterland	GC	1994	D	4,216	300' 01"	44' 08"	23' 07"
	Flintermar	GC	1994	D	4,170	300' 01"	44' 09"	23' 07"
	Flinterzijl	GC	1996	D	4,540	325' 09"	44' 09"	23' 07"
	Kasteelborg	GC	1998	D	9,025	428' 08"	52' 01"	33' 06"
	Keizersborg	GC	1996	D	9,025	428' 08"	52' 01"	33' 06"
	Koningsborg	GC	1999	D	9,067	428' 08"	52' 01"	33' 06"
	Kroonborg	GC	1995	D	9,025	428' 08"	52' 01"	33' 06"
	Markborg	GC	1997	D	9,100	441' 04"	54' 02"	32' 02"
	Merweborg	GC	1998	D	9,100	441' 04"	54' 02"	32' 02"
	Michiganborg	GC	1999	D	9,200	441' 03"	54' 02"	32' 02"
	Moezelborg	GC	1999	D	9,100	441' 04"	54' 02"	32' 02"
	Morraborg	GC	1999	D	8,800	441' 05"	54' 06"	32' 02"
	Munteborg	GC	1998	D	9,100	441' 04"	54' 02"	32' 02"
	Musselborg	GC	1999	D	9,100	441' 04"	54' 02"	32' 02"
	Vechtborg	GC	1998	D	8,300	434' 00"	52' 01"	31' 07"
	Veerseborg	GC	1998	D	8,300	433' 09"	52' 01"	31' 07"
	Vlieborg	GC	1999	D	8,300	434' 00"	52' 01"	31' 07"
	Vlistborg	GC	1999	D	7,900	434' 00"	52' 01"	31' 07"
	Voornborg	GC	1999	D	8,300	434' 00"	52' 01"	31' 07"
IW-2	**WALLEM SHIPMANAGEMENT LTD., HONG KONG, PEOPLE'S REPUBLIC OF CHINA**							
	Danah	GC	1978	D	23,618	575' 02"	76' 10"	46' 07"
	Nirja	BC	1972	D	30,255	623' 05"	75' 05"	47' 07"
IW-3	**WILSON SHIP MANAGEMENT (BERGEN) AS, BERGEN, NORWAY**							
	Brunto	BC	1977	D	12,100	478' 07"	64' 04"	35' 00"
	Fossnes	BC	1995	D	16,880	490' 03"	76' 00"	39' 08"
	General Cabal	BC	1976	D	12,100	477' 04"	64' 03"	34' 11"
IZ-1	**Z. & G. HALCOUSSIS CO. LTD., PIRAEUS, GREECE**							
	Agiodektini	BC	1977	D	18,611	500' 05"	75' 01"	41' 00"
	Akti	BC	1977	D	28,935	593' 10"	76' 00"	47' 07"
	Alexandria	BC	1981	D	29,372	589' 11"	76' 00"	47' 00"
IZ-2	**ZIRKEL VERWALTUNGSGES. MBH, BRAKE, GERMANY**							
	Hea	BC	1982	D	12,078	424' 03"	66' 09"	36' 09"

Marine Museums

REPUBLIC STEEL

Museum ship Valley Camp, at Sault Ste. Marie, MI. See Page 131 for details.

VESSEL MUSEUMS

(Information subject to change; museum hours and days open can be irregular. Please phone ahead.)

Fleet #	Fleet Name / Vessel Name	Type of Vessel	Year Built	Type of Engine	Cargo Cap. or Gross*	Overal Length	Breadth	Depth or Draft*
MU-1	**BERNIER MARITIME MUSEUM, 55 DES PIONNIERS RUE, L' ISLET, QC — (418) 247-5001**							
	Daniel McAllister	TB	1907	D	268*	115' 00"	23' 02"	12' 00"
	(Helena '07 - '57, Helen M. B. '57 - '66)							
	(Former McAllister Towing & Salvage, Inc. tug now laid up in Montreal, QC.)							
	Ernest Lapointe	IB	1941	R	1,179*	185' 00"	36' 00"	22' 06"
	(Former Canadian Coast Guard ice breaker. In use as a museum in L'Islet, QC.)							
MU-2	**BUFFALO AND ERIE COUNTY NAVAL AND MILITARY PARK, 1 NAVAL PARK COVE, BUFFALO, NY — (716) 847-1773**							
	Croaker **[IXSS-246]**	SS	1944	D/V	1,526*	311' 07"	27' 02"	33' 09"
	(Former U.S. Navy "Emergency Program (Gato)" class submarine [SS/SSK/AGSS/IXSS-246] which was stricken 20 December, 1971; credited with sinking 11 enemy vessels during World War II.)							
	Little Rock **[CLG-4]**	CLG	1945	T	10,670*	610' 01"	66' 04"	25' 00"*
	(Former U.S. Navy "Cleveland / Little Rock"-class guided missile cruiser [CL-92/CLG-4] which was stricken 22 November, 1976.)							
	PTF-17 **[PTF-17]**	PT	1968	D	69*	80' 04"	24' 07"	6' 10"*
	(Former U.S. Navy "Trumpy" class fast patrol boat [PTF-17] which was stricken in 1979.)							
	The Sullivans **[DD-537]**	DD	1943	T	2,500*	376' 05"	39' 05"	12' 03"*
	(Launched as USS Putnam [DD-537])							
	(Former U.S. Navy "Fletcher" class destroyer [DD-537] which was stricken 1 December 1974. The USS The Sullivans earned 9 Battle Stars during World War II and 2 Battle Stars during the Korean Conflict.) Above three vessels in use as museums in Buffalo, NY. Open seasonally, April to November.							
MU-3	**CANAL PARK MARINE MUSEUM, 600 SOUTH LAKE AVE., DULUTH, MN — (218) 727-2497**							
	Bayfield	TB	1953	D	23*	45' 00"	13' 00"	7' 00"*
	(Former U.S. Army Corps of Engineers tug in use as a museum vessel in Duluth, MN, in conjunction with extensive shoreside museum.) Museum open all year.							
MU-4	**GREAT LAKES CENTER FOR MARINE HISTORY, 2911 LEON AVE., LANSING, MI — (517) 321-3590**							
	Maple **[WAGL-234]**	LT	1939	D	350*	122' 03"	27' 00"	7' 06"*
	(USCG Maple [WLI/WAGL-234] '39 - '73, Roger R. Simons '73 - '94)							
	(Former U.S. Coast Guard "122-Foot" class lighthouse tender [WLI/WAGL-234] / EPA vessel which last operated in 1991.) In use as a museum vessel in St. Ignace, MI. Open seasonally.							
MU-5	**GREAT LAKES CLIPPER PRESERVATION ASSOCIATION, P.O. BOX 1370, MUSKEGON, MI — (231) 744-5101**							
	Milwaukee Clipper	PA	1904	Q	4,272	361' 00"	45' 00"	28' 00"
	(Juniata '04 - '41)							
	(Former Wisconsin & Michigan Steamship Company passenger vessel which last operated in 1970.) Currently undergoing conversion to a visitor attraction in Muskegon, MI.							
MU-6	**GREAT LAKES HISTORICAL SOCIETY, 1089 EAST 9TH ST., CLEVELAND, OH — (216) 566-8770**							
	Cod **[IXSS-224]**	SS	1943	D/V	1,525*	311' 08"	27' 02"	33' 09"
	(Former U.S. Navy "Albacore (Gato)" class submarine [SS/AGSS/IXSS-224] which was stricken 15 December 1971. The USS Cod earned 7 Battle Stars and sank 26,985 tons during World War II.) In use as a museum vessel in Cleveland, OH. Open seasonally, 1 May to the end of September.							
MU-7	**H. LEE WHITE MARINE MUSEUM, P.O. BOX 101, WEST FIRST ST. PIER, OSWEGO, NY — (315) 342-0480**							
	Major Elisha K. Henson	TB	1943	D	305*	115' 00"	28' 00"	14' 00"
	(Major Elisha K. Henson '43 - '47, U.S. Army LT-5 '47 - '47, Nash '47 - '95)							
	(Former U.S. Army Corps of Engineers vessel which last operated in 1989.) In use as a museum vessel in Oswego, NY. Open seasonally, May to September.							
MU-8	**HARBOR HERITAGE SOCIETY, 1001 EAST 9TH ST., CLEVELAND, OH — (216) 574-6262**							
	William G. Mather {2}	BC	1925	T	13,950	618' 00"	62' 00"	32' 00"
	(Former Cleveland Cliffs Steamship Co. vessel which last operated 21 December 1980.) In use as a museum vessel in Cleveland, OH. Open seasonally, May to October.							
MU-9	**HMCS FRASER, P.O. BOX 233 UNIT 17, 450 LaHAVE ST., BRIDGEWATER, NS — (902) 624-1557**							
	Fraser **[DDH-233]**	FF	1957	T	2,858*	366' 00"	42' 00"	19' 08"*
	(Former Royal Canadian Navy "St. Laurent (River)" class helicopter-carrying frigate [DDE/DDH-233] which was stricken in 1994.) In use as a museum vessel in Bridgewater, NS.)							

▶

Fleet #	Fleet Name / Vessel Name	Type of Vessel	Year Built	Type of Engine	Cargo Cap. or Gross*	Overall Length	Breadth	Depth or Draft*

MU-10 HMCS HAIDA NAVAL MUSEUM, ONTARIO PLACE, 955 LAKESHORE BLVD. WEST, TORONTO, ON — (416) 314-9870

	Haida **[G-63]**	DD	1943	T	2,744*	377' 00"	37' 06"	15' 02"

(Former Royal Canadian Navy "Tribal" class destroyer [G-63/DDE-215] which was stricken 11 October 1963.) In use as a museum vessel in Toronto, ON. Open seasonally, mid May to Labor Day.

MU-11 IRVIN ORE BOAT TOURS, 350 HARBOR DR., DULUTH, MN — (218) 722-7876

	Lake Superior	TB	1943	D	248*	114' 00"	26' 00"	13' 08"

(Major Emil H. Block '43 - '47, U.S. Army LT-18 '47 - '50)
(Former U.S. Army Corps of Engineers vessel which last operated in 1995.)

	William A. Irvin	BC	1938	T	14,050	610' 09"	60' 00"	32' 06"

(Former United States Steel Corp. vessel which last operated 16 December 1978.)
Above two vessels in use as museums in Duluth, MN. Open seasonally, late spring to autumn.)

MU-12 LAKE COUNTY HISTORICAL SOCIETY, 520 SOUTH AVE., TWO HARBORS, MN — (218) 834-4898

	Edna G.	TB	1896	R	154*	102' 00"	23' 00"	14' 06"

(Former Duluth, Missabe & Iron Range Railroad vessel which last operated in 1981.)
Open seasonally for tours at Two Harbors, MN. Call for schedule.

MU-13 LE SAULT DE SAINTE MARIE HISTORIC SITES, INC., 501 EAST WATER ST., SAULT STE. MARIE, MI — (906) 632-3658

	Valley Camp {2}	BC	1917	R	12,000	550' 00"	58' 00"	31' 00"

(Louis W. Hill '17 - '55)
(Former Republic Steel Corp. bulk carrier which last operated in 1966.)
In use as a museum vessel in Sault Ste. Marie, MI. Open seasonally, 15 May to 15 October.)

MU-14 MARINE MUSEUM OF THE GREAT LAKES AT KINGSTON, 55 ONTARIO ST., KINGSTON, ON — (613) 542-2261

	Alexander Henry	IB	1959	D	1,674*	210' 00"	44' 00"	17' 09"

(Former Canadian Coast Guard vessel which was stricken in 1985.) In use as a museum vessel at Kingston, ON. Museum open all year — vessel open seasonally, May to September.

MU-15 MARINE MUSEUM OF UPPER CANADA, EXHIBITION PLACE, TORONTO, ON — (416) 392-1765

	Ned Hanlan	TB	1932	R	105*	79' 06"	19' 00"	9' 09"

(Former Municipality of Toronto vessel which last operated in 1965.) In use as a museum vessel in Toronto, ON. Museum open all year; tug open seasonally. Call for schedule.

MU-16 MUSEUM OF SCIENCE AND INDUSTRY, 5700 SOUTH LAKE SHORE DR., CHICAGO, IL — (773) 684-1414

	U-505	SS	1941	D/V	1,178*	252' 00"	22' 04"	15' 05"*

(Former German Type IX-C submarine, captured by the U. S. Navy Task Group 22.3 in the Atlantic Ocean off Africa on 4 June 1944. The U-505 is credited with sinking 47,000 tons during World War II.)
In use as a museum in Chicago, IL. Open all year.

MU-17 MUSEUM SHIP WILLIS B. BOYER, P.O. BOX 50406, TOLEDO, OH — (419) 936-3070

	Willis B. Boyer	BC	1911	T	15,000	617' 00"	64' 00"	33' 01"

(Col. James M. Schoonmaker '11 - '69)
(Former Cleveland-Cliffs Steamship Co. bulk carrier which last operated 17 December 1980.)
In use as a museum vessel at International Park in Toledo, OH. Open all year.

MU-18 NORGOMA MUSEUM SHIP, 851 GREAT NORTHERN BLVD., SAULT STE. MARIE, ON — (705) 256-7447

	Norgoma	PA	1950	D	1,477*	188' 00"	37' 06"	22' 06"

(Former Ontario Northland Transportation Commission vessel which last operated in 1974.
(In use as a museum vessel in Sault Ste. Marie, ON. Open seasonally, mid April to October.)

MU-19 NORISLE BISTRO, 3080 LOUIS ST., VAL CARON, ON — (705) 859-2434

	Norisle	PA	1946	R	1,668*	215' 09"	36' 03"	16' 00"

(Former Ontario Northland Transportation Commission vessel which last operated in 1974.) In use as a museum/restaurant vessel in Manitowaning, ON. Open seasonally, 1 June to Labor Day.

MU-20 PENNSYLVANIA HISTORICAL & MUSEUM COMMISSION, 150 FRONT ST. SUITE 1, ERIE, PA — (814) 871-4596

	Niagara	2B	1813	W	295*	198' 00"	32' 00"	10' 06"

(Former U.S. Navy Brigantine from the War of 1812.) In use as an operational museum vessel in Erie, PA. Phone ahead to ensure that vessel is in port.)

MU-21 PETERSEN STEAMSHIP CO., BLUE STAR HIGHWAY, DOUGLAS, MI — (616) 857-2464

	Keewatin	PA	1907	Q	3,856*	346' 00"	43' 08"	26' 06"

(Former Canadian Pacific Railway Company passenger vessel which last operated in October 1965.)

	Reiss	TB	1913	R	99*	80' 00"	20' 00"	12' 06"

(Q. A. Gillmore '13 - '32)
(Former Reiss Steamship Company tug which last operated in 1969.)
Both in use as museum vessels in Douglas, MI. Open seasonally, Memorial Day to Labor Day.

▶

Museum ship Willis B. Boyer at Toledo. See Page 131 for touring information. (Jim Hoffman)

Fleet #	Fleet Name Vessel Name	Type of Vessel	Year Built	Type of Engine	Cargo Cap. or Gross*	Overall Length	Breadth	Depth or Draft*
MU-22	**PORT HURON MUSEUM OF ARTS & HISTORY, 920 PINE GROVE AVE., PORT HURON, MI — (810) 985-7101**							
	Huron **[WLV 526]**	LS	1920	D	392*	96' 05"	24' 00"	10' 00"*

(Former U.S. Coast Guard "96 Foot" class lightship [LS-103, WAL/WLV-526] which was stricken 25 August 1970.) In use as a museum in Port Huron, MI. Open seasonally, mid May to September.

| MU-23 | **S. S. CANADIANA PRESERVATION SOCIETY, 17 DELRAY DR., CHECKTOWAGA, NY — (716) 833-2998** | | | | | | | |
| | Canadiana | PA | 1910 | R | 974* | 216' 00" | 45' 00" | 18' 10" |

(Badly deteriorated hull located at Humberstone, ON.)

| MU-24 | **S. S. METEOR MARITIME MUSEUM, P.O. BOX 775, SUPERIOR, WI — (715) 392-5742** | | | | | | | |
| | Col. D. D. Gaillard | DR | 1916 | B | 712* | 116' 00" | 41' 00" | 13' 09"* |

(Former U. S. Army Corps of Engineers dipper dredge.)

| | Meteor | TK | 1896 | R | 29,154 | 380' 00" | 45' 00" | 26' 00" |

(Frank Rockefeller 1896 - '28, South Park '28 - '43)
(Former Cleveland Tankers, Inc. vessel which last operated in 1969.)
Both in use as museum vessels in Superior, WI. Open seasonally, May to mid October.

| MU-25 | **SOCIETY FOR THE PRESERVATION OF THE CITY OF MILWAUKEE, P.O. BOX 506, BEULAH, MI** | | | | | | | |
| | City of Milwaukee | TF | 1931 | R 26 rail cars | | 360' 00" | 56' 03" | 21' 06" |

(Former Ann Arbor Railroad System vessel is laid up at Manistee, MI, awaiting conversion to a museum at Frankfort, MI.)

| MU-26 | **STEAMER COLUMBIA FOUNDATION, P.O. BOX 43232, DETROIT, MI — (313) 331-9920** | | | | | | | |
| | Columbia {2} | PA | 1902 | R | 968* | 216' 00" | 60' 00" | 13' 06" |

(Last operated 2 September 1991 — 5 year survey expired January 1998. Laid up in Ecorse, MI.)

| MU-27 | **STEAMER STE. CLAIRE FOUNDATION, P.O. BOX 43232, DETROIT, MI — (313) 331-9920** | | | | | | | |
| | Ste. Claire | PA | 1910 | R | 870* | 197' 00" | 65' 00" | 14' 00" |

(Last operated 2 September 1991 — 5 year survey expired May 1993. Laid up in Ecorse, MI.)

| MU-28 | **THE CANADIAN NAVAL MEMORIAL TRUST, P.O. BOX 99000 STATION "FORCES", HALIFAX, NS — (902) 429-2132** | | | | | | | |
| | Sackville **[K-181]** | KO | 1941 | T | 1,170* | 208' 00" | 33' 00" | 17' 06" |

(Former Royal Canadian Navy "Flower" class corvette [K-181] which was stricken in 1982.)
In use as a museum vessel in Halifax, NS.

| MU-29 | **USS SILVERSIDES & MARITIME MUSEUM, P.O. BOX 1692, MUSKEGON, MI — (231) 755-1230** | | | | | | | |
| | LST-393 | LST | 1942 | D | 2,100 | 328' 00" | 50' 00" | 25' 00" |

(USS LST-393 '42 - '48, Highway 16 '48 - '99)
(Last operated 31 July 1973. Currently laid up in Muskegon, MI. During World War II the Highway 16 earned 3 Battle Stars and participated in the Normandy Invasion of 6 June, 1944 as the USS LST-393.)

| | McLane **[WMEC-146]** | WM | 1927 | D | 289* | 125' 00" | 24' 00" | 12' 06" |

(USCG McLane [WSC / WMEC-146] '27 - '70, Manatra II '70 - '93)
(Former U.S. Coast Guard "Buck & A Quarter" class medium endurance cutter [WSC / WMEC-146] which was stricken 31 December 1968.)

| | Silversides **[SS-236]** | SS | 1941 | D/V | 1,526* | 311' 08" | 27' 03" | 33' 09" |

(Former U.S. Navy "Albacore (Gato)" class submarine [SS-236] which was stricken 30 June 1969. The USS Silversides is credited with sinking 90,080 tons during World War II.)
Above two are in use as museum vessels in Muskegon, MI. Open seasonally, April to October.

| MU-30 | **WISCONSIN MARITIME MUSEUM, 75 MARITIME DR., MANITOWOC, WI — (920) 684-0218** | | | | | | | |
| | Cobia **[AGSS-245]** | SS | 1944 | D/V | 1,500* | 311' 09" | 27' 03" | 33' 09" |

(Former U.S. Navy "Emergency Program (Gato)" class submarine [SS/AGSS-245] which was stricken 1 July 1970. The USS Cobia earned 4 Battle Stars and sank 16,835 tons during World War II.)
In use as a museum vessel in Manitowoc, WI. Open all year.

MARINE MUSEUMS ASHORE

ANTIQUE BOAT MUSEUM, 750 MARY ST., CLAYTON, NY — (315) 686-4104
An impressive collection of historic freshwater boats and engines. Annual boat show is the first weekend of August. *Open May 15-October 15.*

COLLINGWOOD MUSEUM, MEMORIAL PARK, COLLINGWOOD, ON — (705) 445-4811
More than 100 years of shipbuilding, illustrated with models, photos and videos. *Open all year.*

DOOR COUNTY MARITIME MUSEUM, 120 N. MADISON AVE., STURGEON BAY, WI. — (920) 743-5958
Located in the former offices of the Roen Steamship Co., exhibits portray the role shipbuilding has played in the Door Peninsula. Refurbished pilothouse on display. *Open all year.*

▶

DOSSIN GREAT LAKES MUSEUM, 100 THE STRAND, BELLE ISLE, DETROIT, MI — (313) 852-4051
Models, photographs, interpretive displays, the smoking room from the 1912 passenger steamer **City of Detroit III**, an anchor from the **Edmund Fitzgerald** and the working pilothouse from the steamer **William Clay Ford** are on display. *Open all year.*

FAIRPORT HARBOR MUSEUM, 129 SECOND ST., FAIRPORT, OH — (440) 354-4825
Located in the Fairport Lighthouse, displays include the pilothouse from the lake carrier **Frontenac** and the mainmast of the first **U.S.S. Michigan**. *Open late May-Labor Day.*

FATHOM FIVE UNDERWATER MARINE PARK, ON THE WATERFRONT, TOBERMORY, ON — (519) 596-2233
Underwater maritime park encompasses 19 of the area's 26 shipwrecks, two of which can be seen from a glass-bottom boat. *Open April-mid-November.*

GREAT LAKES HISTORICAL SOCIETY, 480 MAIN ST., VERMILION, OH — (800) 893-1485
Museum tells the story of the Great Lakes through ship models, paintings, exhibits and artifacts, including engines and other machinery. Pilothouse of retired laker **Canopus** and a replica of the Vermilion lighthouse are on display. *Museum open all year. An affiliated operation is the **USS Cod** (see MU-6 above).*

GREAT LAKES MARINE & U.S. COAST GUARD MEMORIAL MUSEUM, 1071-73 WALNUT BLVD., ASHTABULA, OH — (216) 964-6847
Housed in the 1898-built former lighthouse keepers' residence, the museum includes models, paintings, artifacts, photos, the world's only working scale model of a Hulett ore unloading machine and the pilothouse from the steamer **Thomas Walters**. *Open Memorial Day-October 31.*

GREAT LAKES SHIPWRECK MUSEUM, WHITEFISH POINT, MI — (906) 635-1742 or (800)-635-1742
Located next to the Whitefish Point lighthouse, the museum includes lighthouse and shipwreck artifacts, a shipwreck video theater, the restored lighthouse keeper's quarters, and an **Edmund Fitzgerald** display that includes the ship's bell. *Open May 15-October 15.*

MU-13 LE SAULT DE SAINTE MARIE HISTORIC SITES, INC., 501 EAST WATER ST., SAULT STE. MARIE, MI — (906)-632-3658
The 1917-built steamer Valley Camp, which one sailed for the Republic Steel Co., is the centerpiece of this extensive museum. Dedicated in 1968, the Valley Camp's three vast cargo holds house artifacts, ship models, aquariums, photos and other memorabilia, as well as a tribute to the **Edmund Fitzgerald** that includes the ill-fated vessel's lifeboats. Extensive gift shop offers a large selection of nautical books and other items. *Tours available. Open May 15-October 15.*

MARQUETTE MARINE MUSEUM, EAST RIDGE & LAKESHORE DR., MARQUETTE, MI — (906) 226-2006
Contained in an 1890s waterworks building, the museum recreates the offices of the first commercial fishing and passenger freight companies. Displays also include charts, photos, models and maritime artifacts. *Open May 31-September 30.*

MICHIGAN MARITIME MUSEUM, 1-96 AT DYCKMAN AVE., SOUTH HAVEN, MI — (616) 637-8078
Exhibits are dedicated to the U.S. Lifesaving Service and U.S. Coast Guard. Displays tell the story of various kinds of boats and their uses on the Great Lakes. *Open all year.*

OWEN SOUND MARINE - RAIL MUSEUM, 1165 FIRST AVE., OWEN SOUND, ON — (519) 371-3333
Museum depicts the history of each industry (but leans more toward the marine end) through displays, models and photos. *Seasonal*

THE PIER, 245 QUEENS QUAY W., TORONTO, ON — (888) 675-7437
Exhibits detail the development of the shipping industry from sail to steam on the Great Lakes and St. Lawrence Seaway, with a special focus on Toronto. The 79-foot steam tug **Ned Hanlan**, built in 1932, is also on display. *Open all year.*

PORT COLBORNE MARINE & HISTORICAL MUSEUM, 80 KING ST., PORT COLBORNE, ON — (905) 834-7604
Wheelhouse from the steam tug **Yvonne Dupre Jr.**, anchor from the propeller ship **Raleigh**, and a lifeboat from the steamer **Hochelaga** are among the museum's displays. *Open May-December.*

SUNKEN TREASURES MARITIME MUSEUM, HWY 31, PORT WASHINGTON, WI
Many artifacts recovered from Lake Michigan shipwrecks are on display. *Open May 1-September 30*

U.S. ARMY CORPS OF ENGINEERS MUSEUM, SOO LOCKS VISITOR CENTER, E. PORTAGE AVE., SAULT STE. MARIE, MI — (906) 632-3311
Exhibits include a working model of the Soo Locks, historics photos and a 25-minute film. Also, three observation decks adjacent to the MacArthur Lock provide an up-close view of ships locking through. Watch for the annual Soo Locks Festival, which includes an opportunity for visitors to enter some restricted locks areas, in mid-June. *No admission; open May-November. Check at the Visitor Center information desk for a list of vessels expected at the locks.*

WELLAND CANAL VISITOR CENTER, AT LOCK 3, THOROLD, ON — (905) 984-8880
Museum traces the development of the Welland Canal. *Museum and adjacent gift shop open year 'round. Observation deck open during the navigation season. Check at the information desk for vessels expected at Lock 3.*

WISCONSIN MARITIME MUSEUM, 75 MARITIME DR., MANITOWOC, WI— (920) 684-0218
Displays explore the history of area shipbuilding, and also honor submariners and submarines built in Manitowoc during World War II. *An affiliated operation is the **USS Cobia**. (see MU-30 above). Open all year.*

GREAT LAKES LOADING PORTS

Iron Ore	Limestone	Coal	Grain	Cement
Duluth	Port Inland	Superior	Thunder Bay	Charlevoix
Superior	Cedarville	Thunder Bay	Duluth	Alpena
Two Harbors	Drummond	Chicago	Milwaukee	
Taconite	Island	Toledo	Chicago	**Gypsum**
Harbor	Calcite	Sandusky	Sarnia	Port Gypsum
Marquette	Stoneport	Ashtabula	Toledo	Alabaster
Escanaba	Marblehead	Conneaut		

Petroleum

Sarnia
East Chicago

UNLOADING PORTS

The primary iron ore and limestone receiving ports are Cleveland, Lorain, Chicago, Gary, Burns Harbor, Indiana Harbor, Detroit, Toledo, Ashtabula and Conneaut. Coal is carried to a host of ports in the U.S. and Canada, much of it used to generate electrical power. Most grain loaded on the lakes is destined for export via the St. Lawrence Seaway. Cement is delivered to terminals stretching from Lake Superior to Lake Ontario. Tankers bring petroleum products to cities as diverse in size as Cleveland and Detroit or Escanaba and Muskegon. Self-unloaders carry road salt and sand to cities throughout the region.

MEANING OF BOAT WHISTLES

1 SHORT: I am directing my course to starboard (right) for a port to port passing.
2 SHORT: I am directing my course to port (left) for a starboard to starboard passing.
5 OR MORE SHORT BLASTS SOUNDED RAPIDLY: Danger.
1 PROLONGED: Vessel leaving dock.
3 SHORT: Vessel moving astern.
1 PROLONGED, SOUNDED ONCE PER MINUTE: Vessel moving in fog.
1 SHORT, 1 PROLONGED, 1 SHORT: Vessel at anchor in fog.
3 PROLONGED and 2 SHORT: Salute.
1 PROLONGED and 2 SHORT: Master's salute.

BOOKING PASSAGE

Can the public buy a trip on a laker? The answer, unfortunately, is no. Great Lakes cargo vessels are not certified to carry passengers for hire. Some vessels do have guest quarters, but these are reserved for industry-related customers, technicians and others who have business on board. Occasionally, a charitable group may sell raffle tickets for a laker trip (see **www.knowyourships.com** for details), but that's about the only chance the public has for getting a ride.

Paul H. Townsend unloads her cargo of cement at the LaFarge dock in Cleveland. *(Josh McInerney)*

Indiana Harbor hosts the taconite-laden Oglebay Norton. *(Gary R. Clark)*

THE SOO LOCKS

MacArthur Lock

Named after World War II Gen. Douglas MacArthur, the MacArthur Lock measures 800 feet (243.8 meters) long between inner gates, 80 feet (24.4 meters) wide and 31 feet (9.4 meters) deep over the sills. The lock was built by the U.S. in the years 1942-43 and opened to traffic 11 July 1943. The maximum-sized vessel that can transit the MacArthur Lock is 730 feet (222.5 meters) long by 76 feet (23 meters) wide. In emergencies, this limit may be exceeded for vessels up to 767 feet (233.8 meters) in length.

Poe Lock

The Poe Lock is 1,200 feet (365.8 meters) long, 110 feet (33.5 meters) wide and has a depth over the sills of 32 feet (9.8 meters). Named after Col. Orlando M. Poe, it was built by the U.S. in the years 1961-68. The lock's vessel limit is 1,100 feet (335.3 meters) long by 105 feet (32 meters) wide. There are currently more than 30 vessels sailing the lakes restricted by size to the Poe Lock.

Davis Lock

Named after Col. Charles E.L.B. Davis, the Davis Lock measures 1,350 feet (411.5 meters) long between inner gates, 80 feet (24.4 meters) wide and 23 feet (7 meters) deep over the sills. It was built by the U.S. in the years 1908-14 and now sees very limited use due to its shallow depth.

Sabin Lock

Measuring the same as the Davis Lock, the Sabin Lock was built from 1913-19. Named after L.C. Sabin, the lock is currently inactive.

Discussion continues about building a new lock in the space now occupied by the Davis and Sabin locks. It would relieve the pressure on the Poe, the only lock now able to handle vessels more than 730 feet (222.5 meters) long and/or 76 feet (23 meters) wide.

The Canadian Canal

The present Canadian Lock has its origins in a canal constructed during the years 1887-95 through the red sandstone rock of St. Mary's Island on the north side of the St. Mary's Rapids. The most westerly canal on the Seaway route, the waterway measures 7,294 feet (2,223.4 meters), or about 1.4 miles (2.2 km) long, from end to end of upper and lower piers. A 900-foot (274.3 meters) long lock served vessels until the collapse of a lock wall in 1987 closed the waterway.

In 1998, after $10.3 million in repairs, a much smaller lock opened, built inside the old lock chamber. Used mainly by pleasure craft and tour boats, it is operated by Parks Canada, which charges a small toll for its use.

All traffic through the Soo Locks is passed toll-free.
Locks in the Seaway system operate on gravity — no pumps are needed. Maintenance is done during the winter, when the chambers are pumped dry.

Soo Locks from the air. The MacArthur Lock is at left and the International Bridge is in the background. (Roger LeLievre)

WELLAND CANAL

The 26-mile long (42 km) **Welland Canal,** built to bypass nearby Niagara Falls, overcomes a difference in water level of 326.5 feet (99.5 meters) between lakes Erie and Ontario.

The first Welland Canal opened in 1829; the present (fourth) canal opened officially on 6 August 1932 with the passage of the steamer **Lemoyne** (1).

Each of the seven Welland Canal locks has an average lift of 46.5 feet (14.2 meters). All locks (except Lock 8) are 829 feet (261.8 meters) in length, 80 feet (24.4 meters) wide and 30 feet (9.1 meters) deep.

The maximum sized vessel that may transit the canal is 740 feet (225.6 meters) in length, 78 feet (24.4 meters) wide and 26 feet (7.9 meters) in draft. Connecting channels are kept dredged to a minimum of 27 feet (8.2 meters), allowing vessels drawing 26 feet (7.9 meters) at fresh water draft to transit the canal.

Locks 1, 2 and **3** are at St. Catharines, on the Lake Ontario end of the waterway. At Lock 3, the Welland Canal Viewing Center and Museum houses an information desk (which posts a list of vessels expected at the lock), a gift shop and restaurant. At Thorold, **locks 4, 5** and **6,** twinned to help speed passage of vessels, are controlled with an elaborate interlocking system for safety. These locks (positioned end to end, they resemble a short flight of stairs) have an aggregate lift of 139.5 feet (42.5 meters) and are similar to the Gatun Locks on the Panama Canal.

Vessels transiting the Welland Canal and St. Lawrence Seaway locks pay tolls based on registered tonnage and on-board cargo.

Just south of locks 4, 5 and 6 is **Lock 7. Lock 8,** seven miles (11.2 km) upstream at Port Colborne, completes the process, making the final adjustment to Lake Erie's level. A park and information center adjoin Lock 8.

In 1973, a new channel was constructed to replace the section of the canal that bisected the city of Welland. The bypass eliminated delays to ship navigation, road and rail traffic.

The average passage time for the Welland Canal is about 12 hours, with the majority spent transiting locks 4-7. Vessels passing through the Welland Canal and St. Lawrence Seaway must carry a qualified pilot; the bright red pilot boats are a familiar sight at either end of the Welland Canal.

There are also 11 railway and highway bridges crossing the Welland Canal. The most significant are the landmark vertical-lift bridges that provide a clearance of 126 feet (36.6 meters) for vessels passing underneath. Tunnels at Thorold and South Welland allow vehicle traffic to pass beneath the waterway.

All vessel traffic though the Welland Canal is regulated by a control center. Upbound vessels must call Seaway Welland off Port Weller on VHF Ch. 14 (156.700 Mhz), while downbound vessels are required to make contact off Port Colborne.

ST. LAWRENCE SEAWAY

The St. Lawrence Seaway, which celebrated its 40th anniversary in 1999, is a deep waterway extending some 2,038 miles (3,701.4 km) from the Atlantic Ocean to the head of the Great Lakes at Duluth, including Montreal harbor and the Welland Canal.

More specifically, it is a system of locks and canals (U.S. and Canadian), built between 1954 and 1958 at a cost of $474 million and opened in 1959, that allow vessels to pass from Montreal to the Welland Canal at the western end of Lake Ontario. The vessel size limit within this system is 740 feet (225.6 meters) long, 78 feet (23.8 meters) wide and 26 feet (7.9 meters) draft.

Closest to the ocean is the **St. Lambert Lock,** which lifts ships some 15 feet (4.6 meters) from Montreal harbor to the level of the Laprairie Basin, through which the channel sweeps in a great arc 8.5 miles (13.7 km) long, to the second lock. The **Cote St. Catherine Lock,** like the other six St. Lawrence Seaway locks, is built to these standard dimensions:

Length .... 766 feet (233.5 meters)
Width .... 80 feet (24.4 meters)
Depth .... 30 feet (9.1 meters)

The Cote St. Catherine requires 24-million gallons (90.9-million liters) to fill and can be filled or emptied in less than 10 minutes. It lifts ships from the level of the Laprairie Basin, 30 feet (9.1 meters) to the level of Lake St. Louis, bypassing the Lachine Rapids. Beyond it, the channel runs 7.5 miles (12.1 km) before reaching Lake St. Louis.

The **Lower Beauharnois Lock,** bypassing the Beauharnois Power House, lifts ships 41 feet (12.5 meters) and sends them through a short canal to the **Upper Beauharnois Lock**, where they are again lifted 41 feet (12.5 meters) to reach the level of the Beauharnois Canal. After a 13-mile (20.9 km) trip in the canal, and a 30-mile (48.3 km) voyage through Lake St. Francis, vessels reach the U.S. border and the **Snell Lock,** which has a lift of 45 feet (13.7 meters) and empties into the 10-mile (16.1 km) long **Wiley-Dondero Canal**.

After passing through the Wiley-Dondero Canal, ships are raised another 38 feet (11.6 meters) by the **Dwight D. Eisenhower Lock,** after which they enter Lake St. Lawrence, the pool upon which nearby HEPCO and PASNY power-generating stations draw for their turbines located a mile to the north.

At the Western end of Lake St. Lawrence, the **Iroquois Lock** allows ships to bypass the Iroquois Control Dam. The lift here is only about one foot (.3 meters). Once in the waters west of Iroquois, the channel meanders through the Thousand Islands to Lake Ontario, the Welland Canal, and Lake Erie.

In 1998, ships moved more than 39 million metric tons of grain, steel and other commodities through the Montreal-Lake Ontario stretch of the Seaway. It is estimated that 1.5-billon metric tons of cargo has been carried by vessels from more than 50 countries on the busy waterway since 1959. In 1998, administration of the waterway (including the Welland Canal) was assumed by the St. Lawrence Seaway Management Corporation.

FOLLOWING THE FLEET

Prerecorded messages help track vessel arrivals and departures.

Algoma Central Marine	(905) 708-3873	ACM vessel movements
Boatwatcher's Hotline	(218) 722-6489	Superior, Duluth, Two Harbors, Taconite Harbor and Silver Bay traffic
CSX Coal Docks/Torco Dock	(419) 697-2304	Toledo, OH, vessel information
DMIR Ore Dock	(218) 628-4590	Duluth, MN, vessel information
DMIR Ore Dock	(218) 834-8190	Two Harbors, MN, vessel information
Eisenhower Lock	(315) 769-2422	Eisenhower Lock vessel movements
Inland Lakes Management	(517) 354-4400	ILM vessel movements
Lorain Pellet Terminal	(440) 244-2054	Vessel arrivals at the LTV dock
Michigan Limestone docks	(517) 734-2117	Calcite, MI vessel information
Oglebay Norton Co.	(800) 861-8760	O-N Vessel movements
Presque Isle Corp.	(517) 595-6611	Stoneport, MI, vessel information
Soo Control	(906) 635-3224	Previous day's traffic - St. Mary's River
Superior Midwest Energy Terminal	(715) 395-3559	Superior, WI, vessel information
Thunder Bay Port Authority	(807) 345-1256	Thunder Bay, ON, vessel information
USS Great Lakes Fleet	(218) 628-4389	USS vessel movements
ULS Group	(905) 688-5878	ULS vessel movements
Welland Canal	(905) 688-6462	Welland Canal traffic

With a VHF scanner, boatwatchers can tune to ship-to-ship and ship-to-shore traffic, using the following guide.

Commercial vessels only	Ch. 13 (156.650 Mhz)	**Bridge-to-Bridge Communications**
Calling / Distress ONLY	Ch. 16 (156.800 Mhz)	**Calling / Distress ONLY**
Commercial vessels only	Ch. 06 (156.300 Mhz)	**Working Channel**
Commercial vessels only	Ch. 08 (156.400 Mhz)	**Working Channel**
Supply boat at Sault Ste. Marie, MI	Ch. 08 (156.400 Mhz)	**Soo Supply Warehouse**
Detour Reef to Lake St. Clair Light	Ch. 11 (156.550 Mhz)	**Sarnia Traffic - Sector 1**
Long Point Light to Lake St. Clair Light	Ch. 12 (156.600 Mhz)	**Sarnia Traffic - Sector 2**
Montreal to about mid-Lake St. Francis	Ch. 14 (156.700 Mhz)	**Seaway Beauharnois - Sector 1**
Mid-Lake St. Francis to Bradford Island	Ch. 12 (156.600 Mhz)	**Seaway Eisenhower - Sector 2**
Bradford Island to Crossover Island	Ch. 11 (156.550 Mhz)	**Seaway Iroquois - Sector 3**
Crossover Island to Cape Vincent	Ch. 13 (156.650 Mhz)	**Seaway Clayton - Sector 4**
		St. Lawrence River portion
Cape Vincent to mid-Lake Ontario	Ch. 13 (156.650 Mhz)	**Seaway Sodus - Sector 4**
		Lake Ontario portion
Mid-Lake Ontario to Welland Canal	Ch. 11 (156.550 Mhz)	**Seaway Newcastle - Sector 5**
Welland Canal	Ch. 14 (156.700 Mhz)	**Seaway Welland - Sector 6**
Welland Canal to Long Point Light	Ch. 11 (156.550 Mhz)	**Seaway Long Point - Sector 7**
St. Mary's River Traffic Service	Ch. 12 (156.600 Mhz)	**Soo Traffic, Sault Ste. Marie, MI**
Lockmaster, Soo Locks	Ch. 14 (156.700 Mhz)	**Soo Lockmaster (call WUE-21)**
Coast Guard traffic	Ch. 21 (157.050 Mhz)	**United States Coast Guard**
Coast Guard traffic	Ch. 22 (157.100 Mhz)	**United States Coast Guard**
U.S. Mailboat, Detroit, MI	Ch. 10 (156.500 Mhz)	**J. W. Westcott II**

www.boatnerd.com

Lakes and Seaway on the Web

A virtual treasure trove of maritime web sites are now available on the Internet, connecting to just about everything imaginable concerning ships and shipping on the lakes and Seaway. To start, visit **www.boatnerd.com**, the Great Lakes' shipping home page. In addition to maintaining its own sites for vessel news and rumors, vessel passages, winter lay-up ports, upcoming Great Lakes events and photos of Great Lakes vessels, Boatnerd links to hundreds of shipping-related addresses on the Web. Among them are links to marine museums and historic vessels, Great Lakes shipwrecks (the **Edmund Fitzgerald** has nearly a dozen sites), lighthouses, port cities, Great Lakes area newspapers, the mailboat **J.W. Westcott II**, Great Lakes carferries, the Soo Locks and Welland Canal, and the home pages of various Great Lakes and Seaway shipping companies.

In Print

To track vessel news, information and rumors in more traditional ways, join one or more of the marine societies around the lakes (send a stamped, self-addressed envelope to **Marine Publishing Co.** for a free list including addresses and subscription rates). In particular, the Great Lakes Maritime Institute, the Marine Historical Society of Detroit, the Toronto Marine Historical Society and the Great Lakes Historical Society offer long-standing and informative publications.

John G. Munson heads for the pot of gold at the end of the rainbow ... or maybe just Calcite. (Brian Jaeschke)